If hovercraft can go anywhere,
how did we end up here?

Contributors

Russ Bagley's working years have been spent in the world of hovercraft as designer, pilot, engineer and trainer, first with Pindair and later at Griffon Hovercraft. He is now retired and lives a hovercraft-free life in Hampshire with his two children and his wife Kathy Brogan, who wrote this book.

John Barker has a background in design and a passion for sailing and boats. A mistaken call to a hovercraft company led John to a thirty year career in the industry. John is still travelling the world with hovercraft and lives in Hampshire with his wife, Sue Shennan.

Kathy Brogan worked for twenty years as a teacher and has now retired in order to write. She has written a novel called 'Catch Me' in which, she would like to make clear, hovercraft play no part whatsoever.

This book would not have been written without Sue Shennan. Fuelled by naps on the sofa she has contributed energy and wisdom without which the project would soon have run out of steam. She also knows where to buy extremely good chocolate biscuits.

About this book

The events described in this book are real. The names of some people and places have been changed. The 'big picture' chronology is accurate but some smaller events have been rolled together for the sake of brevity and wit.

The idea to write a book about their experiences with hovercraft was conceived on the day that John and Russ found themselves snow-bound near the Arctic Circle. This project provided a reason for Russ and his wife Kath to get together regularly with John and his wife Sue, with the intention of writing stuff down in a focused and business-like way. In reality, we drank a lot of tea, coffee, beer and wine, ate chocolate biscuits and laughed a great deal. Sometimes we did a bit of writing. Before we knew it, six years had passed and people were asking to see some evidence of our labour. Luckily, Kath had all along been shaping a book out of the jumble of disparate stories, anecdotes and yarns. *If Hovercraft Can Go Anywhere, How Did We End Up Here?* is the result.

Published by Shivering Sheep
First Published May 2018
Copyright © Kathy Brogan 2018

ISBN 978-1-9999302-1-9
www.ifhovercraftcangoanywhere.com

Cover design by Studio 6 Design and Print
Printed by Studio 6 Design and Print
www.studio-6.co.uk

Dedicated to Mike Pinder and John Gifford.
Who were there at the beginning, took a chance on us
and made all these adventures possible.

Thank you

To John Gifford who employed Russ and John for many years and for taking time to read and comment on this book.

To Mike Pinder for giving Russ his first hovercraft job, for his interest and suggestions, and for the photographs.

To Sue and Rob Martin for their constant encouragement and tireless proof reading and to Rob for his help with the photographs.

To Lindsey Maguire and Sarah Lowson at Studio 6 Design and Print who have been so helpful with their advice and encouragement.

CONTENTS

Introduction

'So what do you do?'

There are a few stock reactions when you tell people you work with hovercraft. Some are a bit impressed. (Although, on reflection, this applies mainly to small boys and bearded men.) Some ask, 'Are they still going then?' Others nod and smile brightly but if you look closely you will see that their eyes are scanning the room for the nearest escape just in case you turn out to be an anorak or a boffin, both of which, let's be honest, the world of hovercraft has more than its fair share. If your listener's eyes take on an unnatural intensity, they probably *are* one of those fanatics or boffins, in which case it is best to escape before you find yourself drawn into conversation about the merits of a loop-and-segment skirt versus the bag-and-finger system.

The hovercraft was part of that bright, fresh optimism of the 1960s. To little boys raised on *Thunderbirds* and *Tomorrow's World*, this brand-new invention had a place reserved in the marvellous Future: the day would come (just about now, probably) when we'd all be hovering around town propelled by power-packs and wearing silver suits. Air-travel still had a whiff of glamour about it in those days and early hovercraft services aimed for a similar chic but, let's face it, 'stylish' or 'fashionable' are not the first adjectives which attach themselves to the word 'hovercraft'. It was no accident that Monty Python chose to lament: 'My hovercraft...' (rather than my boat, plane or train) '...is full of eels'. By the time the sixties were over, its place in British culture and the public imagination had been secured – no longer as an icon of an exciting, sunny future but as the archetypal plucky underdog, the ugly duckling. Suddenly everyone knew it was less bovver with a hover. Hovercraft were officially funny.

Nevertheless, it is a rather wonderful invention. Neither boat nor plane, but both. It flies and floats, it is an amphibian, a compromise, a hotchpotch, neither one thing nor the other. But the instant the hovercraft subsides onto a beach or slipway, people materialize: crowds of children, compulsive questioners ('What's it made of?' 'How fast does it go?') and always a few solitary men who stare in silence. They all wander over to take a look, lingering for that moment when it will rise up and cross the threshold of land and sea as if they are not separate elements but one and the same thing.

A lot has changed since the sixties. There are now more than three flavours of crisps, no-one hitch-hikes any more, cars don't rust and you can't buy an Afghan coat anywhere. But the production of hovercraft has never stopped because in the right conditions, which usually means in rugged and far-flung parts of the world which you would never choose to visit or ever want to go back to, nothing else will do the job.

And that makes the hovercraft a success.

For posterity and in case it should be forgotten, here are some stories about hovercraft, not about their technical merits or how they work or their history, which have all been covered elsewhere, but the human side of hovercraft and, in particular, two people who travelled the world to keep some of them running.

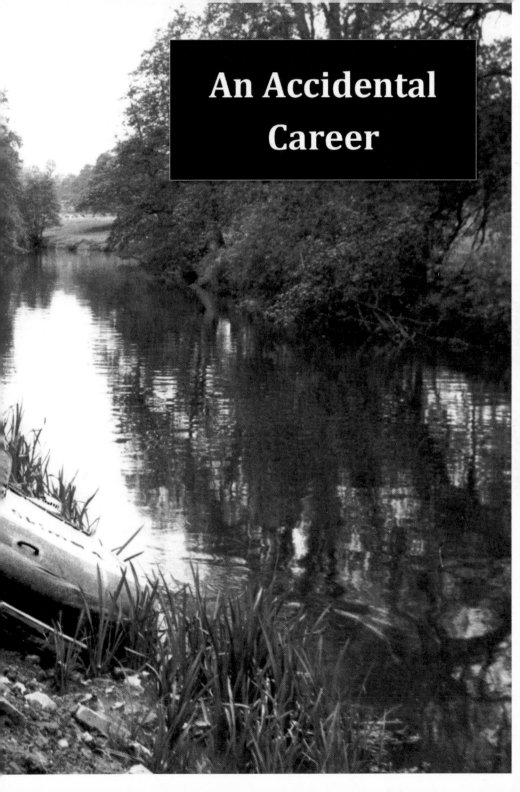

An Accidental Career

Chapter 1
An Accidental Career

Russ Bagley: England 1976

'Wanker!' The cry rose high and distinct above the ragged booing and jeering, setting off a wave of laughter from the crowd. If I'd had time to think about it, I might have taken a moment to mourn the sudden passing of my new career. It was, after all, only three weeks since that auspicious day when I'd seen the ad in the Job Centre and been taken on by Pindair, a local hovercraft manufacturer, all in the course of one afternoon. But these thoughts were swamped by the immediate terror of wrestling with the controls of the Skima 2 as it plummeted down one steep river-bank and headed at full speed towards the other.

I had jumped at the chance to help out at Water 76, a trade fair held for the water industry at Stoneleigh, Warwickshire. We were there to demonstrate the versatility of our two smallest craft, Skimas 2 and 4. My new boss, Mike, was an amiable character who evidently had a touching amount of faith in me. As we set up camp, I heard him say, '... and after Mac's done his bit, Russ, you can take the Skima 2 through the obstacles and then down onto the river...' I protested vigorously, reminding him that I had only driven a hovercraft for about five minutes on wide areas of flat and featureless water, and then under close supervision. Undeterred, he told me how easy it was to drive these craft, and added that the commentators would be explaining over the PA what a novice I was while I masterfully drove the course. It would be easy - and a great selling point for the craft. With severe misgivings I agreed, my anxiety slowly increasing as hundreds of discerning spectators started to arrive and throng the perimeter of the arena in anticipation of seeing the hovercraft put through their paces.

Mac, who was more experienced in the practical points of hovercraft, clearly believed it was not going to be as easy as Mike wanted it to be. He took me aside for words of advice on what might go wrong (quite a lot apparently), handling tips for negotiating the tricky steep drop into the river and some last-minute do's and don'ts regarding throttles and rudders. Unfortunately, as my brain had seemingly stopped processing information, he seemed to be speaking in a made-up language; and having lost the power of speech myself, all I could do was watch his lips move and nod.

More gobbledegook over the PA, then the crowd burst into applause as Mac did his bit: a faultless slalom run in the larger Skima 4 mk2 (see appx. 1), figures-of-eight, sixpence turns... He manoeuvred around the course perfectly. You could almost see the enthusiasts reaching for their wallets.

My turn. By then I had passed through terror and paralytic fear and come out the other side into a zombie-like state of calm. I started the engines, took a firm grip on the tiller and headed for the row of stakes through which Mac had just serenely weaved the Skima 4. The first stake seemed to disappear as I approached. Then the next. Indeed, so systematic was my flattening of the course, I could sense the crowd's confusion: was this meant to happen? Like a strike in a bowling alley? With any confidence I might have had now draining away, I found myself drifting sideways as I came up to the end of the

course. Perhaps it was my heightened state of awareness but for a brief moment, the blur of the crowd separated out into real people with frightened faces. Correcting my heading to avoid a group of fleeing women and children, I completed the turn and found myself faced with the demolished course. Panic set in. What should I do? With nothing to slalom through, the return run was now pointless. I would just have to hover over the flattened stakes and head straight for the river. After I had made this decision, many things seemed to happen at once. The river, which was twenty or thirty-foot-wide, was already looming towards me at a surprising speed. I knew I had to slow down but in my haste twisted the throttle the wrong way and suddenly I was hurtling headlong towards the water, kamikaze-style. The bank was 8 or 10 feet high and sloped at an angle of about 45 degrees. In my defence I should say that successful negotiation of this sort of terrain is a difficult and advanced manoeuvre: you need to approach the gradient slowly, and during the descent begin turning the craft upstream, then power up the river as soon as it hits the water. That isn't what I did. Instead, I plunged down the bank at top speed, failed to turn, hurtled across the river and was thrown sprawling over the bow as the craft buried its nose in a large hawthorn bush on the opposite bank.

It is difficult to remain nonchalant in such a situation. To my credit, however, studiously ignoring the hoots of derision and sundry insults, though scratched and bleeding, I did manage to extricate the craft from the bush and actually finish the demo, driving up and down the river as if it had all been planned.

Then I went to face my future.

I decided I would offer to make my own way home – leave there and then rather than suffering the ignominy of travelling back with the others after failing in such spectacular fashion. I would look for another job.

But the shock of the collision was playing tricks on my mind. Here was Mike, coming to meet me, with a look of pleasure on his face, proffering his outstretched hand, saying, 'Well done, Russell. Good show. Come and have a beer.' And here was Mac, also smiling, passing me the can and patting me on the back. Having lost all faith in reality, I stayed quiet and downed the beer in a dreamlike state.

I figured it out later: Mike and Mac were probably the only two people in the showground who hadn't seen what happened. Mike had found his way to the beer tent in the arena, where he had been dispensing corporate hospitality; Mac, of course, had been driving away from me in the other craft and had only seen my triumphal finale of driving up and down the river, the one bit I hadn't messed up. I stayed to share a couple of beers then went back and surreptitiously removed the few incriminating pieces of vegetation which remained on and in the craft, still not quite able to believe that my catastrophic performance could be so easily overlooked.

Nevertheless, I was sure my days at Pindair were numbered and that it would be only a matter of time before the real account of my disastrous debut somehow made its way back to Mike. He would ask me to leave - nicely, of course, and rather sorrowfully - and that would be that. It was the seventies so there were plenty of jobs around. In the past year alone, I had lugged sacks of toxic chemicals from lorry to warehouse and vice versa, placed new TVs on a trolley as they arrived off an unrelenting conveyor belt, and positioned lumps of dough, destined to become buns, onto a baking tray the size of a barn door. Sadly, with the decline of manufacturing in the UK, many of these important skills may have been lost forever.

Some weeks passed, however, and the demo was not alluded to. I was at last beginning to forget my fears when Mike turned up unexpectedly one Friday just as we were finishing and signalled across the noisy workshop that he would 'like a word'. I was sure that my public failure was about to come back to bite me; the game was up. Wondering whether I should put up a fight or just go quietly, I took a long time finishing whatever small task I was working on then reluctantly sought him out in the untidy little booth which acted as an office.

'Russ,' he began, rather too cheerfully I thought, in the circumstances. 'Are you doing anything tomorrow?' Thinking that the weekly laundry and lying in bed didn't really amount to 'anything', I cautiously admitted that I wasn't. 'I've got rather an important demo and I could do with some help. Can't pay you I'm afraid, but thought you might like to come along for the ride.'

I was so relieved that he wasn't sacking me, I would have agreed not only to come, but to pay him for the privilege. On the other hand, although the trauma of the last demo was slowly beginning to lessen – the nightmares came only every other night now – it was still very much with me and I felt sure that if I didn't shape up this time, that would be the end of my career.

'Is it a - er - big venue?' I asked, picturing Wembley, perhaps, or Earls Court.

'Not big,' admitted Mike. 'But local. It's important to get local interest - that's one of my key marketing strategies.'

'So where...?'

'Hamble Village Regatta,' he explained. 'Great fun. Be sure to bring your swimming trunks.'

This seemed like a great idea. It was shaping up to be a record-breaking, drought-ridden summer; already temperatures had been in

the 30s most days and the whole country had a distinctly un-English, holiday feel. The next day, decked out for the regatta, Hamble foreshore looked glorious, more reminiscent of the south of France than the south of England. We unloaded the craft on a beach, drawing the usual crowd of watchers. I had dutifully brought my swimming gear and was already thinking longingly about the cooling dip I would have once the craft was inflated. This is not what Mike had in mind.

'Okay,' he said, a few minutes before the demo was due to start. 'Get into your trunks and swim out somewhere near that buoy.' He pointed a long way out, towards the middle of the river.

I started to feel worried. 'Why?' I asked, not unreasonably.

'So that I can run you over with the hovercraft... as part of the demo,' he explained, as if it was the most natural thing in the world to ask someone to do. Mike must have detected some lack of enthusiasm on my part. 'It went down a bomb last year! The crowd are expecting it. They'll be disappointed if we don't do it,' he continued, 'and it does illustrate the hovercraft's amphibious capability so well.' I sighed resignedly. Here was a chance to prove my mettle and bank up some good points against the day the truth about the Stoneleigh debacle finally came out.

Mike absolutely loved his demos. Some months before, he had talked his way into doing a live one on local television. The grand finale was to run Mac over. As a slight nod to health and safety and the 'don't try this at home' brigade, Mac had donned a full-face crash helmet before lying down on the studio floor. Slowly and steadily the craft went over him so that his body gradually disappeared then re-emerged from the back of the craft. Then it stopped. Mac's limbs writhed briefly and violently then he leapt to his feet and stood with his arms raised like Lazarus, evidently unharmed by the experience. Only the more observant viewers would have noticed that the crash helmet was not on his head; perhaps the more perceptive ones would have realised that this was because it was still under the hovercraft, hopelessly entangled in the inner skirt.

So Mike ran me over with the hovercraft. The experience is actually rather anti-climactic: seeing a large vessel approaching at speed, one expects an impact, and a lot of noise, and possibly pain. The hardest thing is to keep still and have faith. After that, it is as unremarkable as walking through a line of washing. There is a brief silence as the craft passes overhead, another brush with the laundry, and normality returns.

Having survived the running over and savoured the round of applause this elicited from the spectators, I was soon dry and dressed, on the shore again and ready for home. But Mike had another wheeze in mind. 'Shall we see how far we can get the craft up the river? It'll only take an hour or so and I don't think anyone has done it before.'

We knew the navigation finished a few miles upstream and was only accessible to canoes not far beyond Bursledon, but the river continued much farther. Mike drove, leaving me time to muse on how I could talk up the story of being run over for my mates in the pub that night. There was a four-knot speed limit all the way up river, but hovercraft are peculiar in that they make more wash and spray at low speed until they reach 10-15 knots when the waves they make are negligible. It was generally accepted at the time (by us at least) that it's better for a hovercraft to ignore the speed limit and go faster. Of course, not everyone understands this.

It was a jolly outing on such a beautiful afternoon. The Skima 4 Mk2 we drove was a small open craft, powered by three very noisy (ok, deafening) two-stroke engines. As we sped north, enjoying the cooling breeze, the river narrowed and meandered through beautiful meadows, parched now after weeks without rain. We admired the expensive, exclusive and very quiet waterside properties as they flashed past. Then, as we swept on by some sort of smallholding, an angry-looking man appeared and began gesticulating to us with frantic urgency. Obviously, we couldn't hear what he was saying because of the noise so we could only wave back cheerfully. Unperturbed, we continued at a good lick for another five miles, eventually arriving at Botley. At this point, a small road bridge with narrow spans finally put an end to our foray to the source of the Hamble. We could go no further.

Satisfied with our small achievement, we turned back. It was almost impossible to think, let alone talk, over the racket of the three engines. They were the type found in chain-saws and the din they made would certainly be a fitting soundtrack to accompany the fleeing of animals and toppling of ancient Amazonian trees. I was just wondering whether our exploit would be worthy of a place in the *Guinness Book of World Records* when, rounding a bend, we caught sight of our farmer friend again, hopping up and down. Mike suggested that he might be doing a rain-dance. We waved back. Incensed, he held up four fingers of one hand, mouthing (well, probably bellowing): 'Speed limit four knots. FOUR KNOTS!' At this point, we might have stopped and politely explained that we had permission from the Harbour Master to exceed the speed-limit but such thoughts instantly evaporated the moment we saw the gun - a shotgun, and it was aimed at us!

Mike increased his speed and carried on. Then he did something which is probably way down the list of suggestions for calming an unpredictable gun-wielding psychopath. He called back to him 'WE'RE ONLY DOING TWO KNOTS!' – a fact he clarified by showing the appropriate number of fingers. A thousand thoughts raced through my mind simultaneously: Is that it? Are we going to die today? Should I dive to the bottom of the craft for cover? How thick was the skirt? Would buckshot bounce off rubber? It would be all over the papers: 'Hamble Hovercraft Murder Mystery'... the police would eventually find our bodies rotting in a barn beside the burnt-out hovercraft...

Without changing his speed or course, Mike drove on. All I could do was tense myself, anticipating gunshots at any second. They never came. We rounded another bend in the river and I breathed again, feeling a rush of gratitude like a man reborn, as if everything under the heaven was in its rightful place.

We were still a good distance from our starting point but luckily quite far from the gun maniac when the Skima 4 puttered to a halt, out of petrol. Trying not to imagine the bloodbath if this had happened ten minutes earlier, I immediately volunteered to go back to the Land Rover for a jerrican. This was not an entirely altruistic gesture: it occurred to me that I would be safer walking away than sitting alone and unprotected in the craft – you never know how persistent some people are. In the solid heat of the late afternoon, I set off back along the riverbank wearing my hi-vis orange jacket, leaving Mike to sun himself in the craft, perfectly happy to take his chances with the gunman.

I was soon sweltering. Flies were everywhere. I took off my jacket and used it to swish away the pesky insects as I walked. At first, I thought the thundering noise was just the echo of the hovercraft engines in my head. My next thought was that it could it be the angry gunman pursuing his quarry. A casual glance behind suggested strongly that this was not the case. The bull was large and disproportionately angry. As he charged, gouts of mud and grass flew out from his massive hooves, steam puffing out of cavernous nostrils which were flared in outrage. I had two choices: stand my ground and face him out, or run like hell. While I was weighing up these choices, my body took unilateral action and I found myself clearing in a few giant strides the distance which separated me from a four foot barbed-wire fence. Adrenalin is a wonderful chemical: for my second lucky escape, this time with no crowd to witness my achievement, I cleared the fence like an Olympic hurdler, in one graceful leap.

Back at the hovercraft, Mike did not seem impressed by the account of my heroic escape. In the time I had been away, he had rigged up a makeshift shelter and turned a livid shade of pink – I'm not sure in what order – and I think he suspected that I had made up the story in order to deflect his attention from the suspicion that I had stopped off at the beer tent before returning with the petrol. I had, of course, but only in an attempt to stave off dehydration.

With the fuel tank now replenished we made the last leg back to Hamble foreshore where I dismantled the craft. An earnest, solitary man (known in the 1970s as a 'nutter') detached himself from the usual handful of onlookers and went to talk to Mike. As I was loading up the trailer, I heard Mike say, 'So can you buy feathers in bulk?' A long, earnest discussion followed.

The light was fading as I drove us home although Mike was clearly visible in the passenger seat as a faint pink fluorescence. Mike always had a keen nose for a money-making scheme and it seemed that the chap wanted to charter a craft to test out a long-standing dream he had for using feathers to mop up oil spills on water. (Yes, some people do have dreams like this and a fair proportion of them like hovercraft as well.) This stemmed from the observation that oil is attracted to feathers, as borne out by the images of stricken sea-birds so often shown in the wake of an incident of oil pollution. He was therefore keen to experiment with spreading chicken feathers over the oil which would, in theory, soak it up and then could be scooped up as a coherent mass before any harm was done to the environment. A hovercraft's lift system, he decided, would be the perfect mechanism to distribute the feathers onto the surface. Like many of the most hare-brained schemes, this one had a ring of plausibility about it.

Consequently, one hot afternoon a few weeks later, on a slipway in Portsmouth Harbour, we were to be found loading a Skima 12 (see appx. 3) with half a dozen large boxes crammed full of chicken feathers (apparently, they are obtainable in

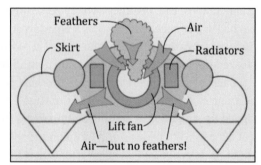

bulk but it's a niche market). It was hot work and I was glad to put to sea. I don't remember feeling that we were doing anything wrong as we poured the crude oil over the surface of the sea – remember, this was before the days of bottle-banks and poop-a-scoops when the world was covered in discarded plastic bags and lengths of cassette tape festooned the trees. We drove across the spreading slick in the hovercraft while a volunteer (yes, me) threw armfuls of chicken feathers into the lift-fan intake, through which they would be dispersed onto the oily surface. This was surprisingly hard work. We were expecting to see the feathers lying on the surface behind the craft within a few seconds, greedily soaking up the oil, but there was no sign of them. Could feathers sink? And if so, how did the water-bird population work round this? The last boxful hit the fan and we watched intently, still hoping for a glimpse of a feather on the water, when the driver shouted:

'The engine's overheating, I have to stop!'

For the next half an hour, with the engine stopped and the craft drifting across the busy harbour, we took it in turns to contort ourselves into the narrow fan bay and scrape enough of the feathers from the inside of the engine cooling radiators to be able to drive the craft back to base. It was a hot sweaty job and we were soon covered in ragged plumage as the feathers stuck to our arms, got in our eyes and wormed their way to other unlikely parts of our anatomy only to reveal themselves several days later. The actual scale of the feather disaster was already horribly apparent: attracted by the wet surfaces, every centimetre of the underside of the craft, the inside of the skirt and all the rest of the structure was caked with a thick layer of downy fluff. It is debatable whether any of the feathers actually left the hovercraft.

Were you there that day? Cast your mind back. In the scorching summer of '76, a hovercraft limps across the harbour and subsides onto Quay Lane slipway. Inside are three figures, all reminiscent of Big Bird from *Sesame Street* in the moulting season. Nobody says anything much: they are probably too occupied absorbing the disappointment, reflecting that the role of feathers in cleaning up oil-spills has a limited future.

In the space of one month, I'd been made a laughing stock and forced to face a jeering crowd like a gladiator; I'd somehow survived a head-on collision with a river bank, been deliberately run over, threatened by a madman with a gun, chased by a monstrous bull, been made to pollute Portsmouth Harbour with a mini oil-slick and been given just a glimpse into what it must feel like to be tarred and feathered. Added to that, I was underpaid, sometimes not paid at all.

But hey – every day I got to play with hovercraft. At twenty-three, how could life be any better than that?

From Venice Beach to Spitfire Quay

Chapter 2
From Venice Beach to Spitfire Quay

John Barker, The World

I always thought I would have a career in design but as a gormless teenager I chose the wrong kind of design. Based on winning a school poster competition and not knowing any different, I'd thought graphic design would be the career for me. But after three years of art college and six years working in a busy London graphic design office, I became pretty disillusioned with that idea. I was young, idealistic and craved adventure and not so keen on the nine-to-five office routine. I decided to save up and go to California, where something more adventurous would surely be available and at least the climate would make for a better life. Two years later I arrived in Venice Beach with the money I'd managed to save.

I'd always loved the freedom of sailing. Coming from the Isle of Sheppey, as a teenager I'd spent most of my weekends

exploring the muddy tidal waters of the Thames Estuary, aboard my Dad's little sailing boat and really missed it when I moved to the city. The waters off the California coast couldn't have been more different from those I was used to at home. Rather than cold, brown water and low marshy shores, here was endless sunshine and the sparkling blue Pacific stretching to a distant horizon. I was fascinated by the thousands of boats moored in nearby Marina Del Rey: everything from the sleek yachts of the super-rich to patched-up home conversions. Every day, boats would take off for idyllic bays, beaches and islands up and down the coast. Even more tantalisingly, I would watch one head out over the horizon, bound for Hawaii or Mexico.

It occurred to me that had the Beach Boys been born on the Isle of Sheppey they would have had far less to sing about.

I spent so much time in the marina that I was offered a job with a yacht charter company carrying out maintenance on their fleet of boats and cleaning up after charters. It's the sort of work where you meet lots of new people and there was always plenty of sailing, mostly evenings and weekends up and down the coast. Things were better, but still not quite there.

A year later I heard about a yacht needing crew to sail around the world. Perfect. I spent the next eighteen months hitch-hiking boats across the Pacific, finally ending up in Australia.

Along the way, in some of the remotest islands, I saw first-hand the loss of traditional boatbuilding skills and the increasing reliance on imported mass-produced boats and outboard motors which no-one knew how to maintain or repair. I was particularly affected by the story told by a fisherman on a remote atoll in the Cook Islands.

In the old days, when they paddled their canoes out into the lagoon, he and the other fishermen would take a couple of hours each evening to catch enough fish to share among them all. They would eat well and sleep well. Then they were given outboard motors by an aid agency, but the noise of the outboards scared the fish away, so they had to keep fishing all night and still the catch was poor. They neither ate nor slept well.

Then they used the money they were given to buy detonators which they threw into the water. This stunned many more fish that they needed, but they could just scoop up what they wanted. The rest went to waste or got eaten by the seabirds, but at least the fishermen ate and slept well again. After a few years of this though, the lagoon was all but fished out. The coral was irretrievably damaged. Piles of broken outboards lay everywhere, immobilised by simple things like broken starter cords or spark-plug leads. Heart-breaking. There had to be a better way.

I pondered these things as I meandered from island to island across the Pacific, in a loose westerly direction to stay ahead of the hurricane season. My only goal was to meet up with an old school friend who had married an Australian girl and settled in Brisbane. 'Come and stay with us if you get here,' Martin had said. That gave me a focus. When I got there, I should really start to plan for the future. But that was a long way ahead and I had no idea how long it would take. And anyhow, I was living the dream.

The Chaos Theory proposes that most things in life are unpredictable and occur as a chain of accidental events, each tiny event changing the world in a unique way. When a butterfly flutters its wings, so it's said, this insignificant act sets up a chain reaction which could reach to the other side of the world. The butterfly is merely an example, of course; in my case, it was a parrot.

I had tried without success to be friends with Dry Rot, a surly creature with green plumage and evil eyes, the beloved pet of Michelle who, with her partner Bill, co-owned *Seafarer*, a beautiful wooden ketch I had crewed from Mexico across the Eastern Pacific to the remote Marquesas Islands and Tuamotus, before finally reaching Papeete, the capital of Tahiti.

Dry Rot, who had been bought in Mexico, regarded any friendly overture or kindly meant tit-bit from me with cynical suspicion and lost no opportunity to repay these gestures with a sharp nip. The one consolation was that he hated everyone on board equally, although a slight preference for Michelle was evident in the way that he bit her less frequently and was less likely to draw blood.

The day which decided my future began in the same languid way as any other I had spent aboard Seafarer. Bill and Michelle would have a leisurely breakfast while I tinkered around, paying my way by taking on any of the numerous maintenance tasks involved in keeping a wooden boat operational. There was always something to do.

A few weeks earlier, the inflatable dinghy, our only means of getting ashore in remote anchorages, had sprung a bad leak and the relative civilisation of Papeete offered the opportunity of having it professionally repaired. That morning it was dropped back on the quayside in an uninflated heap.

'OK, Jharn, let's blow that thing up,' said Bill. From the experience of the last several weeks I knew this meant: You blow it up while I stand around telling interminable stories of my previous life as a Private Investigator, mostly in 'repossession work' – taking goods back from people who had defaulted on payments. These stories, which were darkly comic the first time around, became intolerable with repetition. Bullying, intimidation and strong-arm tactics were all part of the game and each depressing tale was concluded with the same gleeful punchline: 'You shoulda seen the look on their faces!' These tales were interspersed with kindly phrases of encouragement like 'pump harder' or 'more in this one'. It was going to be a long job in a temperature much more conducive to lazing about.

Soon Michelle came down the gang-plank. 'I'm going into town for supplies,' she said as she walked off along the quay. Not long after, a large, brightly dressed, hippy-looking woman approached. 'What a beautiful boat!' she declared. Flattered, Bill engaged her in conversation and the pair wandered a little further along the quay, out of earshot, to get a better view of the undeniably handsome vessel. I kept my head down and went on pumping solidly, occasionally changing legs as one got tired.

It was true, *Seafarer* was a fine-looking classic boat, but also very high maintenance. During the voyage the refrigerator had failed, the engine died intermittently, the heat of the sun had blasted her once beautiful varnish work; now her painted decks had started leaking. They all needed fixing. She was, as the Americans say, a money pit.

Their conversation continued out of earshot and after a while they sauntered back to where I was working. Bill announced: 'Jharn, we're going aboard,' and he ushered his new best friend ahead of him, being exaggeratedly gallant as she waddled up the gang-plank. Admiring glances were taken of the sweeping decks and lofty rigging before they disappeared below – intriguing.

After twenty minutes of continuous pumping, I saw Michelle reappear with bags full of shopping. 'Hi, Jharn,' she said, breezing past me and disappearing into the cabin. She hadn't been below for more than a few minutes before an agonised cry came from the hatchway, followed by an intense, unintelligible argument. After a while the shouting died down and Michelle emerged on deck in tears.

This unfolding drama was being played out in public. Seafarer was just one of many yachts moored stern-to against the quay, their crews lounging and chatting in cockpits or up on deck doing the odd bit of light maintenance; they all had front row seats for the action. Things were usually pretty quiet around these itinerant floating suburbs. Realising she was the focus of attention, Michelle got off the boat and went and sat on a nearby bench, still sniffing back her tears.

Despite my aching legs, I kept pumping until the dinghy was inflated to its fullest extent and in danger of bursting if I carried on. I was uncomfortably sweaty and in need of a drink but I was in a quandary about what to do next: I couldn't go below with Bill and 'the other woman' down there; I wondered whether I should talk to Michelle but thought better of it, remembering the hot temper she displayed in the blazing rows that she and Bill had at regular intervals. So I contented myself tinkering aimlessly about on deck and when I looked around I realised that everyone was doing the same thing, all waiting for the next instalment.

After a while, Michelle composed herself and came back aboard, avoiding the cabin, ignoring me and going right up to the bow and out onto the bowsprit, as far from Bill and 'the intruder' as it was possible to get, on a 50-foot boat.

Unable to contain my curiosity, I joined her. 'What's up?' I enquired. 'He's going to sell the boat,' she said curtly. Jointly owned, *Seafarer* had been their dream, but their charter business just wasn't making a profit, and the boat needed lots of work – there had been talk of selling up but now it seemed that Bill, the moment he was left alone, had gone ahead and virtually agreed to sell *Seafarer* to Florence, our bohemian visitor, as-seen, right there and then. Michelle was furious.

As her story tailed off, my eye was caught by something bright green moving in the rigging. Dry Rot. Under cover of all the commotion, or perhaps because of it, he must have snuck from his usual perch in the corner of the cabin, up on deck and into the rigging.

Now, he had alighted on the crosstrees, ten metres up. It seemed he was going to make an undoubtedly long-planned bid for freedom. But had he, in his little bird brain, thought it through?

To limit his range and confine him to the boat, his flight feathers were regularly clipped, rendering his wings incapable of supporting him. But only a few hundred metres away, across the quayside, palm trees swayed enticingly, no doubt rekindling a nebulous sense of nostalgia for a jungle he had once lived in. He shuffled from side to side on his lofty perch, clearly preparing himself for a launch and then, with an almost audible intake of breath, he jumped. At that very same moment, a sharp offshore gust of wind caught him and sent him, not towards the safety of shore, but out over the water of the harbour.

It couldn't really be called a flight, more a controlled descent – but without the control. He was flapping his stubby wings faster and faster with less and less effect, trying to ward off the inevitable. The cruel breeze carried him further and further in the wrong direction, like a weak swimmer in a strong current. Michelle and I looked on transfixed as he splashed heavily into the water, well off our bow and for the second time that day, Michelle's anguished cry rang out, a sound which finally bought Bill lumbering inquisitively up on deck. Following her gaze and desperate pointing, he looked out across the water and, without a moment's hesitation, dived over the side.

As the ensuing tidal wave subsided, he swam strongly forward, covering the not inconsiderable distance with powerful strokes. On reaching the desperately floundering Dry Rot, he grabbed him in one hand and holding the little limp body aloft, kicked strongly back to the boarding ladder. He was a remarkably buoyant man.

With much struggle, Bill clambered back aboard and the bedraggled green scrap was carried reverently below and wrapped in a tea towel advertising Jamaica rum, then laid gently on the cabin table. A wet parrot is a desperately sorry sight. Dry Rot was not a creature of beauty even when he was fully-preened, but I don't think any of us could quite take in how ugly he looked, or how little of him there actually was. He looked like a discarded green dish-mop. His tiny body shivered violently and then he was sick. Sick as a parrot. Finally, with an ominous shudder, he lay still. Bill and Michelle, reunited in grief, made some clumsy attempts to detect a pulse.

Throughout it all, at the head of the table, with an inappropriately beatific smile, sat Florence.

When Dry Rot showed no evidence of vital signs, Michelle sobbed hysterically, at which point, Florence took her moment and arose. 'Allow me,' she said firmly. She scooped up the limp green body and held it to her, whereupon the creature was almost lost from sight, somewhere in her ample bosom. She laid her right hand on him and cocked her head to one side. After a dramatic pause, she breathily announced: 'His aura is weak.' Bill and Michelle looked crestfallen, then more hopeful as she continued: 'But there is still life force within him!' Bill and Michelle gazed at her with imploring, expectant eyes. 'If we all hold hands...'

This was too much for me. From the moment the parrot had been brought back aboard it had been obvious to me that there was only one way this was going to end. The lines from the Monty Python sketch had now firmly taken hold inside my head: He's an ex-parrot. He's shuffled off this mortal coil! He's gone and joined the choir invisibule. Hello Polly! I bit my lip and looked sternly at the floor. If he wasn't nailed to the perch... hysterical laughter was too close to the surface for me to hold back much longer, I'd had enough of this macabre charade. Suppressing a wave of spluttering laughter, I detached myself from the group and made my way up on deck. I emerged into the sunshine and gasped in some air. Outside it was just another beautiful day in paradise. I'd go for a walk, clear my head, get some perspective. I stepped onto the gangplank and glanced down at the quayside. My gaze was met by another pathetic sight – the dinghy had gone flat, all that pumping for nothing. That was the last straw. I decided there and then, that when I got to Australia I'd get work, save my money and go home.

29

Six months later, on the plane, I thought hard about what I wanted to do. Yes, I wanted to design boats, but commercial yacht building seemed a bit decadent. My still idealistic self wanted to do something worthy. I'd become in interested in EF Schumacher's ideas that western aid was not always the answer, and his ethos of 'Appropriate Technology', particularly certain projects which had helped traditional fishing communities regain their boat-building skills. A report by Dr Edwin Gifford in *Design* magazine about such a project he had supervised in southern India had particularly grabbed my attention: I'd actually been carrying the torn-out page around with me for some time. It showed a picture of a boat called a 'Catfish' being sailed against an industrial backdrop by a kindly looking man with white hair and beard. The caption read: 'Catfish, designed by Gifford Technology'. The boat was designed to be built by Indian and African fishing communities.

Not having the qualifications to take a yacht design course I signed up for the 'Yacht and Boatyard Management Course' at Southampton Institute of Higher Technology. This was a sandwich course which included two six-month periods working in the industry for firms of our choice. I had been in Southampton for some time and was coming to the point where I needed to find my first six-month work placement. So far, searching for a job had been a somewhat fruitless experience, then one day I looked again at the faded article. I realised that the industrial site in the picture had to be part of Fawley oil refinery whose huge ugly chimneys, as anyone who has visited the city knows, dominate the head of Southampton Water. Did this mean that Gifford Technology was a local company? Did it even still exist? I looked in the phone book and there it was: Gifford & Partners. I rang the number from a phone box.

'I'm looking for some work which might involve me in foreign projects,' I said.

'Afraid not,' said a genial voice on the end of the phone. 'Those projects only come up occasionally when some funding becomes available. There's nothing at the moment.'

'Oh,' I said, disappointed. 'I read the Catfish article and...'

'Oh, this isn't Catfish,' said the voice. 'This is Griffon Hovercraft.' Griffon Hovercraft? It transpired that I was in fact talking to John Gifford, the MD, who was Dr Gifford's son. We chatted.

'What about getting involved in a project to take a group of doctors to the source of the Yangtze River in China, implementing a vaccination programme along the way?' he suggested.

My heart leapt, then fell again. 'In a hovercraft?' I enquired cautiously.

'Of course,' he replied. 'Hovercraft can go anywhere.'

Two Go Mad
in Sweden

Chapter 3
Two Go Mad in Sweden

John and Russ: Sweden 2012

Fast forward thirty years – thirty years in which John and I had worked all over the world for the same company without ever going on a trip together.

Griffon Hovercraft was a small company which had to grow or shrink depending on the order-book so the people who worked there had to be versatile and adaptable. There was no culture of bloated expense accounts, nobody had a flash company car. Creature comforts meant nothing to JG, our boss, and it didn't occur to him that they were important to anyone else. I discovered this when I accompanied him on a trip to Belgium. He booked us on the 11 o'clock Sunday night ferry, which meant leaving home on Sunday afternoon. True, he did reserve a cabin but as the ferry was due to berth at 4am, we weren't in it for very long. I soon found out that there's not much to do on a wet Monday in Ostend at 4 am and that railway benches are even less comfortable to sleep on than you might suspect. We emerged exhausted, dishevelled and unshaven to find the rain lashing down and a strong wind whipping up the sea. Nevertheless, we had to be ready to carry out acceptance trials for the Belgian Army at 9 o'clock. The terse note at the bottom of the diary entry for this trip reads: *Never let JG make the travel arrangements again.*

This explains why John and I had never gone together on our trips abroad: it was much cheaper to send one person, and over the years we had become accustomed to the need for total self-reliance especially where communication home was impossibly expensive, or just impossible, and resigned to eating alone in restaurants.

With only ten days until Christmas, it is not surprising that there was a bit of a stony silence when JG called us into his office to discuss this latest trip.

'Don't worry,' he said, in the determinedly upbeat tone he always used when trying to convince others, or himself, of a bad idea, 'I'm going to make this a two-man job. You can both go to Sweden then you'll be home by Christmas.' Then the line which really set the alarm bells ringing: 'Anyway, it's a straightforward routine job.'

And thanks to Swedish efficiency, it did begin smoothly enough. A warm Volvo rental car was waiting to take us to the Comfort Hotel in Luleå. If it had been light we would probably have taken pleasure in the rows of tidy red-painted houses flanked by a half a trillion fir trees; but it wasn't light, it was dark and was destined to be dark until spring. At the Coastguard base in Svarton, Luleå the next day, everything was already prepared for us: the hangar was well-heated and the craft, a Griffon 2450 (see appx. 9) was already up on blocks ready for its skirt change.

Luleå lies at the northern end of the Gulf of Bothnia where the coastline is speckled with thousands of little islands. Drive east for an hour and you are in Finland. The smooth ice makes it brilliant hovercraft country, perfect when the ice is not reliably strong enough to support weight. A standard part of the design brief for Coastguard craft was a hatch wide enough through which to manoeuvre a stretcher. The Coastguard told us that the first and last fatalities of the winter are usually snow scooter riders. Sadly, the recovered

bodies were often frozen stiff in the sitting position of their last ride so it would have required a very wide hatch to get them on board; in such cases, they had to be strapped onto the outside of the craft. Most of SCG's boats were ice-bound six months a year and over the years, snow scooters and airboats had been tested as alternatives with limited success. The airboats were vessels with punt-shaped hulls, huge air-propellers and powerful, noisy engines; they had a limited ability to go over land but were not very manoeuvrable. One of the airboats I saw at a coastguard base was equipped with a large block of lumber. When I asked about it, I was told that because these vessels are not very good at going backwards, they often get trapped in dead-ends, such as at the head of a narrow creek. If this happened, the only way to turn them was to lift them up on the block of wood and spin the vessel round until it faced out to sea. So they turned to hovercraft instead, trialling them in arduous conditions over many terrains. The crews loved them because they were comfortable and quiet; they could easily tackle most ice and sea conditions. It was a kind of one-stop solution, like having a boat they could use year-round.

The first morning passed uneventfully enough. We set about dismantling the old skirt-shift with no more trouble than might be expected. Leaving the Coastguard base for the one and only occasion we managed to escape for lunch, we were able to see the area properly for the first time. Svarton means 'black town' which probably has a lot to do with its coal-mining past. It is the dock area of Luleå, bristling with machinery and crisscrossed by rail lines. Pylons, cranes and gantries silhouette the sky. Huge ships carrying coal, steel and scrap metal come across the Gulf of Bothnia and dock among the ice-breakers. At this, the darkest time of year, the bio-power station and a chemical factory are darker smudges in a smoky sky across which a huge conveyor belt in continuous use creaks and groans, clattering overhead as it transports coal across the docks. Every so often this background noise is punctuated by a crashing boom as another load of scrap metal is dropped into a vast ringing hold. In an almost entirely white wintry landscape, here and there darker spots of land, devoid of snow, steam gently and mysteriously in the half light.

The afternoon did not go quite as well as the morning. It must be understood that any work with hovercraft has its own particular problems. The space beneath the craft is limited and tight, and it's a mysterious yet well-known fact that it gets tighter as the years go by. Skirts are made of black rubber. Every small movement requires a big effort: manoeuvring on one's back from one part of the skirt assembly to another, the rubber grips at you in a tiresome clingy embrace. None of this was anything new, but something about our mind-set on this job seemed to make all of these usual difficulties worse.

'You know, I think I'm getting too old for this,' said John at one point. I was glad to hear him admit it because the same idea had been going through my mind too. A little downhearted, but not yet despondent, we decided to call an end to our day's labour, driving back to the Comfort Hotel through the quiet streets, made quieter still by a fresh blanket of snow. By five o'clock, it had already been dark for three hours.

That night we discovered another fine Swedish thing - the Bishop's Arms. This was an 'English' pub more English than any left in England, full to bursting with jolly Swedish families celebrating the beginning of the Christmas holidays. The hot food, beer and conviviality restored our spirits. Tomorrow would be better.

But it wasn't.

For reasons now forgotten, an experimental skirt-shift had been fitted on this craft but as it had failed to live up to expectations, one of our main jobs was to replace it with a more conventional system. It seemed determined not to go quietly. Old stuff wouldn't come off; new stuff wouldn't go on; the struts were in the way and needed refitting. Every tool seemed to lie maddeningly out of reach; the garrotting wires which connect the segments seemed to entangle themselves incessantly and malevolently around arms and legs so you were always on the wrong side of them. Then of course protective clothes and equipment always come at a price: gloves are particularly annoying, kneepads slip and twist, goggles steam up.

There was a time when I had found it exciting to take on difficult things and overcome problems like these – there had even been some strange masochistic satisfaction in pitting my wits against the problems these sorts of expeditions threw up. It was too depressing to put my change of heart down to age – Mick Jagger was doing alright, after all – but I had to admit that I had recently been spending a lot of time at my desk, sometimes not even venturing down to the workshop from one week to another. Now here in Sweden, I was paying the price.

This was the beginning of a dispiriting run of days: each started bad and grew worse; darkness came earlier, we worked longer and left the base later in the evening. Hands grew sorer, aches and pains spread to new and surprising areas. Our spells of respite in the Bishop's Arms grew shorter and more taciturn. But it was the curses that flourished the most – always impressively varied they became more frequent, more vehement and more creative every day. It is possible that a whole repertoire of new and untried swear words was born in the *Kustbevakningen*. (Note: this is not a swear word; it is Swedish for 'coastguard'.)

What made it worse was that every piece in our kit of parts required some modification – brackets, for instance, needed to be drilled off and re-welded meaning a trip to the friendly local shipyard most days, which gave one of us a welcome break but wasted time we didn't have. After a while, we did manage to achieve a brutal sort of rhythm: once the first side was done, the second was easier. After another day's solid graft, we had the new hydraulic pump fitted. Micke, Chief Engineer at the Coastguard Base, had been visiting every day to make sure we had all we needed and generally to help out where possible. Coastguards, not surprisingly, are a particularly unflappable breed for whom an inevitable part of the job is killing time and Micke did not seem bothered about our slow progress. He even loaned us a skinny, lank-haired recruit from Kalix called Olaf, whom we nicknamed 'Olaf a minute' due to his dour disposition.

Eventually the skirt was properly on but we still hadn't tested it out. Late afternoon is not an ideal time to start trials, but we had no choice and as it turned out we were barely half way through our working day anyway. As we had both secretly suspected, the existing pump was not man enough for the new system. It did its best but it soon became evident that it was overheating like mad. Okay, for 'overheating', read 'melting'. The problem was, we couldn't get to the pressure-relief-valve adjustment screw, a component which was so inaccessible and in such a tight corner that even a double-jointed conger eel would have struggled. Olaf was the nearest human equivalent, but even hanging upside down, rather unwillingly, he was unable to reach it.

We sent the lad home and worked on and on, trying different solutions, putting off the dreadful moment when we would have to admit that the only way to get round the problem was to undo a whole day's work and take the pump out again. As afternoon (which, let's face it, would be called 'night' anywhere else) turned to evening and the long evening wore on, despite being already on the highest level of expletive output, no curse or profanity seemed to quite hit the spot. Meltdown was finally precipitated by my obstinately stupid decision, against John's firm advice, to try to use an ancient angle-grinder to cut a piece of bar. This would not have been a problem but for the fact that I could only find oversized cutting discs which didn't really fit. What does one do in such a situation? It's obvious – take off the safety guard. In a hurry and a thoroughly bad mood, I switched the machine on and promptly ground what felt like several layers of skin from my knuckles. It hurt. I swore.

I swore at a level I had never sworn at before. It was as if all previous swearing had been a mere rehearsal for this outpouring, this tirade of incoherent ranting. I harangued all hovercraft, individually and collectively, and their very invention. As the red mist cleared, I became aware that John was standing stock-still and staring at me open-mouthed.

'My God, what have you done?' he asked.

I looked down at my hand which looked remarkably normal, slightly grazed but still possessing four fingers and a thumb. 'Nothing,' I said, surprised. 'But it hurt.'

'Let's have a cup of tea,' said John, using the same tone of voice one might use when confronting an escaped mass-murderer in a woodshed. 'A nice cup of tea and a chocolate biscuit...'

A fragile calm had fallen over us by the time Micke arrived. He quickly made a cool appraisal of the situation and said two counter-intuitive things: 'Cut a hole in the hull' and 'Take tomorrow off' but as soon as he uttered them, we knew he was right on both counts. Admittedly, we were tired and shaken enough to agree to anything – if he had said: 'What you need to do is strip naked and wrestle this moose to the floor,' the chances are we would not have argued.

Take – tomorrow – off. The three short words sent a rush of joy through me. To celebrate, we drove back to Luleå and the respite of the Comfort Hotel and used the basement facilities to do our washing.

If you were beginning to think that the life of a hovercraft engineer is not all glamour, your suspicions are now probably confirmed.

'Let's go and look for the Arctic Circle,' said John the next morning.

It sounded like a reasonable suggestion. After all, what else does one do on an unexpected day off in the far north of Sweden in the depths of winter?

To be honest, I had been thinking along the lines of something less strenuous: lots of sleeping interspersed with a little eating, all preferably indoors. However, reasoning that the opportunity might not come again, we turned to the Wikipedia entry for a destination to put into the satnav. The Arctic Circle apparently has no post-code but its latitude is 66° 33' 44" north, although this is not constant as it seems that it moves around a bit, currently drifting northwards at a speed of about 15m per year. So it was that, in an intrepid mood, blinking in the first 'daylight' we had seen for a long time, we set off on a quest to track it down.

It was already snowing heavily, more heavily than I had ever seen myself, a fact I remarked to John.

'Yes,' he said. 'Imagine this in England – the whole country would be at a standstill. The Swedes don't let a bit of snow put them off getting on with things.' We were soon bowling along the empty roads, both in agreement that this was the perfect day to go and look for the Arctic Circle. And no traffic! We found a heavy-metal station on the radio and turned it up loud.

Sweden has lots of trees. I thought this to myself as we motored on along the empty roads. Trees, trees and more trees. More trees than people. More pine needles than grains of sand. We drove for long stretches of road which looked exactly like the last long stretch of road. Sometimes there was a bend. Our game of I-Spy was over very quickly.

After a while, I realised that we had been silent and concentrating hard for a long time. John had turned off the radio. Neither of us liked to voice what we were thinking: that the weather was deteriorating

quickly. Indeed, the outside world had suddenly turned into a disturbing optical illusion, a mesmerising vortex of whiteness, sucking you in. The wipers slapped time as the snow fell. And fell and fell. The grey day with its low ceiling of cloud had closed into darkness even though it was still early afternoon.

John cleared his throat. 'Getting a bit heavier – the snow.'

'Mm.'

'Really coming down now.'

'Hm.'

'Those wipers are certainly working overtime.'

'Can't – see – that – well, actually.'

'Whoaaa... bit slippy. That's better, facing the right way now.'

'Is that the road?'

'Er, no, think that bit's... not road. Hard to see.'

I swallowed as I remembered the dramatic description of a Force 10 sea-state I had once read in *The Boys' Book of Weather*: 'Impossible to distinguish sea from sky.' Ever after, it held a fascination which still struck fear in my heart.

'Rough tough types, these Swedes, guess they're used to these conditions.'

'Haven't seen many actually.'

'Many...?'

'Swedes. You know – driving about.'

'No... At church maybe.'

'What's that?' John was about to explain about churches when something ahead loomed out of the whiteness. Something that wasn't white!

'God, what's that?'

'Better stop, maybe.'

'I am stopping.'

Indeed, I could see John's foot firmly on the brake but not much was happening on the stopping front. The whirling white veil cleared a little to reveal the startling splash of colour getting nearer, coalescing into a vehicle straight out of *Monster Machines*, tons of hard, bright metal, lights flashing, and now some people, another vehicle, a car... still we were slithering and I could see that John's face was another white thing in a white landscape, entirely white except for the huge thing ahead of us.

Our car came to a gentle gliding near-halt metres from the scene. We could see a Saab crumpled against a tree. The big coloured splash of red and yellow was a snow-plough as large as a small barn and beside it stood a little knot of people watching gloomily as the driver attached a tow-bar to the stricken dinky toy. We could understand none of the impenetrable language but I think I worked out the gist of what they were saying.

'Terrible conditions.'

'Dreadful. I only risked it because we'd completely run out of food and the children were crying. I had no choice.'

'Same here. If my old dad hadn't needed to attend his vital hospital appointment, I would be happily indoors toasting my toes on the fire. No-one but a fool would willingly go out in this atrocious weather.'

By now John was executing a 12-point turn with extreme caution, without eye contact and humming a little – always a bad sign. One of the women nodded in our direction. '*Hej*, do you think those two are English?'

'They have an English look about them. I wonder what terrible emergency has befallen them to venture out in that base model Volvo. Shall we...'   We can only guess the end of the conversation because by then we were gingerly trundling back the way we had come. How could we have justified our folly? 'Madam, myself and my colleague are here on an emergency hovercraft expedition to relocate the Arctic Circle. It has drifted 49ft in the last year and is in danger of slipping off altogether. If the world was not in peril, believe me, we would be sitting by the fire in the Bishop's Arms.'

Leaving the accident behind us, we passed a sign which said Jokkmokk 40km and I mentally made a note to add it to the list of strange place-names I had been collecting over the decades. Deadhorse in Alaska had been at the top for some time, recently toppled by the delightful Normalville in Pennsylvania, but four 'K's in one word had to be impressive. Just then, I caught a glimpse of a more welcome sign, in English too, which proclaimed jauntily:

'Welcome to Sven's Restaurant and Cabins!'

John slowed.

'Traditional Swedish Restaurant!' it read. At last, a refuge in the storm. We drew onto the forecourt then stepped out of the whiteness into a cosy wood-panelled interior where a wood-burning stove blazed next to a Christmas tree. Otherwise, there was no sign of life unless you counted the moose heads and photos of bearded men posing proudly with large dead fish. Perhaps it was the cold or delayed shock of the near collision but, not for the first time in my life, a surreal feeling swept over me. How did we end up here? It was as if a random hand had dropped me from the sky and gone 'Oops! Oh, well, never mind.'

'Looks a bit empty,' remarked John. 'Could murder a coffee.'

'Coffee or not, I'm not going back out there until it stops,' I said. Despite my low mood, the view outside was beautiful, a Christmas card snow-scene with big soft flakes fluttering against a backdrop of fir trees whose branches were picked out by the swinging lights. But I still felt miserable and homesick. The job which still awaited us back at the coastguard base was far from finished. It had already seemed like a huge enough obstacle standing between me and home, now here we were snowbound in the middle of nowhere.

'Aha,' said John. 'That sounds more promising.' From the murky depths of a long corridor we heard footsteps approaching. Could this be Sven himself? I knew very little Swedish apart from a few emergency phrases, including the term for coffee and cake – *fika* – and I was prepared to use it. There was no need: most Swedes have an English-Detector mode in their heads and Sven's had just lit up at the sight of us.

'Hello gentlemen, I see you have got caught out in the storm. Did you set out before the weather warnings were issued? Due to the terrible conditions, and the advice that everyone should stay indoors, I am afraid I did not expect many customers so my menu is limited. But I can offer you...'

'*Fika?*' I asked hopefully.

'Indeed. Would that be okay?'

We assured him that it would and sat down in the corner by the stove and looked out on the blizzard, feeling quite cosy now we were not in it. And when sitting before a blazing log fire with snow falling outside, what else can one do but reminisce?

'The winter of 1990,' said John. 'Do you remember? I still think the coldest place I have ever been was on that slipway on the Itchen.'

'You take this one and I'll take the other'

Chapter 4
'You take this one and I'll take the other.'

John: Thailand 1991

Standing on the dockside in Bangkok in the spring of 1991, I watched a pair of hovercraft being lowered by crane into the sluggish brown water of the Chao Phraya River. I had known these craft since they were just a twinkle in a designer's eye and I couldn't but help feel a sense of proprietary pride at the sight of them now – fully-fledged, sleek and powerful, ready to make the final leg of the journey. The freezing, bleak winter wastes of the River Itchen could not have seemed further away.

The winter of 1990-91 had been a hard one, and not just in the meteorological sense. As a newcomer, there had been times when it had seemed to me that this hovercraft lark was nothing like I'd imagined – rather than swanning off to find the source of the Yangtze (an expedition which had happened, but without me) I found myself plunged into managing a brand-new project - a lucrative order for two twin-engine 30-seater Griffon 3000TDs (see appx. 10), our biggest craft to date. It was a prestigious contract with future orders depending on its success, so from the very start, I'd had to learn quickly.

The snag was that Griffon's pokey workshop, barely more than a barn in the New Forest, was neither big enough, nor well enough equipped to build craft of this size. Luckily however, the remnants of a hovercraft industry from an earlier age still existed around the Solent. Hovermarine had premises in Southampton and Hoverwork had a maintenance and construction facility on the Isle of Wight. Hovercraft plied their way across the Solent and, along the coast at Dover, the huge SRN4s carried cars and hundreds of passengers across the Channel to France. Favours were easy to pull in. A plan came together: Griffon would build one craft using the Hovermarine workshops and the other would be built by Hoverwork.

Griffon was a small company, but it was rich in enthusiasm, talent and ideas. The team was inventive and versatile, a small group of hard-working and committed souls. The design department was John Gifford, the MD, and Malcolm Cox, an independent consultant and brilliant engineer who was an expert in fan, propeller and skirt design, while Russ and I worked as detail designers and draftsmen. In the workshop, we also had good people: a GRP mould-maker, a mechanic and an electrician. But this was not enough: we needed more skilled people, so we set to hiring metal fabricators, welders, outfitters, painters and all the trades-people for whom jobs were scarce at the time.

Hazel Road in Woolston used to be a tatty place, the unfashionable end of Southampton: boatyards and car repair workshops cheek by jowl with big, anonymous industrial units, hemmed in between the Itchen River and the railway line. The rutted road was always busy with trucks and fork-lifts. In the middle of it all, rising up in decaying art-deco splendour was the old Vickers Supermarine works, a massive hangar built for manufacturing Spitfires during the Second World War. This was where we rented workspace for the duration of the project. Ten years previously Hovermarine, who occupied half of the huge yard, had been in its heyday, building dozens of sidewall hovercraft, many of which were still operating in Hong Kong harbour. Now the huge shed was almost empty and down at heel.

Russ, as well as doing most of the drawings, was more or less running the rest of the show. The first craft was to be built to a very tight schedule and as a result, and as ever when time is short, we were up against it, every day a fresh challenge to face and something new to learn.

After a few weeks working on the design, the aluminium hull was delivered to the Hovermarine premises. It was built by a specialist fabricator in the Isle of Wight and had been floated across to the mainland. Russ and I drove over to have a look. In the middle of the big dark space, the shiny metal hull stood like a gleaming beacon, something new amongst the grime and decay. I felt naively optimistic, excited to start building. I had yet to learn that every build is simply a series of problems to solve – some of our own making, many due to elements beyond our control – all of this exacerbated by the tight deadline of the shipping date.

Part of my role was overseeing and co-ordinating the newly-hired workers and making sure they always had enough to do. Among the sundry characters who were taken on for the duration of the build was a laminator called Stuart. I had picked up early on that laminators are of a particular breed – maybe because their work is difficult and monotonous; the materials of their trade are sticky, itchy and unpleasant and give off noxious fumes. The saying goes, 'If you can urinate, you can laminate but not everyone can piss straight'. Given all he had to put up with, perhaps it's not surprising that Stuart had a gloomy disposition and always wore the same lugubrious expression – except, that is, when the ancient telephone rang, which it did regularly throughout the day with endless calls from suppliers and sub-contractors.

The entire workforce was alerted to an incoming call by a loud bell, installed high on the wall at one end of the vast echoing hangar which, when it rang, easily drowned out the low hum of industry below. No-one within that workplace, even those using the noisiest tools in the remotest parts, were unaware of a call. Despite this, the bell was to Stuart what a bolt of lightning was to Frankenstein's monster: on the first ring, he came to life and using a tone not dissimilar to a ship's fog-horn, but many times louder, helpfully bellowed 'Telephone!'

It was always me, when in the middle of something else, who had to drop what I was doing, run from wherever I was in the workshop, through two pairs of double doors, outside and into the scruffy Portacabin which served as the Griffon office, in a desperate bid to reach it before it stopped ringing. I'd grab the phone and breathlessly intone 'Griffon Hovercraft, how can I help you?' in most cases only to be greeted the dial tone. I found Stuart such an immense source of irritation that I was almost provoked to violence had he not been six inches taller than me and a lot wider. Many years later I'm still traumatised by loud ringing bells and involuntarily start running when I hear them.

After three months of hard work, the sea-trials were due to start, and we were making a last concerted effort to get everything ready. With the customer, the owner of a Thai bus company, scheduled to inspect the craft the next day we were, as usual, working right up to the wire, well into the evening on a wintry Sunday. It was already dark when we made the decision to take the craft out on the water. The huge hangar doors were rolled open and the craft moved under its own power for the first time. It was towed out into the gathering gloom, across the yard to the slipway. With JG at the controls, the hovercraft set off down-river, when as if on cue, a heavy downpour obscured it from our sight.

Russ and I were just about to trudge back to the shelter of the hangar when something caught our eye. Squinting into the darkness through the rain, we could see the craft emerge again, heading back towards us – slowly – something was wrong. As it drew nearer, we realised that one engine had stopped and instantly foresaw that it would be a struggle to get the craft onto the slipway and back into the workshop.

JG is probably the best hovercraft driver there is, but as the nose mounted the slipway the wind and tide suddenly joined forces, took hold of the back end of the craft and slewed it sideways, leaving the front on the concrete and the rear hanging over the edge, the skirt flapping ineffectually. The escaping lift air blew a fine muddy spray high into the drizzly air, but the craft would no longer lift: it was well and truly stuck, and with the tide still dropping, we would have a long wait until the water returned and it would be able to hover again.

Defeated, wet, cold and muddy, we retreated to the shelter of the workshop. It wasn't until the small hours of the morning that nature relented its assault on us. The wind dropped a little, coinciding with the rising tide which gave us the opportunity to move the craft back onto the slipway and above the high-water mark.

This last-minute set-back was devastating: not only was the customer already in town and looking forward to a ride in their brand-new craft but they were to be accompanied by the Lloyds' surveyor. At first light, Russ and I were back, trying to work out exactly what had gone wrong. We began with the premise that there was probably a loose connection somewhere on the fuel system. But was it air leaking in or fuel leaking out? A drip of fuel is visible but air being pulled in is harder to spot. Either way, a lot of detective work would be needed.

The stormy Sunday night became a miserable Monday morning, still cold and raining, with a brisk wind whipping up the river. The craft had ended up in an exposed position far from any shelter or electricity, but it was the furthest we could get up the slipway for the time being. We rigged up a tarpaulin and set to, systematically working through the fuel system, checking and tightening the dozens of fittings and connections in an attempt to track down the leak. All the while, the tarp tugged and rattled furiously above our heads and our fingers were soon numb from handling cold steel tools.

With the customer due to arrive at any minute and no obvious fault to be found, we came to realise that we would have to pressure-test the entire system. This is an involved and difficult process, even in a warm, dry workshop. At the end of a freezing slipway it became a feat of determination and ingenuity. We would need power and a supply of compressed air for the test so, as the various garages and engineering workshops in Hazel Road started their working week, we begged, borrowed and scrounged a ragged daisy-chain of air-lines and power cables until we reached the stricken craft, all the time looking out for the customer. This wasn't the way we had planned it to be.

By mid-morning, just as we had everything set-up, the big Jag belonging to Graham, our Sales Director, pulled up at the top of the slip. Inside were the customer, his family, and the marine surveyor. JG followed on in his Land Rover. The group alighted from the cars and made a dash for the craft. Direct from tropical Thailand, the customer's party looked pinched with cold, their smart clothes affording no protection from the grim English winter as they came gingerly down the slipway towards us.

We kept our heads down while Graham took over the situation like a true pro. Loftily ignoring the flapping tarpaulin at the back of the craft and the furtive, greasy-handed pair crawling around under it, he explained it was far too unpleasant to take the craft out, and besides, there were still a few minor adjustments to be made. With extravagant gestures he jovially ushered the party into the cabin out of the rain, where he demonstrated the comfy seats and bright fabrics... and here was the delightful little galley, where the crew could prepare hot drinks for the passengers.

Although Graham's magic worked on the customers who had little interest in the mechanics of the craft, only a fool would try to charm a marine surveyor. His expertise was not in hovercraft, but in ships

and he knew the rule books back to front. During the build he had made his regular visits. 'This is not the way ships are built,' he would chide us, shining his ever-present torch onto some notably un-shipshape item. But, we would reason, hovercraft are not ships.

We tried to look very preoccupied as he emerged from the cabin and sauntered towards the back. 'Everything OK back here?' he enquired. The tarp flogged violently as an icy blast whipped up the river. 'Fine!' we cheerfully replied in unison, biting our lips and keeping our heads down, studiously avoiding his beady eye. 'What are you up to then?' he continued. We kept working and mumbled in non-committal terms: 'Just checking things over.' The grim weather finally worked in our favour as the thick drizzle turned to heavy rain, sending him scuttling back to the shelter of the cabin before he could do any more probing or questioning.

Over the next couple of days, we learned that the end of the slipway on the Itchen River is without doubt the coldest place on earth. While the rest of the country was merely cold, down on the hovercraft a unique micro-climate prevailed. The gale constantly whipping down the channel sent the wind chill factor off the scale. The work went slowly as we had several hundred yards to walk between the craft and the workshop. Every forgotten tool or spare part meant a long, icy trudge.

'I'm going back for the torque wrench and I may be some time,' Russ would say as he set out, bent into the wind like an Arctic explorer. It was so cold we wore two hats. This became our measure of temperature. When people asked what it was like, we'd say: 'It's a two hatter!'

On the second morning the gales had abated only to be replaced by plunging sub-zero temperatures. The entire craft was frozen, the decks covered with deep frost and the water-pipes in the galley had burst. As if we didn't have a big enough problem, now another thing to repair.

Eventually though, we were ready to test the system. We gave it an hour, and there was no drop in pressure and, following a short sea-trial, no engine cut-outs. Success! Even though there had been no moment of truth or epiphany where we'd been able to point accusingly at the problem part, we believed the fault was cured.

As the launch day for the second craft was looming, we began to spend more time on the Duver in Hovertravel's workshop on the Isle of Wight. This involved many days of commuting using their commercial hovercraft ferry service from Southsea to Ryde. On yet another wintry evening, we'd had a long day making last minute adjustments and setting up the craft's systems. It grew so late that neither of us felt it was worth making the journey home to the mainland when we would need to be back again in a few hours. All being well, we would be returning to Southampton the next day in the new craft. Nevertheless, we were badly in need of some warmth and sustenance. Then one of the lads from Hovertravel told us about a B&B within walking distance.

As we knocked on the door, like all travellers before us, we felt hopeful of finding the simple pleasures of a hot meal, a cosy fire and a comfortable bed. But the owner was clearly one of those people who has been forced against his will into the hospitality industry when his true calling was to any walk of life where your purpose is to make people feel unwelcome - a nightclub bouncer or a traffic warden, perhaps. Yes, he had vacancies, he admitted grudgingly. He would let us two rooms but the terms were tough: cash up front, no eating in the room and, although we would be gone before breakfast, we paid the same rate as if it was B&B rather than just B. Pooling our cash we managed to scrape together £11.43 which fell woefully short of the over-inflated price. Yes, it had to be cash in advance. Was there a cashpoint machine nearby? Yes, in Cowes, ten miles away which isn't nearby in any respect but especially on the Isle of Wight, which is only 26 miles long anyway. With no transport of our own we borrowed the Hovertravel van and drove halfway across the island to discover the cashpoint was out of order. Never mind, there was another one a couple of miles further on. By this time, everything else was closed, not even a pub to be found, all closing their doors early on account of Sunday hours. I daresay all the Isle of Wighters were already tucked up in bed. Our friendly landlord made a point of telling us that if we'd come five minutes later, he would have been, for sure. By the time we were shown to our quarters, we had given up any idea of food. The cosy fire was also a non-starter; instead, we resigned ourselves to the chill of the dull, unheated rooms, grateful that we at least had a bed. A lumpy one.

Finally, by mid-morning the next day, everything was finished and we were ready to go. We looked forward to a pleasant, uneventful crossing back to Southampton in our own craft – surely, we were due some plain sailing? But as soon as we left Bembridge Harbour we ran into thick fog. Since there was no radar on the craft, good old-fashioned 'eyeball' navigating would be required. We decided to go on, slowly hugging the shore, cautiously peering through the fog, keeping the land close to our left. Approaching Ryde, we joked about colliding with the Hovertravel ferry. Ha ha – wouldn't that be just typical?

Russ checked his watch. 'Actually...'

There was a Hovertravel timetable on the dashboard. I quickly flicked through it.

'When's it due?' Russ asked.

'Er - about now,' I replied, just as a familiar rumble, distant but growing louder, was heard.

We slowed to a crawl and opened the windows.

'Sounds close,' I said, my voice a little higher than usual. Tense and silent, we tried to locate its position, looking everywhere at once but seeing only a dull grey curtain of fog. The sound grew louder and louder. Was it in front of us or behind? It was impossible to tell, but it was getting very close.

'Oh, look, there it is,' Russ squeaked. The big craft passed right ahead of us. We felt some relief to actually see it, but maybe not at quite such close quarters. It was near enough for us to make eye-contact with the surprised passengers who happened to be looking out the window at that moment. We could only stare dumbly as it quickly disappeared again and imagine the conversations on board:

'Did you see that?'

'I thought I did... a hovercraft? Smaller than this one? It just sort of loomed out of the mist and... melted away.'

'Two ghostly figures aboard, their expressions fixed, faces unnaturally white.'

'Could it be... a ghost hovercraft? You know the sort of thing - endlessly hovering around the Isle of Wight, never coming to land, only momentarily visible when the sea-fog rolls in from the west.' The passengers shook their heads at the thought – it was too awful to contemplate. As if the daily commute wasn't bad enough.

After Ryde pier, we turned and made for the mainland, cautiously crossing the shipping channels until we suddenly burst out of the fog into the bright sunshine of a glittering new world. Leaving the Isle of

Wight somewhere behind us, still swallowed in the mist, we opened the throttles and headed smoothly into Southampton Water.

JG had the other craft out on the river and for a while we had two identical craft running alongside each other in the sunshine. Russ and I looked over at 'our' craft. It was a fine-looking thing, we felt proud: our months of hard work had really paid off.

Weeks later in Bangkok, it felt like a different world as I stood and watched the crane lower the first craft into the river. Despite the industrial setting, everything felt warm and exotic. A colourful butterfly landed on the holstered gun of the security guard. Life was good.

At the start of this, my very first trip abroad with Griffon, I had been told: 'Miles is going to do all the driving and you'll just help out'. This was good – Miles Rosko was an old hand, a bit of a maverick, tall and imposing, every inch the experienced pilot. The heavy tweed jacket he wore may have been rather scruffy and from a bygone era, but when he spoke, he sounded like a BBC announcer from the 1940s. Integral to Miles was the pipe clamped permanently between his teeth which caused his eyebrows to dance up and down with every word as if they were on separate strings. Hovercraft filled just one of the many compartments of his life: he spent months at a time at his remote croft in the Highlands where he periodically went walk-about, traipsing alone through the countryside, sometimes for weeks on end.

Over the years, we'd employed him from time to time and when he came to Southampton he lived in an old green van in the car-park which you entered at your own risk, so noxious were the fumes of Rough Cut Shag. Once the craft was engaged in sea trials in Southampton, he had arrived and taken up residence in order to familiarise himself with the new craft.

One day he decided we needed some additional equipment on board, so he and I took the company car out for a tour of local chandlers. During the trip we drove by a motorbike shop and he suddenly insisted we stop, 'I need to buy a motorbike' he proclaimed, like it had suddenly occurred to him that he could no longer live without one. We went into the glossy showroom and Miles went straight over to the top-of-the range BMW tourer, a very expensive machine. He pondered the gleaming bike while lighting his pipe and made appreciative mumblings, accompanied by a lot of eyebrow action. He was clearly smitten.

The salesman spotted us and came over. 'You're not allowed to smoke in here, sir,' he proclaimed officiously.

Miles slowly turned to face him, took a deep puff on his pipe, took it from his mouth and using the stem as a pointer said, 'How much for this one?' The salesman must have sensed that this was a serious enquiry and made no more mention of the smoking policy. He started explaining that this show-model had a number of expensive extras fitted and another would take a couple of week's delivery. Unfazed, Miles persisted, 'But how much for this one?'

Nonplussed, the salesman blurted out a very high figure. Miles reached inside his jacket and drew out his cheque book. 'I'd like to pick it up tomorrow.' There was a moment of silence, then the salesman gathered himself. 'Of course, sir.' He managed to maintain his professional veneer as we left the shop but no doubt there were high-fives and whoops of joy once we had gone.

The next day Miles rode into the yard astride his new steed, dressed in new boots, jacket and helmet. Protruding beneath the visor, clamped between determined jaws, was his pipe.

Now standing here chatting with him in Bangkok, I realised to my surprise that the crane driver had started to lift the second craft. 'Is this right?' I said, although Miles probably knew less than I did about the logistics of the trip. 'We were going to launch one at a time.'

Miles shrugged. 'Well, I'd say it was too late for that, wouldn't you?' The second craft was already swinging over the water. We could only watch as the crane driver placed it gently in the river

where it bobbed about, gleaming in the sun, looking good. 'Here we go then,' said Miles. 'You take this one and I'll take the other.'

In the moment it took for the implications of this to sink in, Miles was already claiming the first craft. A knot of fear took hold of my stomach. My inner self started to bluster self-righteously. 'Excuse me, but this isn't what I was told to expect,' it wanted to say. 'I'm supposed to be the crew.' But it was no good – events were moving swiftly. With the two craft unloaded and taking up valuable quay space, they needed to be moved immediately, no choice.

I found myself breathing steadily, trying to calm my nerves. I could do this, it would be OK... After all, I had been driving hovercraft on and off for a while by then, having been introduced to the black art soon after joining Griffon. I was given lessons in the peculiarities of craft operation and its esoteric phrases. The emphasis on 'trim'. The mysterious 'hump speed' and the importance of staying 'over hump'. The mention of the ominous 'plough-in' and the need to avoid it at all costs. All this gave the impression of a unique skill, something completely beyond any experience of handling cars and boats. Something which would take a long time to learn.

But on the first occasion I'd driven one of these Thai craft on trials in the Solent, everything started to fall into place. This was more like it! Unlike the twitchy, nervous smaller craft I had wrestled with before, these big twin-engine machines felt stable and benign. I began to relax and enjoy it and feel this was something I could master. Whenever the work schedule allowed, Russ would let me take the controls on our regular trips across to Bembridge to supervise the construction of the second craft. Once he had done the skilful part of getting off the slipway and down the Itchen River, out in open water, I would take the controls and drive the straight line across to the island. Russ would then retake the controls for entering the harbour and landing on the tricky slipway at the Duver.

But I was still a novice and now this was for real, a brand-new hovercraft on a river crowded with every type of vessel imaginable... and where were we going? On the river Chao Phraya there is nowhere to park a hovercraft and it isn't good to leave them afloat for too long. They are lightly built and the rubber skirt, when not inflated, hangs in the water like a heavy black curtain. This causes a lot of drag and collects any junk floating by. Ideally, they should be driven out of the water and parked on dry land. But here the banks were all taken up with private docks and buildings and no unoccupied space, let alone a slipway. The only place the customer had been able to find for us to stay overnight was 20 kilometres up river, through the city, where we would moor alongside a big motor yacht belonging to an American friend of the owner. The craft would be afloat, true, but up there the river was calmer and less busy. I told myself it would be fine: we would cover that distance in an hour at the most, before dark.

We set off as the sun was getting low, me following Miles line-astern. At first the river was wide and straight and the going was easy. I started to relax. We cruised along past the docks lined with ships from around the world with containers and cargo loading and unloading. I felt comfortable and in control. The industrial landscape thinned out as we left the docks and approached the city where densely packed wooden houses now lined the shore. Big ships gave way to smaller craft and the river-traffic got denser. Brightly coloured long-tail boats were the local mode of water-transport, ranging from personal craft to water buses. These were basically long covered canoes powered by a car engine mounted on the stern, driving the boat with a long external propeller shaft amongst long lines of heavily loaded barges, pulled by stocky little tugs, chugging up and down. Second-guessing where they were headed and how to navigate between them was a constant challenge, but an enjoyable one. It was fun, an adventure.

The two hovercraft were to be used as ferries to Ko Samui, a holiday island off Surat Thani in the gulf of Thailand. At this time Ko Samui had an extremely polarised clientele. At one end of the scale were young, mostly Aussie and American back-packers who were content to take the long bus journey south from Bangkok to Surat Thani, and then catch the crowded local ferry boats out to the island, where they stayed at cheap hostels, spending their days on the beach and nights in the bars and clubs. At the other end were the well-to-do visitors, who either chartered a boat or came aboard their own yachts. They stayed in the more upmarket resort hotels at the other end of the island.

The bus company, whose owner had visited us on that dismal wintry day in Woolston, had come up with a third way to reach the island, thus increasing the commercial potential of the resort. Arriving at Bangkok, visitors would take the short internal flight to Surat Thani, where they would be transferred to the hovercraft by air-conditioned bus, then whisked out to the beach nearest to their hotel. As we went smoothly up the river, it occurred to me that piloting these craft would be a pretty good job to have.

Just as this thought entered my head, the craft slewed sharply to one side and slowed down rapidly. I wrestled with the steering as

Miles kept going, pulling into the distance, unaware of my plight. Boats poured into the growing gap between us until I lost sight of him altogether. I felt panicky, filled with an ominous sense of deja-vu. I grabbed the radio.

'The bloody port engine's stopped!' I told him.

'We have to keep going,' came the calm reply. 'I'll cut my speed and keep just ahead of you to clear the way. Do what you can.'

So on we went, Miles patiently leading me along at a crawl which caused both craft to send up billowing plumes of spray. Having only one engine running meant not just that the craft would go very slowly but was also pulling strongly one way. Only by holding the steering hard over would the craft go in a straight line. Turning to starboard was very slow and unpredictable but turning to port was just a case of letting go.

The long lines of barges we had overtaken earlier now started to overtake us. The sun set just as we approached the centre of the city. Tropical darkness fell quickly and Bangkok lit up with bright street lights and coloured neon signs which reflected off the water. Seen through the spray-soaked windscreen of the hovercraft, everything merged into a brightly coloured mess. The river had now become more winding and much busier. Numerous ferries criss-crossed our path, adding to the confusion.

The International Maritime Organisation has strict rules regarding the lights vessels should show at night. This enables you to identify the size, direction and purpose of other vessels. In Bangkok, none of these rules applied. A row of approaching multi-coloured fairy lights turned out to be a tug towing several hundred yards of barges. The flashing jumble of green to starboard resolved itself into a neon sign which proclaimed 'Club Zodiac'. The thing with flashing blue and orange lights was a souped-up long-tail, which came zipping up, checked us out, then disappeared among the floating flower barges. I felt exhausted from the effort of concentration I had to expend to work out what was land, what was reflection and what was moving on the water.

As we crawled along and after a few close calls, I remembered the intermittent nature of the fault we thought we had cured back in England. Was it still that? I tried restarting the dead engine - it burst into life immediately - hooray! We sped through the teeming city, once again under full control and able to manoeuvre at will – until after about 15 minutes the engine spluttered and stopped again. We slowed back down to walking pace. Disappointing, but at least we were clearing the city and entering more rural surroundings: soon the traffic thinned to only the occasional barge and long-tail. The bright lights faded and it was easier to distinguish the river from the land. A pattern emerged for the troublesome engine: after 20 minutes of inactivity, it would start and run for about 15 minutes, inevitably stopping at the most inconvenient time.

At one point we were able to make a shortcut through a canal, cutting off a big loop in the winding river. The canal was narrow and lined with houses on stilts. I turned the key and the engine started, so we sped up the canal at 25 knots. The sudden speed in such a restricted space was exciting, but brief, as the end of the short canal rapidly approached. Not wanting to lose any precious time, we shot back into the wide river. Here my lack of driving experience showed itself. I threw the craft into the turn only to find it travelling sideways and heading for the far bank – neither of which I particularly wanted to do. Stilted houses emerged through the darkness. I eased back the throttles and turned the steering more, but the craft remained slewed sideways and carried on. Like skidding on ice, it just wasn't turning. With buildings looming large, I remembered something I had been told, but never really investigated: 'Keep the power on in a turn.' Through desperation rather than logic, I opened the throttles wide - it was the only thing left to try. In a majestic, drifting arc the craft responded with a sweeping sideways turn, just missing the houses, but drenching them with blown spray.

After three hours of slow, boring progress punctuated by scary bursts of speed, our destination loomed out of the darkness - a big, white, 1960s motor yacht moored alongside a barge. It was 10pm. Lines were taken. Friendly American voices greeted us, then Miles' clipped tones as he shook my hand saying, 'Well done, you deserve a medal!' The fear instantly evaporated, replaced by the sense of elation I would experience from then on, every time a passage was safely completed.

A wiry American man who introduced himself as Frank, handed me a cold beer. We sat chatting on the deck, Frank going through all the sights and attractions we must not miss in Bangkok. But Miles and I had arrived a few days before the hovercraft, so we'd already done the tourist thing. We'd hurtled around in tuk-tuks in and out of eight lanes of smoggy traffic which somehow, right at the last second, parted magically like water to let us through. We'd admired what we could see of the temples and gardens through the throngs of Japanese visitors who piled out of coaches for five minutes at a time in their matching baseball caps.

Still, our American host insisted on taking us to the notorious Pat Pong Road. I was tired, and the last place I wanted to be was in a crowded noisy street full of sleazy bars with near-naked girls gyrating behind glass shop fronts. Frank suggested we go inside one of the bars. I was really not keen but I stifled my misgivings and told myself it would be fun to see a little local colour. We pushed open the door and the girls immediately covered up. It was early and we were the only people there. We were offered drinks, sat at a table and the show began.

Four tiny, slender girls came onto the small stage in front of us, dancing mechanically to loud music, their faces blank and their movements well-rehearsed. They were teenagers. When they caught our eye, they would turn on radiant come-on smiles. Slowly, they shed the little clothing they had and gyrated some more. Then two of them stepped off the stage and danced in front of us, a private show, and my discomfiture grew with every move they made. The writhing and shimmying became more suggestive, the smiles more predatory. Finally, they both reached down and produced, to my surprise, a ping pong ball from between their legs which they handed to us. It was hard to know what to do with such an unexpected gift. The show reached its finale with the other two dancers pulling strings of razor blades from between their legs – a strangely un-erotic act. The whole episode left me feeling no more than embarrassed. Even then, against my better judgement we allowed ourselves to be talked into buying drinks for our companions. It was all so fake, so clichéd. I felt I'd like to say something to them, just one human being to another, but they didn't speak English.

One of the girls enticed Miles on the small dance-floor where they jigged around awkwardly although the discrepancy in their heights was almost comical. Another girl was sitting on Frank's lap, giggling. A third had draped herself over my shoulders; she whispered something indecipherable, but nevertheless perfectly understandable, in Thai. Frank leaned over to me. 'How about you take this one and I'll take the other?' he suggested.

But the girls were indicating that more drinks had to be bought. Out of sheer embarrassment I became uncharacteristically authoritative. No more drinks; this wasn't fun. As if a switch had been flicked, the girls turned sulky and sour. The next thing we knew, an oversized bill was slapped down in front of us. Miles picked it up with an expression of disbelief.

'This is utterly intolerable. We are not paying this!'

The proprietor came over and remonstrated. Behind the bar, a woman started screeching. 'Completely outrageous!' continued Miles, now mounted firmly on his high horse. The little naked girls started twittering and looked aggrieved.

Frank reached into his pocket and slapped some money on the table; Miles added a few more notes, announcing, 'That's all you are getting from us!' although it looked like a generous wad of Baht to me.

My two companions strode towards the door. I tagged along with the agitated crowd following behind. As we burst into the street, I fully expected our followers to come too but the door slammed shut.

The next morning, I awoke in a narrow berth on Frank's motor-boat to a high sun and a calm river. Our stressful maiden voyage and the other tawdry adventures seemed as if they had happened to someone else. I poked my head through the hatch and found myself in the middle of a timeless landscape. Traditionally-dressed men and women toiled in fields with hand tools. Oxen trudged by, pulling carts. Only the noisy long-tails placed us in the 20th century.

We spent the morning fiddling about with the fuel system. I realised that I had done this job in what seemed like the coldest place on earth and now here I was doing it in the tropical heat; it was too close a call to say which was the more uncomfortable. We went through the same old routine although, just to ring the changes, this time we also fitted new filters. We didn't find anything amiss. In the afternoon we took the craft for a test run. It started promptly and we ran up and down the river for almost an hour. We had fixed it! Then, approaching our berth, the engine stopped again.

We devised a plan. We would take the craft down the coast one at a time, the good one first and leave the troublesome one alongside the yacht. We would devote some time to fixing it once the other was safely delivered. In the meantime, we had to get a craft down to Surat Thani to start the ferry service.

Preparations were made. The whole crew would be coming with us and the 400-mile trip would take three days with two overnight stops. The first day was spent winding our way back down the Chao Phraya river, past the city and docks and out to the river mouth, reaching there in the late afternoon. We anchored for the night, and sat on deck watching the sun go down in perfect stillness, as the brown water swirled slowly around the craft. After a short, hot, uncomfortable night it was a relief to be up before sunrise and heading out to sea.

If hovercraft can go anywhere, how did we end up here?

Following the red and green flashing lights which marked the winding channel, we twisted and turned and watched the land slowly recede behind us. After one tight left hand bend the channel turned right. The craft continued to turn left. I looked over at Miles. 'Bloody steering's jammed,' he called, 'I can't turn to starboard.' We stopped the craft and I went around to the stern. The sky was brightening, although the sun was still not up. In the gloom, the problem revealed itself. One of the six rudders had come loose and was jamming the others. What to do? 'Take it off!' said Miles, 'It'll steer well enough with five.' He was right and it was a pretty easy job as it turned out; with the offending rudder stowed in the cabin, we were on our way again.

Our navigation was simple and basic: it entailed ticking off the various landmarks on the chart as we progressed. One of the young, friendly Thai crew offered me a toffee. We were approaching Hua Hin where we could see a beautiful beach with palm trees and loungers under palm-leaf parasols, and a grand hotel among the trees behind. Miles and I agreed that we simply couldn't pass this up – it would be a great place to stop for a break, have a drink and stretch our legs. I chewed happily down on my toffee thinking of what might be available in the way of lunch. It was then I found that my jaws wouldn't open – they were locked fast together. We were still in the middle of making a perfect approach to the beach but I had no means of saying so.

Surreptitiously trying to prise my jaws apart, I started to get a bit panicky, although nobody seemed to have noticed my embarrassing plight. The crew, who were all seated together in the cabin, were talking uncharacteristically earnestly, but it seemed to be something on the shore that they were interested in. After much discussion, they glanced furtively in my direction and it looked like one of them was being pushed forward by the others. I tried to avoid them by going up to the cockpit to join Miles, refusing to let them catch my eye. It was always me they came to for questions. Like most people, they were a little in awe of Miles with his aloof manner and constant pipe-sucking – they certainly hadn't offered him a toffee.

One man, Sarawut, detached himself quite unwillingly from the others and came up to join us. I tried to pretend that I was busy navigating. Despite this he firmly said something in broken, heavily-accented English which I was unable to interpret. He tried again.

'Urs um ugburb,' I mumbled airily, hoping this might be interpreted as a non-committal response. The chap stared uncomprehendingly, gave a little nervous twitch but stood his ground, waiting expectantly. I tried to look firm and confident, turning away as if I had some important task to attend to. The Thais were so polite, I was sure he would not persist: he would probably give me some privacy now and I would find a way of freeing my jaws. But instead of this, the situation seemed to be escalating. The others were pushing their way into the cockpit and there was waving of arms and some very excitable pointing towards the shore.

Across at the controls, I could see Miles was holding his steady course to the beach, pipe clamped tightly between his teeth, signalling a concentration which must not be disturbed. Another crew member approached, speaking sharply to Sarawut who had not been deterred and was still waiting dumbly for some response from me. 'Landing not permitted here,' said the newcomer quite clearly. 'No landing.' He stared straight at me, permitting no prevarication. 'Reerry?' I replied, trying to feign an expression of thoughtfulness. Sarawut nodded vigorously, backing up his colleague. 'No landing,' he repeated.

They were eyeing Miles with something like fear, expecting me to pass the message on. With one last unnatural effort, I forced my locked molars apart and after a short fit of choking and one or two false starts, regained my powers of speech sufficiently to relay the crew's message rather faintly to Miles. Typically, Miles ignored all this and headed on. Uproar! All the crew-members were now clamouring at Miles, bunched on the couple of steps leading up to the driving seat, adamant – we must turn and leave immediately! But too late: the craft was already heading up the beach.

By now all the Thais were white-faced with anxiety, wringing their hands – no, no, we couldn't stop, there would be serious repercussions. It was the ghastly look on their faces that finally convinced the strong-willed Miles to put the craft into a tight 180-degree turn; we zoomed back into the water in a flurry of sand and spray. Although my jaws were unglued, my toffee was still resistant to being swallowed; I resorted to severe sucking rather than chewing. Looking behind me, I could see loungers and parasols being scattered up the beach, the palms bending in our prop wash.

'What was that about?' I asked the cowering crew members. 'This is one of the places where the King stays,' they explained, 'to proceed would cause much trouble.' It was exactly at this moment that my tongue found something hard and metallic stuck in the sweet goo. One of my gold crowns. It felt like a bad omen.

Robbed of the chance of a pleasant break ashore by the crew's insistence, we carried our way on along the coast. I decided not to explore the incident any further just then.

Late in the stifling afternoon, we arrived at a military base where we planned to stop overnight. After three attempts, we made a tricky landing on a steep beach and were led up to some barracks. My clothes stuck to me. I found that I was sweating in places which I never knew could sweat, such as ear-lobes and ankles. Our accommodation comprised long bunkhouses, an Asian toilet – and a bathroom of a sort I hadn't seen before, consisting of a chest-high cistern, a tap, a jug and nothing else. At the end of a long hot day and a night sleeping on the craft, I was pretty desperate for a shower but unsure of the etiquette of using this rather alien facility. Wait and observe, I thought, always a good strategy. Before long, Sarawut entered and I could hear him inside generating a terrific amount of noise – splashing, hawking, spitting, sloshing and energetic clanging of the metal jug. When the door eventually opened, the tiny room was drenched. I got the idea.

Although refreshed after a good sloshing myself, I still felt miserable about my dislodged crown. What a hassle! Now I would have to go through the trip being careful how I ate; I would probably get toothache or worse. It was bound to be difficult and expensive to get it fixed. Back in England it would mean 'going to the dentist' and all that involved. The dread. I'd have to make an appointment and wait for days. Then spend hours in a grim waiting room and the job might take several visits.

Sarawut came over for a chat. I hadn't spoken to any of the crew since the incident. 'Would you have got into trouble if we had gone in to the Royal resort?' I asked. 'Is not so much that, but is extreme disrespect,' he said haltingly. I felt ashamed of the ignorant way we had presumed to ignore the exhortations of the Thais in this matter. We had obviously caused them distress and offence. The people's love for their King was touching and completely genuine. His name was King Bhumibol Adulyadej, or Rama IX, and he reigned over the country from 1946 until his death in 2016, longer than that of any other Thai monarch. His face appeared on pictures and posters all around the country, like a well-loved family member. Bank notes, every denomination of which have his face on them, are not folded but carefully smoothed out as a sign of reverence and esteem. Every evening at 6 o'clock the National Anthem is played in public places and everyone stands to show their respect.

I confided the problem of my tooth and Sarawut listened sympathetically then went to consult his colleagues. Within half an hour, another member of the crew had escorted me to a nice Thai dentist, in a clean bright surgery. She glued the crown back in place for a handful of Baht.

The next morning, I was once again in fine spirits. We had a long way to go if we were to reach Surat Thani before dark so we pushed on in good conditions and made easy, uneventful progress. The sun was low as we approached the large shallow bay of Ao Ban Don. Dozens of fishing boats criss-crossed our path and, more worryingly, the area bristled with long bamboo fishing stakes driven into the sea bed, sticking up a metre above the surface. Due to the wind and current these were angled towards us, like spears, threatening to damage the skirt if we ran over one. I don't know how he did it, but Miles somehow managed to avoid them all, an amazing feat because we arrived in Surat in complete darkness.

My elation at the safe delivery of craft number one was overshadowed by the thought of the infuriating engine problem awaiting us back in Bangkok. We went straight to the craft when we arrived back in the city, took it out and everything seemed fine. Then the engine died. Again, we went through the fuel system. Even with an extremely calm, logical and systematic approach, we got no nearer to the cause of the trouble.

As well as the usual routine of tightening, checking or replacing the components, time and again I had peered through the dinner-plate sized inspection hatch into the cavernous fuel tank, hoping to find something – I wasn't sure what. I knew the fuel was good quality so it couldn't be that. One of my first checks had been to ensure that there was no water under the fuel, caused by condensation. Even so, after another morning of drawing a blank, I felt compelled to lift the cover again, this time shining my torch into the nearly full tank. Nothing. As I went to replace the cover, something white caught my eye. I peered in more closely - yes, there was something drifting around on the bottom. I gingerly reached down into the warm oily diesel fuel, until my arm was at full length. I felt blindly around. Nothing. A trick of the light, perhaps. Withdrawing my dripping arm, I noticed something stuck to my wrist. A rectangle of paper, its oily sheen making it almost transparent. It had printing on it, the wording in English and perfectly legible.

In a flash, I understood everything. Taking hold of the scrap of paper, I jumped up, knowing now what it was: a label - a sticky label used to identify the metal panels that make up the tank. The welder hadn't noticed it. The diesel fuel would have dissolved the glue leaving it free to drift around the tank. While the engine was running it would have eventually been sucked towards the engine pick-up pipe where it would block the flow, starving the engine of fuel. And each time it did this, the engine would stop. And then the label would float away again until we restarted the engine and the whole process would repeat itself.

Miles wandered over and I could tell by the rate at which his pipe was puffing that he was as fed up and stumped as I had been only minutes before. He took the oily trophy I was holding out for him to see. He looked at it, frowned, then removed the pipe from his mouth as his expression turned from gloom to a broad smile. 'Part No 6645,' he read. 'PORT BAFFLE.' He gave a shout of laughter and stabbed the air with his pipe. 'Well it bloody well baffled me!'

Our repeat voyage was pleasantly uneventful, giving me lots of time to reflect on my career in hovercraft so far. The build had been hard-going but I felt it had paid off now as keeping close to the coast, we passed serenely through an oriental painting of steep, tree-fringed cliffs, backed by misty hills. We get better at things. For instance, it became policy to never take a new craft to sea without an hour of tethered running; never again did we leave labels inside a fuel tank. We just had to learn from our errors... there was no culture of blame about these things.

Apart from when it came to Stuart, that is. Reason told me that he had nothing to do with the fuel tank, but I still harboured a suspicion that it was somehow Stuart's fault. It was his inane bellowing about the telephone that had distracted the person who should have removed the label. I pondered on these things as the miles slipped by: with the craft behaving faultlessly, there was very little else to do. As we passed close by to King's residence at Hua Hin everyone looked straight ahead. Yes, I thought: we learn from our mistakes.

With the two craft successfully delivered and commissioned, Miles flew on home. There was one more thing for me to do before leaving Thailand: a year or so before, Griffon had built three small craft for the Royal Thai Navy. They were for flood relief and interestingly one was fitted with a special seat, set higher than the others, so the King could ride in it: no-one was allowed to sit higher than the King in his presence. The warranty was about to run out so, as I was in the country, I had promised to make a courtesy visit and fix a couple of minor problems.

I was beginning to develop a real affection for Thailand as I understood the culture better. There is a merriness about ordinary people which I found charming, and a friendliness in people's attitude to foreigners. As I had discovered, there is also a great sense of propriety and modesty about much of Thai society, and it is necessary to understand the things that are considered socially unacceptable. It is offensive to touch anyone on the head, for instance. You must never show the soles of your feet to anyone or use your feet to point at something. One time I made a terrible gaffe when I scooted a box out of the way with my foot. There was a collective gasp as a frisson of shock went through the room. I looked up to see ten pairs of eyes on me, then ten pairs of eyes fixed on the floor. Nobody said anything but I never did it again.

The Navy craft were stationed at a naval base in Sattahip, south east of Bangkok. This involved a long, crowded bus ride past the holiday resort of Pattaya, sitting among the backpackers and groups of surprisingly noisy monks, another thing that delighted me about this country. I arrived at the naval base late in the afternoon and was shown the craft, sitting under a corrugated iron roof. It was stiflingly hot and as the warranty jobs were pretty straightforward, I decided to do them in the morning when it would be a bit cooler. In the meantime, I needed to find somewhere to sleep so one of the naval guys kindly dropped me off at the only local hotel.

This was unlike any hotel I had seen before, and I found it puzzling. It seemed to be more of a motel, in fact, but the parking spaces were under cover, with heavy curtains across the entrances, so the cars couldn't be seen. As I checked in, I was eyed suspiciously and without the usual friendliness. No credit cards, only cash. Where was my car? The admission that I did not have one seemed to throw everyone into confusion. I was grudgingly shown to a large room which seemed almost pitch black. After stumbling around in the dark for a bit, I finally located the switch for the ceiling light but this only held a dim red bulb which, rather than throwing a rosy glow over the furnishings, gave the room a blood-red creepy cast like something out of the Adams Family mansion. My uneasiness grew as I discovered shiny black sheets on the bed, ornate mirrors on the ceiling and a huge TV on the wall. Sleep was a long time coming and even then it was frequently disturbed by various bumpings and moanings coming from the adjacent rooms, which crept into my dreams as I tossed and turned, tangling myself up in the slippery sheets.

In the morning, feeling less than rested, I questioned the guys at the base about my strange accommodation. It was a 'love hotel', I was told. I had just stumbled across another custom in Thailand: apparently, it is not unusual for successful men, such as businessmen and military officers, to have a series of liaisons. They marry their first wife young and have children. Then, as time goes on, they take a succession of younger mistresses to hotels which are there for the purpose of facilitating these clandestine encounters, even providing a place to discreetly hide your car – hence the curtains. These places are money-spinners: one room in a love hotel can earn a lot of money as customers change frequently – often seven to eight in one day. But their anonymity – no cameras nearby, and no requirement to show an ID card, passport or any other identification – make them good covers for all sorts of other criminal activity.

All this was explained to me by the guys as I worked through the jobs on my list. If I wanted, they could, you know… arrange something for me. It would be no problem.

I shook my head. Today was my last day. A quick calculation told me that my plane was due to take off in precisely eight hours, leaving me no time at all for even the briefest love-encounter.

'I'll put it on the bucket list,' I promised.

Sweden 2012

The tropical warmth of Thailand seemed a million miles away from the wintry wastes beyond the window of Sven's Restaurant and Cabins. But John's story prompted me to recall my initial taste of working abroad.

'My first foreign trip was to Spain,' I told him. 'Probably the best one I ever had.'

'Really?' John raised a sceptical eyebrow. 'When was that?'

I did a quick mental calculation and was surprised to discover that it must have been in 1980 – thirty-two years before. My accidental career in hovercraft had been going for about four years by then, mostly on a steady downward trajectory, a repeating pattern in which I would work for a few months then jack it in to do a bit of travelling, run out of money and start again on the bottom rung of the career ladder.

Then out of a low grey sky came the sort of opportunity my 27-year old self could only dream about.

Trouble in Paradise

Chapter 5
Trouble in Paradise

Russ: Marbella, Spain 1980

I was making hovercraft at Pindair in Gosport. In geographical terms, or any other, I hadn't really come that far. The company order book was pretty full but the work was actually quite unchallenging at times and I was wondering what future there was in hovercraft. Some friends had asked me to go cruising with them for the summer and the thought of some time out in the Med was a tempting prospect. I decided to give it a few weeks then make the decision whether to stay on.

1980 was the beginning of the Video Age. Video hire shops were springing up in every high street. Until this time, there had been no way of watching a film again once it had done its rounds in the cinemas unless you were able to catch it by chance some years later on TV. For the first time ever, it was now possible to watch a film of your choosing whenever and wherever you wanted, and even to record TV onto video tapes, which were the shape and size of a large paperback, to watch at your own convenience. This was a clunky, hit-and-miss process which involved pressing lots of fiddly buttons and much room for error. The disappointment of coming to the end of a double episode of *Inspector Frost* only to discover that the last five minutes containing the vital denouement is missing, or settling down to watch *The Hitchhiker's Guide to the Galaxy* but finding that you have recorded *Songs of Praise* from Harrogate by mistake cannot be over-estimated. MTV channel played wall-to-wall music videos. The genre of the day was New Romantic. Bands who had shot to sudden fame through the pop charts and had only recently left their day jobs as plumbers and shop assistants suddenly found that they were expected to dance like Barry Gibb or Olivia Newton-John as well as playing two chords on a keyboard. The results are still out there on YouTube: grainy over-dubbed footage of bewildered people with mullet hair-dos and no dance skills whatsoever gamely writhing and jiving in leg-warmers, or acting out the lyrics as if they are playing a game of charades.

Gadgets were shrinking in size and their prices were plunging, meaning that everyone could afford a Japanese camcorder which would fit in your pocket, so anyone could produce a video. And because everyone else was doing it, Mike, my boss, decided that we needed to do it too. This at least provided some diversion from the usual daily grind of the workshop.

As well as advertising the fact that the Skimas were cheap, versatile, fast, manoeuvrable and easy to drive, we wanted this video to give them a racing-car, jet-set image. Unfortunately, our budget was low and the drizzly mud-flats of Portsmouth Harbour were an uninspiring setting, not the usual milieu of the carefree elite. Nevertheless, we set to with enthusiasm and over the next few weeks, only interrupted by the weather and other inconveniences like having to build hovercraft, our opus magnus began to take shape.

The finished product is of its time. Opening shots of the Skima living up to its name and skimming over a fast-flowing weir are quite impressive. Then up starts the muzak – a jaunty tune which somebody probably found on an old C90 cassette tape in the bottom of a bin, rejected by an ITV sit-com. Inexplicably wearing a large white woolly hat, like a cartoon bandaged head to which the eye can't help being drawn, Trevor appears in the driving seat of the Skima 4 mk3 (see appx. 2), 'undeterred by rocks' and going places, we are told, that boats 'dare not'. Apparently, after only five minutes' instruction two British actors (actually Bodie and Doyle from *The Professionals* which coincidentally also had a bad theme tune) managed to cross The Channel, the first time anyone had done so in an

inflatable hovercraft. With the exaggerated flourishes of magicians' assistants, Mac and I are seen smirking and assembling a craft, a process which the commentary boasts takes 'less than two hours'. We see people stepping 'dry-shod' from the craft wearing the type of normal everyday clothes you might wear on a bus. (An explanatory word or two about life at the time is required here: tank-tops were normal in the late 70s and yes, two hours to assemble the craft might seem like quite an epic, but in those days people had longer attention spans and a higher boredom threshold on account of there being hardly anything to do.)

There are shots of a bright orange Skima containing four people zipping back and forth across shallow water. They sweep on past a Land Rover stuck in the mud, waving carelessly and not bothering to stop. The alighting passengers are shown looking happy and relaxed after experiencing a 'smooth and comfortable ride'. They display no signs of having been deafened by the ear-splitting screech of engines but in fact seem quite perky, evidently cheered up by the fun they had pointing at some poor people who had gone aground in an old boat.

One day the sun emerged and we took two craft out – Mac and Mike in the Skima 12 (see appx. 3) while Trevor and I filmed them from the smaller Skima 4. As we swept along with a keen following wind, Trevor, not one for new gadgets, was trying to get some action shots with his much-treasured Super 8 cine camera. At over six foot in height, perhaps his sudden impulse to stand up to film had something to do with our alarming and unexpected plough-in, an ignominious and unfortunate event which hovercraft people do not really like to talk about. A propensity for this was a characteristic of the Skimas which we definitely hadn't intended to capture on film.

This was a text-book plough-in: the nose dug into the water, the craft slewed sideways and stopped. The sudden halt created a momentum that launched Trevor head-first into the harbour although by the time I noticed his departure only his white-socked legs were visible. I fervently hoped he was still filming – at least he should be getting some good 'Jacques Cousteau' style footage. 'See 'ow the 'overcraft, now silent, looms majestically above us...' But disappointingly Trevor seemed more intent on getting out of the water. The others arrived as he surfaced, holding the camera determinedly above his head, more anxious for its safety than for his own. Unfortunately, his heroism was in vain – we found later that the film was ruined. The next day, however, Trevor was no doubt amused to see a pair of large flippers next to his boots in the cloakroom and even managed to raise a wan smile at the cluster of barnacles which had been mysteriously glued to his woolly hat. Although he was a mild-mannered chap up to a point, when pushed too far he had a short fuse so the seaweed-festooned trident left propped against his maroon Skoda was probably a step too far – it may only have been made of plastic but when wielded by an angry red-faced man approaching the end of his tether, the effect was quite frightening.

One of the unintended knock-on effects of health and safety and political correctness, both of which are fine things, must surely be the demise of the work-place practical joke. Mac particularly enjoyed these and as the newest member of the work-force I was a victim to quite a few, culminating in the mysterious disappearance of my old moped one Friday evening when I was the last to leave the premises and in a particular hurry to get away. I was stumped to find it had vanished from the car-park. Suspecting a trick from the beginning, I spent a fruitless half an hour searching in all the corners of the workshop and the adjacent boatyard but could find no trace of it. Really worried by this time, I was wondering whether to report it missing when I noticed that the workshop hoist had been in use. My eyes followed the chain into the apex of the roof where my red Garelli swung gently twenty-five foot above the ground. I managed some feeble retaliation the following week when I filled Mac's gloves with Swarfega. Apart from these amusing interludes, and the small diversion of driving Father Christmas down Gosport High Street in a Skima 4, life wasn't very exciting.

One day, when Mike asked me in an offhand way if my passport was in date, I continued rubbing down the mould or whatever mundane task I was working on and said yes, thanks, I thought it was

in date. In that case, Mike continued, would I mind going abroad for the company? A small job had come up, to commission a new private craft for a millionaire in a 6-star marina in Marbella on the Costa del Sol. I was determined not to be taken in.

'Oh, really? Who is it? Barry Gibb? The Aga Khan?'

But although he had a penchant for performing magic tricks at the office party and when 'entertaining clients', a phrase he seemed to have taken literally, Mike was not a practical joker. He looked puzzled. 'No, just a customer. He wants someone to fly to Spain on his private plane and... but I can ask somebody else if you want.' I put down my sandpaper. This was for real.

'I'll go and pack,' I said.

Now everyone at that time had heard of private Lear jets, thanks to the Pink Floyd track *Money*, and I had seen all the movies where the secret agent or Swiss banker is delivered by a Limousine which sweeps across the tarmac right up to a plane staffed by a waiting line of beautiful air-hostesses. When I got to Heathrow, I strode self-importantly past the harassed tourists waiting in long queues at the Freddie Laker bag-drop and went instead to the 'Special Airport Services Desk', my gateway to a world of comfort and luxury far removed from the crowded check-in halls. A clerk greeted me, rather indifferently I thought, and directed me out of a side door not to a Limousine but to a minibus which drove for miles around the perimeter road to a remote apron where stood half a dozen rather flimsy-looking light aircraft. Flying in such a small plane turned out to be not much fun at all: it was freezing, it took four hours instead of two and although all airline food was quite disgusting at that time, at least opening all the little individually wrapped packets helped while away the time whereas I had only a round of cheese sandwiches to relieve the boredom. But I wasn't going to let that lessen my excitement or interfere with the story when I got home. I had been dropped into Paradise to drive a small hovercraft for a millionaire, in one of the most exotic resorts in Europe.

The wealthy hovercraft owner had a holiday villa in Marbella and a yacht in the Marina Puerto José Banús. He had acquired a Skima 4 to use as a tender to his sleek 40-foot motor-yacht. This 4-seat hovercraft was carried on davits at the stern of the yacht, and stored in the purpose-made boathouse of his villa. He was there in Spain for a summer holiday with his family. I became part of the entourage staying in his villa, had fantastic meals in the best restaurants, drank in the swankiest bars and spent our days having a blast with hovercraft. He even put his Porsche at my disposal. In 1980, Marbella and José Banús were still classy; they catered for the rich and beautiful with top-class restaurants and exclusive clubs. There was also another element – crime – which ran excitingly just under the surface of all of this, fuelled by the many opportunities for drug-smuggling and money laundering. Some celebrated British criminals had luxury hide-aways along the coast and the tabloids nick-named it 'The Costa del Crime'. But nobody talked about that.

The following week was all Fun: the craft behaved perfectly, the customer was happy and the new driver Scott (also the skipper of the luxury yacht) was very good. We drove the hovercraft up and down the Costa del Sol in our swimsuits in the Mediterranean sun. So for me this was it - I had finally found my career niche, the life I was born to lead. No more 9 to 5 drudgery for me.

Marbella was a much more photogenic location than Portsmouth Harbour. Mike was keen that I should take advantage of the upmarket backdrop and get some good publicity shots both for the video and our new brochure. I mentioned this to Scott and at the word 'video' he set to immediately and practically wrote a screenplay. Then he turned his mind to the casting. I was to play the driver, a role I felt quite comfortable with even if it was a little typecast. Also recruited were Scott's girlfriend, the owner's wife and her sister. The plot was complicated, involving glamorous bikini-clad hitch-hikers being picked up – maybe even kidnapped – by a passing hovercraft. I began to wonder how this was going to further the image of the Skima.

'Want a getaway vehicle that really draws a crowd? Why not try a Skima 4? Here on the Costa del Sol it's the preferred choice for the criminal community.' 'It's fast, light and reliable,' says a spokesman for the Russian mafia.

By the time we were into the third day of filming, we had started to attract a regular audience. The story had become quite convoluted, and a bit like a 'Pirates of the Caribbean' film which I saw many years later and in which the concept of cause and effect seemed to be entirely missing, I would defy anyone to explain the plot, so I gave up trying. Instead, I did a lot of driving of skimpily-clad girls, which was easy, especially as it was sunny and calm and I was getting paid for it. By the fourth day I began to detect some unrest among the cast: certain people being given bigger parts, others stuck with limited roles, unable to showcase their range of acting abilities... Artistic differences about genre – film noir or pseudo-realistic – caused more arguments. Some of the onlookers had already decided what sort of film we were making, however.

'When do the birds get their kit off?' enquired a particularly regular attendee. By then, things had become impossible, with two of the women flouncing off in opposite directions. Then it began to rain. I never did see any of the footage and it is probably just as well that no-one else did either.

Of course, all this fun soon came to an inevitable halt. The summer ended, I went back to my mundane existence building hovercraft for a living until a couple of months later Mike, my boss, got another call from our customer saying he was having some technical problems with the craft, and he would like Russ (yes, he asked for me by name) to come to fix it up. My second arrival was similarly grand. This time, instead of a private plane to Malaga, I was sent a first class air ticket to Gibraltar (infinitely more comfortable) and given instructions to take a taxi to the marina and meet Scott on board the yacht. After a leisurely lunch, and some sightseeing we cruised the 50 odd miles back to Marbella in grand style.

If hovercraft can go anywhere, how did we end up here?

The hovercraft was having some minor skirt problems – some of the attachments were failing and I had to replace about 500 tiny plastic studs with slightly larger plastic nuts and bolts. Under most circumstances this could have been a fairly dull and fiddly job but doing it on a Mediterranean beach amongst the topless sunbathers made the task more bearable and probably take longer. After a day of this, the skirt was seaworthy. I took to sea and headed a couple of miles up the coast to the villa's boat-house where the craft would be kept for the winter.

It was late autumn and the Med was changing its mood from the friendly, balmy blue ocean I'd known a few months before. The going was slower than I had thought, with a sharp wind ruffling the waves. Keeping an eye on the shore, I realised the beach was actually pretty empty for once. Nearing the villa at last, I could see that there was a half-hearted game of beach volleyball going on; the players broke off to watch the hovercraft do its stuff, but the usual sail-boarders and small craft were nowhere to be seen. Before I knew it, a breeze sprang up and with it a lumpy sea was running. A life-guard was pacing the beach. He raised his hand. Suddenly I knew that I should get the craft ashore. I quickly headed in.

Surf was breaking all around as I approached the shelving beach. I did almost make it in, but then, just yards from the shore, one particularly angry roller swamped the craft, smashing the propeller and stopping the engine dead. In waist-high surf I struggled to haul my stricken water-logged vessel ashore and to safety but I was fighting with the wind and the waves, nearly overwhelmed by the sheer weight of it: it had surely taken half a ton of ocean. The volley-ballers, in bikinis and flip-flops, waded in to help. A handful of surprised sunbathers got to their feet, shading their eyes against the sun. Even the man with a barrow selling bottled water and the Moroccan handbag seller left their wares and came to help. Taking charge, the life-guard shouted instructions in Spanish, organising the diverse but enthusiastic band of rescuers. There was a confused episode of splashing and yelling, during which I went under several times, but clung on manfully until little by little and with an impressive display of international teamwork reminiscent of *Jeux Sans Frontieres*, we managed to drag the craft onto the beach.

Once the excitement was over, the rescuers melted away and I automatically started to bail the water out. Luckily, Scott turned up half way through and he helped me carry the lifeless Skima back to the boathouse. It took a long, long time to empty out the water. Badly shaken but determined to put things right, I then made myself stand back and take stock of the damage, much of which was to my self-esteem. I was completely mortified. I had been asked to do the simplest possible routine job and had succeeded in wrecking the hovercraft. What would the owner say? Not only was the prop broken but the electrics were saturated and there was no spark of life. I set to work: what else could I do?

The single propeller was similar to an air-conditioning fan with replaceable plastic blades. I searched through the stores and found, as I had half hoped, that we had a set of spares. The craft's electrics were the next thing. The ignition coils, having been immersed in salt water, failed to provide a spark, but copious rinsing in fresh water and an hour in a warm oven brought them back to life. The starter motor had not fared so well: it would definitely need a rewind. After some phoning around and a bit of judicious name-dropping, we found a local company who said they could do it – just bring it by. It was getting late so Scott and I borrowed the Porsche, for a bit of extra speed, and drove to a grimy backstreet where Gomez y Hermanos was still open. Would we like to collect the motor tomorrow? No, I said firmly, today, please. While Scott guarded the car, which was attracting some unwanted attention, I stood tapping my fingers on the counter until the repaired part appeared. Then the dash back to the boathouse to fit it and – hey presto! – it all worked.

It was the quickest repair ever. No-one would have guessed that a few hours before the Skima had been a sodden wreck. Then suddenly an attack of nerves hit me like a bludgeon. I can only put it down to delayed shock. Maybe it was finding a shard of the plastic propeller embedded in my shoulder that tipped me over the edge. My condition was quickly alleviated with the help of two or three cuba-libres downed in quick succession in a local bar. By the time the owner arrived to check on the progress of my light repairs, I was quite relaxed. I confessed the mishap, at the same time playing it down. Rather than receiving a bollocking, I was invited to join a party at an exclusive restaurant owned by a famous opera singer, where expensive wine flowed all evening. I am told that the aria the great man delivered at the end of the party was a rare performance, treasured for years to come by those who heard it. I don't think I did, but quite honestly, it's a bit of a blur – all I remember is meeting up with the beach volley-ballers who greeted me enthusiastically, glad to see I was still alive, I guess. It was kind of them to teach me the rudiments of flamenco dancing.

I flew back to a rainy autumnal England, much encouraged and waited for my next enjoyable, undemanding foreign assignment.

I'm sure it will come along soon.

Sweden 2012

By the time I had told the story to John, the blizzard had finally stopped. When we stepped outside, we could see headlights and hear the plink-plink of studded winter tyres from cars passing along the main road. It was time to go.

Sven, the rather dour landlord, had given us shelter from the storm, leaving us more or less to our own devices except to bring fika *at various well-judged intervals. Now that we'd made up our minds to head back we asked to settle the bill. Maybe in his relief to finally get rid of us, he became chattier.*

'I can see you're not fishermen,' he said. I wondered how. Was it the absence of rods and nets about our person? Our complete indifference towards the large stuffed fish on the walls? The absence of any technical fishing vocabulary in our conversation? 'Are you here on business?' We owned up to our connection with hovercraft. He looked sceptical. 'And what use is there for such vehicles today?'

I had often mused about printing a list which could act as an answer to this most FAQ of the hovercraft world. It would look like this:

If hovercraft can go anywhere, how did we end up here?

What have hovercraft ever done for us?

- *Transportation of people, equipment and vehicles across difficult terrain which other vehicles cannot get across*
- *Border patrol*
- *Transportation in environmentally sensitive areas where the ground could be easily damaged*
- *Rescues on swift water, ice, snow, mud flats, deserts, wetlands, shallow water, swamps, bogs, marshes and floodwaters*
- *An affordable, safe way to fly without a pilot's licence*
- *Transportation of people and equipment over specialist grounds such as golf-courses, cricket pitches and tennis courts*
- *Oilfield support*
- *Entertainment such as thrill rides and racing*
- *Wildlife conservation and research when habitats are not easily accessible*
- *Fast versatile ferry services*
- *Travel from land to water where there is no boat dock*
- *Military uses such as assault vehicles and transporting troops*
- *As a means of recovering diving teams*
- *Used in some sorts of agriculture such as pecan and cranberry farming*

Regrettably, I did not have such a list to give to Sven so I just told him that they were great for ice-fishing. He seemed interested in that. We said our goodbyes and once we had decided which heap of snow was our car, dug it out and marvelled that it started on the first attempt, we finally set off. Because of the constant cold, Swedish snow is always fine and powdery, like icing sugar. Our headlights picked out the swirling wisps but not the black road, resulting in an optical illusion which I found unnerving. My low mood was back. With a sinking heart, I realised that our day off was nearly at an end – tomorrow battle would resume. The white-out and the long break in our journey had robbed me of any sense of direction I might have had, but then again if the Arctic Circle drifts aimlessly around, what hope had I?

'Is this the right road?' I asked John.

'Yes,' he assured me. 'I recognise that clump of pine trees.'

The roads were quiet, flanked by snowy forest. It was a long drive home but we were going to take it slowly.

'So my first serious trip,' I said, to take my mind off things, 'was to Bangladesh.'

It was in 1981 that I was quite unexpectedly offered my second taste of exotic foreign travel, this time a job in the Brahmaputra River Delta.

Keep on Running

Chapter 6
Keep on Running

Russ, Bangladesh Feb 1981

My journey to Dhaka took thirty-six hours. I flew Aeroflot. To anyone who knows that name, yes, I can assure you it was every bit as horrible as the picture which has sprung into your mind. The four-hour stopover in Moscow was bearable, with a few beers to while away the time. The terminal had just been rebuilt for the 1980 Olympic Games and was pretty swanky. Unfortunately, the swankiness did not extend to the hidden parts of the airport: to board the plane we had to queue on the tarmac some way from the terminal building in a temperature of minus 10C, a cutting wind and driving snow. I felt sorry for the Bangladeshi passengers dressed in light muslin *kurtas* and *lungis*.

I dozed a little once the flight was underway but woke fuzzy-headed to find the plane descending. Perhaps I had slept through an announcement. I rubbed my eyes and peered out of the window to see brown smudges of land. As we touched down, I saw boxy buildings, piles of shipping containers, a row of snow-ploughs on tarmac, petering out into a bleak landscape of nothing. It was hard to tell if it was dawn, dusk or noon. We seemed to be just about as near to the middle of nowhere as you can get. It was snowing horizontally over stunted trees. We waited. No-one got on or off. We sat for an hour on the stationary plane, during which time all that happened was that it grew dark, then we took off again.

Time wore on. There were two more such stops – unannounced and unexplained – in what looked like military airfields. Tashkent, about half way, was at least scheduled. Here we watched enviously as some lucky passengers were released, last seen hurrying through the snow like a line of extras in a scene from *Dr Zhivago*. Some new passengers got on and to the blank-faced old-handers, those of us who had been on the plane from the outset, these people had fresh optimistic faces and brought with them a curious waft of the world outside, now a distant memory to us.

At one point, we were given cups of water by the burly, dour and dough-faced flight crew whose forbidding expressions did not invite conversation. It occurred to me that they may have been ex-prison warders – after all, they would have the perfect set of skills for dealing with trouble-makers, like the man in the seat in front of me who had asked where we were. Their technique certainly worked: we'd become a docile lot, beyond complaining or questioning, long since reduced to passivity, disoriented, feeble, losing hope of seeing home again. There were several more baffling landings and take-offs by which time the stench from the toilets was awful. A day and a half after I first set off, red-eyed and sallow-skinned, I stumbled off the plane into a proper airport where there were ordinary people and shops. As my feet touched solid ground, I swore I would never fly again. Later I amended that to never fly Aeroflot again. Then I remembered that I had bought a return ticket.

Wherever I had fetched up on the planet (and I felt reasonably certain that I was still on Earth) it appeared to be late at night. Other than that, I had no certainty as to the real time of day, the date, or which hemisphere I was in. The numbers on my watch didn't quite make sense. To my relief, a smiling (ah yes, I remember!) Korean man called Mr Kim was at the terminal to meet me. This seemed like a small miracle – goodness knows how long he had been standing there – but he bore no obvious ill-will and before I knew it I was being whisked away in a small Japanese jeep.

The drive through the city was a different sort of nightmare journey but my exhaustion made me fatalistic. I stared without thought at an endless procession of weird apparitions. A haystack on a bicycle, lorries like swaying shrines, a bus with no lights at all which momentarily bore down on us in the darkness, allowing a quick glimpse of the blank faces of stowaways perched on the roof, then something that was surely a ghostly fairground ride strung with old-fashioned coloured bulbs. Think of *Wacky Races* on acid. At one point, we came to a stop, unable to pass a broken-down lorry on the roadside whose occupants were dismantling its gearbox in the dark and the swirling dust watched by a circle of onlookers. The flares of little open fires were everywhere. Tired now to the point of delirium, I was having trouble remembering my own name. But someone up

there was looking down on me thinking: He's got it a bit easy, hasn't he? Let's add in a bit of challenge here. I know, let's get this Korean chap to ask him lots of difficult questions in an impenetrable accent. That should do it.

So in the midst of this surreal parade, came the questions. I leaned forward, ears straining. I was having real trouble understanding what my Korean colleague was saying to such an extent that I wasn't sure at first whether it was even English; and there are only so many times you can ask someone to repeat their words before a sort of panic sets in.

'Wha' fuer lating be for these engines bogray?'

'Wha' glade of oil?'

'Bogray, wha' is ignition system of engine?'

'How many kirometres, bogray, on one tank of fuer?'

In desperation, I feigned a sudden onset of sleep. What the hell was bogray? I would have to look through my notes.

It was the early hours of the morning when we arrived at the base. Where the Dhaka road meets the Jamuna River, we turned off onto little more than a dirt track which followed the river back up to a passenger ferry terminal called Aricha Ghat. Mr Kim pointed out the camp on the other side of the road – a large fenced-off compound with a busy construction site at its centre. It was deserted now except for some barking dogs and a half-awake security guard. Mr Kim showed me to a wooden hut. Down a corridor with rooms off both sides there was one with an empty bed into which I gratefully collapsed. It could have been ten minutes or ten hours later that someone was hammering on the door shouting: 'Breakfast!'

As Mr Kim showed me around the site that morning, it began to dawn on me what an ambitious and expensive project this was. I was going to be a tiny cog in a huge machine. The plan was to rebuild the whole electrical power distribution network – lines, cables, pylons – across the entire country. This was a particularly tricky section because it had to cross the Brahmaputra River Delta where it joins the Padma River. The contractors were the Korean Development Corporation (KDC) while a British civil engineering company provided the design for the project and were overseeing its completion. There had been problems putting down concrete foundations for the pylons at points where they needed to span several branches of the wide, fast-flowing river. Someone came up with the suggestion that hovercraft would be the perfect way to get quickly around the mixture of shallows, sandbanks and deep water that the power-lines had to cross. It was perfect terrain to show-case the versatility of the hovercraft and demonstrate what it was designed to do – textbook territory.

Except the hovercraft weren't working.

Four Skima 4 mk3s (see appx. 2) made up the fleet. Two of them belonged to KDC who seemed to have lost interest after initial problems; the other two were the property of the Civil Engineering firm who really needed them to get their people around the seven sites dotted across the delta. My duties were to keep the hovercraft running and ferry the engineers wherever they wanted to go. I knew these craft: they were of a design descended from racing hovercraft – the sort that were expected to run flat-out for a maximum of half an hour (although frequently didn't) before being completely reconstructed by an enthusiastic owner. Although they had powerful two-stroke air-cooled engines, designed for snow-scooters, they were built to be light, not robust. Flimsy might be nearer the mark. In short, for a job which needed a hardy camel, we had a slightly neurotic race-horse. Nevertheless, these were the best craft available at the time.

We continued our tour of the site. Mr Kim introduced me to Don, a KDC manager who oversaw the engineering – a craggy 'Marlboro man' type of American with a pock-marked face. In wild-west style, he wore a scarf over his mouth which he pulled down to greet me.

'Welcome to the dust bowl.' It was true: everything you could see was coated in a fine covering of pale dust. We shook hands and I

followed him along the road to the ferry terminal where the Skimas were housed, interested to notice a battered paperback protruding from the back-pocket of his jeans. I am always intrigued about the books people choose to read. A few discreet glances confirmed that it was a copy of *A Town Like Alice*. By this time we had reached the corrugated iron Skima hut. Inside it was sweltering.

'I hear you know something about these,' said Don, indicating the four rather dusty, sorry-looking craft as if they were unruly relatives of mine who had let themselves down. For the first time, I felt a sudden serious weight of responsibility. There was no-one else to rely on out here, no handy shops, no phones or any way of communicating with the UK. The craft looked so familiar but the environment was utterly alien. I wondered if I would be up to the job and almost said as much right there and then. It was a feeling that was to plague me again and again in such circumstances but I set a precedent on that day. I decided to listen a lot and say very little; I would talk to the people around and keep my eyes and ears open to see how everything worked. Don, not surprisingly, was frustrated with the amount of time the Skimas were out of operation, but he acknowledged that the dusty, sandy environment inevitably had much to do with the problems that they encountered.

'But fuel is the biggest problem,' he said. 'When fuel leaves the refinery in the city here it's as pretty well as good as Texan – and that's as good as you'll find anywhere in the world. The refinery sells it to a distributor who wants max profit so what does he do? He cuts it with some dirt-cheap kerosene. Also his tanker is old and rusty - got dirty water in the bottom and bits of crap floating on top. He sells it down the line to the next bastard who plays the self-same trick until, at the end of the chain, what you thought was petrol is no better than piss and only useful for putting out fires.'

I got to work. First, I thoroughly cleaned and stripped down two of the craft and, through a combination of coaxing and brute force, by the second day I had managed to get them both running well enough to begin the other part of my role – driving the six engineers around the project. They were keen to keep the craft running for good

reasons: by the conventional means of boat, foot and jeep, it would take a week for an engineer to inspect all the sites, during which there would be only limited contact with the rest of the team. But if we used the hovercraft, a full 50-kilometre round trip inspection tour would take less than a day after which engineers could report straight back to HQ on progress, and then go off to sleep in a bed, in an air-conditioned room, rather than a tent on a mosquito-ridden river bank. I found the engineers to be friendly, easy-going people who were very much on-side. As the jet-lag faded I began to feel more confident every day.

Then I met Iain.

I had met people like Iain before. We all know them. They complain but never do anything themselves. They are quick to cast blame on others without ever examining their own shortcomings. They expect the worst of people and are constantly on-guard in case someone should get the better of them. They can tell you at length why your ideas won't succeed but never come up with alternative solutions.

In fact, the only good thing about Iain was that he showed up much less often than the other engineers, which is why I didn't get to meet him until the second week. Evidently, he preferred his air-conditioned office to the discomfort and inconvenience of site work. Even the smiling Mr Kim, who liked everybody, avoided Iain.

The first time I met him I had just finished a repair, something I needed to do daily as one part or another failed, although so far I had managed to have at least one craft running every day. As I was tidying up, Mr Kim, looking uncharacteristically out of sorts, came along with a tubby red-faced man. As soon as the introductions were over, Mr Kim made his excuses and left. Iain smirked.

'They saw you coming, then,' he remarked in a Welsh accent. 'You're on a hiding to nothing with those clapped-out heaps of crap if you ask me.'

This set the tone: a whole day of unending sneers and complaints. Mr Kim noticed my mood when I got back to camp. 'You watch your words with Iain,' he warned, 'He rike a sry snake.'

Whatever spectrum Iain was on, Mr Kim dwelt at the other end. He was always cheerful and encouraging and now I'd become attuned to his accent, I realised that his English was very good – certainly better than my Korean – and he liked to practise it whenever he could. He also knew everyone and everything about life on the camp. The meaning of the ubiquitous term 'bogray' still eluded me. It seemed to feature in every conversation so I wondered if it was a special form of address, maybe a Korean custom to show respect. I tackled Mr Kim about it. He looked perplexed at first then laughed.

'Bogray,' he said, clapping me on the arm, 'it's you... Bogray... You are Mister Bogray.'

Ah! Bagley!

Not only were the hovercraft engines being deprived of good fuel, but decent quality marine 2-stroke oil was also hard to find. We had shipped some new cans of 2-stroke out, and decided to adopt a policy of only using factory-sealed bottles from then on. I also spoke to somebody in the KDC procurement section about the contaminated fuel. After a little research, they managed to find a petrol-station

owner in Dhaka who didn't dilute his fuel and kept his pipes clean – 'Honest Hasan' as we nicknamed him. A hair-raising weekly trip to his garage with a dozen jerricans solved the fuel problem. Each journey took two hours, there and back, and probably two years off my life, but saved countless time in lost days due to clogged filters.

Life took on a routine and, as happens, the strange soon became commonplace. The only Westerners and, more to the point, the only English-speakers living on the camp apart from me were Don, the American, and a couple of New Zealanders. I'd guessed correctly from the back-pocket paper-back that Don was an avid reader, never without a book. As an old-hand, he knew the set-up – basically there was nothing to do and nowhere to go – and I could only suppose he had brought a whole container of books with him. I found myself devouring whatever he threw my way, an eclectic mix from trashy westerns with names like *Comanche Bride* or *Death Shadow at Autumn Ridge* to Penguin classics like *Steppenwolf* and *Travels with Charlie.*

Our client's Chief Engineer was Peter Harris, a genial and well-respected chap who served as Chief Engineer on the project. He was extremely enthusiastic about the craft and had played a large part in their procurement. Rather touchingly, Peter had named their craft *Decibelle* and *Sandfly* and he always brought his wife along for the ride when we went to visit any of the sites. The couple were very kind: as expats they were given a monthly liquor allowance which they would share with me in the form of beer and whisky. Peter also wrote me a brilliant reference at the end of the contract.

At that time, Bangladesh was a dangerous and exhausting place to get around. Every year, floods took a terrible toll on the road system. After each rainy season, large sections of road were washed away and the repairs took the whole year. Using whatever material was available the embankments had to be rebuilt by hand, beginning with the process of shaping and firing bricks in kilns at the side of the road; once made, these were then broken up, again by hand, to form a hardcore base. The saying 'many hands make light work' could be Bangladesh's national motto although maybe 'light' is the wrong word – at least, it didn't look like light work for the women I saw sitting by the side of the road in the baking heat breaking up the hot, newly-made bricks.

Of course, the roads were also immensely crowded. At any one time you might expect to find, in order of speed: hand carts, water buffalo, pedestrians, ox carts, bicycles, trucks, buses and cars. Broken-down trucks were everywhere. In the course of even a short journey you would always see at least one accident. The road was so pot-holed it could only be negotiated at a snail's-pace... that is, unless you were a KDC driver in a jeep with an 'important' passenger on board. Then you must drive as fast as the vehicle will go. These cars had an over-speed warning so if they were driven too hard, a repetitive, high-pitched beep-beep-beep was emitted to warn the driver to ease off the gas. For a KDC driver this ear-splitting noise was perceived as a reward for his heroic driving skills, and would only egg him on to go faster.

I dreaded our trips to Dhaka, which we had to make at least once a week. The main road was grandly called the Aricha Highway and it was bad – very, very bad. I never drove in Bangladesh but being a passenger was excruciating. I didn't want to see and I couldn't look away: either option seemed just as terrifying, so I mostly kept my eyes trained on the road like rifle sights, every muscle tensed, my foot taking on a life of its own pressing down on an imaginary brake, only closing my eyes when it seemed like I was entering into the final seconds of existence. I lost count of the number of times I found myself unexpectedly delivered from death by some miracle of chance.

Driving in the dark was especially scary. Late one evening coming back from Dhaka, I was relieved to see a pair of red lights up ahead and relaxed a little – it's always easier for the driver to follow another vehicle. I began to suspect something was wrong when the lights rapidly got bigger and brighter and bigger... My driver made a stomach-wrenching swerve as a bus with two enormous red lights on the front bore down upon us and whooshed off past into the night. I think I was as close to dying at that spot as I have ever been.

As if this stretch of highway wasn't bad enough, the road passed the entrance to the University where an ongoing protest was taking place. Students were always gathered at the gates in groups, chanting and shouting. We had learned to keep our heads down here because if they noticed westerners in the car, they would throw stones. After I'd had my bones shaken to the marrow and contended with violent death several times in quick succession, being stoned by students seemed a bit much. Each journey left me a nervous wreck. The driver, meanwhile, would saunter off as if nothing untoward had taken place; for him, I guess, it hadn't.

Before I went there, I had only ever heard of Bangladesh in the context of George Harrison's 1971 fund-raising Concert for Bangladesh in aid of refugees. What I hadn't appreciated was its huge population. In the sixty years from 1951 to 2011 the population grew from 44,000,000 to 140,000,000 making it the eighth most populous country in the world but effectively it is the most densely populated country in the world by a long way if you discount small heavily built up places like Singapore and Hong Kong. In Bangladesh there are just over 1100 people for each square kilometre compared with 395 in India. Even the second most populated large country, Taiwan, has only 650 people for each square kilometre.

Being able to summon up vast numbers of people relatively easily certainly had its advantages. KDC needed to place several of the pylons in deep water rather than on shallow shifting sandbanks. The way to achieve this was to build a piled coffer dam, a kind of man-made island about 50 metres in diameter which they then filled with sand. In the west, a task like that would have taken two machines a week to fill this vast hole but KDC made use of Bangladesh's biggest resource – its people. They employed several hundred, paid them a

dollar a day and a meal, and had them backfill the hole carrying sand in baskets on their head. The job was finished in a week.

With so much competition for everything, every resource was precious and useful to someone. Recycling and reusing was just a way of life in Bangladesh long before the UK had even thought about its first bottle bank. In my first week, I'd asked Mr Kim what to do with the overflowing bin in the hangar. 'Just leave it outside the shed,' he replied, 'someone will take it.' I assumed he meant there would be a rubbish collection. In less than an hour, every piece had gone, not taken by the dustcart but by the many passers-by, destined to be made into something else. In Bangladesh, there is no such thing as rubbish.

When Peter suggested I should take on a couple of local helpers, someone put the word around Shivalaya, the nearest village that we were looking for a hovercraft pilot and an engineer. The idea was that I should train up two guys to drive and to keep the craft running.

There was no shortage of applicants. It was the first time I had ever hired anyone and I was quite unprepared for the huge number of hopefuls who turned up in person, at all times of day, to offer themselves for work. Most were wildly unsuitable, but I narrowed it down to a few possibles. Sumit was wiry and small but dressed smartly in shirt and trousers; he gave an impression of someone who could wield a spanner. Then came Asad. When I asked about his background, he told me he was a ship's captain, but the kind of 'ship' he commanded was 20 feet long, made from old packing cases nailed together and sealed with 'tingles' made from used golden syrup or ghee tins.

'Have you seen a hovercraft before?' I asked him.

'Oh, yes sir. I am a qualified hovercraft captain with much experience.'

To my knowledge there had been no other hovercraft within 5,000 miles but it was such an obvious lie delivered with such unblinking confidence I was interested to question him further.

'So what kind of hovercraft did you drive, Asad?'

'It was a Bengali-built hovercraft from Dhaka...' he lied, '...a very large one and very fast.'

I left it at that; however, I believed he might be capable and agreed to give him a try. He had a winning smile, accompanied by that confusing sideways shake of the head that leaves westerners wondering if it's an expression of agreement or dissent.

I was putting in long hours – what else was there to do? – yet still the hovercraft continued to go wrong. On a good day, we might have two of the four in action, most days only one, and sometimes, I'm ashamed to say, none. We became experts at stripping the engines down to clean and reset the points. We could change skirt segments and swap out filters in our sleep. Robbing parts from one craft to fix another became a daily necessity as our store of spares dwindled. Constant work helped assuage the intense home-sickness I was feeling, especially around the time that night began to fall – then it

seemed like the loneliest place in the world, so far removed from my usual life that I sometimes wondered whether that world could possibly still be continuing. We heard so little news from outside the camp that anything might have happened.

It turned out that driving a hovercraft did not come easily to Asad, but he showed up every day, unlike Sumit, and was always more than willing to help. One day, we took a spare outboard motor over to one of the sites. In the transfer between the boat and the hovercraft someone lost their grip and the motor splashed into the murky brown water. Without any hesitation, Asad pulled off his shirt and dived headlong into the river with the end of a rope between his teeth. Unbelievably, in 10 feet of brown water he found the motor, tied the rope to it and resurfaced smiling triumphantly. We hauled on the rope and recovered the motor intact.

At this time, Telex was the technology of choice for international communications and the KDC office in Dhaka had a splendid Telex machine. Fax machines, which seem very crude by today's standards, were a rare and expensive commodity. In Bangladesh they were probably unknown: even telephone lines had not reached the base at Aricha. With no phones, if I needed to get a message home I would usually write an airmail letter, give it to someone to take into Dhaka to post and hope that they remembered to do so. Once when I urgently needed some parts, I had to send a message by radio-telephone to the Dhaka office. It was a simple enough process: I wrote it out in long-hand for our radio operator, who broadcast it to Dhaka, where someone transcribed it, and then telexed it to our office in England. Our radio operator was Bengali, the man in the KDC office was Korean, my message was in English... what could possibly go wrong? To my surprise, the correct parts duly arrived and I thought no more about it. Arriving back in Gosport some weeks later, however, I was surprised to see the Telex message again, this time pinned up in the tearoom, obviously a source of much mirth. It began: 'Please issue the following farts...'

The hovercraft hut, known by all as The Hangar, was outside the camp, near the ferry crossing and there I would meet up with the ever-keen Asad and a floating population of about two dozen other total strangers who drifted in from the busy road. As we went about the fascinating business of replacing worn skirt parts, cleaning and changing fuel and air filters, wiping the all-pervasive dust from the points, changing pull-start cords, spraying the ignition system with WD40 and re-tensioning drive belts we were steadily watched by a mixture of school-children, beggars and people on their way to work who would drop by to check on our progress. Some regular attenders turned up every day and became quite knowledgeable to the point where they would offer helpful advice and explain the different procedures to newcomers.

These strangers certainly had a better attendance and punctuality record than Sumit. He turned out to be a less than useful assistant and showed terrifyingly little aptitude for driving the craft. He had been arriving later and later each day, until one day, inevitably, he didn't show at all. I had to tell him he had lost his job. I felt awful about it: we paid him little enough but the small amount of Taka he earned would have kept his family fed. Feeling utterly terrible, after delivering the bad news I offered him a handful of notes as some sort of compensation but he refused and ran off in tears. I never saw him again but I thought about him for days, unable to get the episode out of my head.

Some of the most thrilling moments I ever experienced in a hovercraft were in Bangladesh, flying across the vast dry sand-flats which stretched ahead without any interruption to their emptiness. One day we paced one of the contractor's jeeps and the driver later told me that the hovercraft had clocked over 50mph. The maximum speed of a Skima 4 is only supposed to be 25mph. This could be a record. Such dry and smooth surfaces offer very little friction to a hovercraft, allowing it to literally fly. However, there is a price to this in that the sand brushing so fast past the tips of the skirt segments wears them away much more quickly. To preserve our dwindling supply of spare segments we learned, reluctantly, to rein ourselves in and slow down on those surfaces.

As well as keeping the craft running, my job was to take the engineers wherever they wanted to go on the project. They did not live in the camp but would turn up each morning with a list of sites to visit. I think they rather enjoyed a trip in the hovercraft and took an interest in their operation. In the same way studies have shown that a person left alone in a room with a tea-cosy will nearly always try it on, there aren't many blokes who will ride in a small hovercraft without asking to 'have a go'. I was happy to let them. I would give a quick run-down of the controls, showing how the Skima 4 uses a tiller for steering: it makes the craft turn in the direction you move it, unlike a boat's tiller which works in the opposite way. Some people find it hard to adjust to this control – the reaction time when driving a hovercraft takes some getting used to and the classic mistake is to over-compensate in panic when the craft doesn't immediately respond.

Although Iain had made it quite clear that he had little time for the hovercraft, he was happy to use it. On one trip, we had stopped at the furthest site where there was a canteen – actually a tent situated on the top of a sandbank. Iain was in an irascible mood – it had been raining heavily and now the cook seemed to be taking a long time to make our lunch, neither of which were to Iain's liking. I noticed the waiter walked rather strangely, sidestepping here and there as he came towards us laden with plates. Puzzled, I looked down and noticed for the first time that the mud floor was overrun with tiny froglets, each the size of a thimble. They were a beautiful brilliant green, iridescent and as shiny as if they had been cast in polished resin. I felt touched that the waiter was taking so much trouble to avoid them until I noticed that each side-step he made was actually a detour to stamp on a baby frog, squashing it flat. The sight of this was bad enough but it was the squelching sound which made me lose my appetite and for once Iain and I were of the same mind – we left without lunch.

Perhaps it was this unaccustomed sense of agreement that made him suddenly ask to have a go at driving just as we were crossing a narrow tributary. With a sinking heart, I demonstrated the controls to him and he nodded impatiently. 'Yes, yes, that's simple enough. It's something I've done before.' He indicated for me to make way for him at the steering position and took imperious command of the lever. But for Iain, who was used to getting his own way, the response was nowhere near quick enough so he made the fundamental mistake of moving the control again and again in an effort to make the craft do what he wanted. In the end, though, the craft did what it wanted, which was to embed itself nose-first in the river bank. Jeremy Clarkson once said that it's an irrefutable rule when driving a hovercraft that if you see something you will hit it. Iain was living proof. Who could be stupid enough to drive head-on into a river bank? Brushing away an answering moment of déjà vu, I set about extricating the craft. There was little damage to the hull (one of the great advantages of inflatables) but a lot to Iain's pride. This had an unexpected bonus, however, in that he barely spoke another word to me for the rest of the day and avoided me for some time afterwards.

The next time I saw him was at a large site meeting in the ex-pats' dining room in which all the site engineers were present. Some of the company's senior partners had also flown in from England, their faces showing the sickly pallor which I'd come to realise is the way all Brits look in the winter. I was feeling rather chipper as I walked through the dining room: I had just sorted out a particularly troublesome recurring ignition problem with Sandfly and mentioned that both the craft were in running order again. Iain, who couldn't resist the opportunity to stir up trouble called across the room for all to hear: 'That's a first! About bloody time!'

It is not often that life delivers a moment of complete and utter satisfaction. Hindsight throws up the usual small regrets: the wittier replies you could have made, the perfect cutting and succinct rebuff. But on this occasion, everything went my way. At Iain's remark, Peter Harris paused in mid-sentence, turned to Iain and gave him a long, level look. The two senior partners he'd been talking to stopped in mid-sentence and followed his gaze. The atmosphere changed. 'Iain doesn't spend a lot of time on site,' said Peter, a remark which could be heard by everyone in the charged atmosphere of the suddenly silent room. The two men nodded, only turning their gaze away from Iain's reddening face when Peter called me over to be introduced and tell them what a great job I was doing.

Looking back, this was an astonishingly difficult piece of work KDC had on their hands. For the pylons to remain standing – and they still are – the foundation into the river-bed needed to go down very deep to resist the scouring effect of the fast-flowing river. To achieve this, caissons – 10m diameter concrete tubes – had to be sunk into the fine sand, and using an air-lift system the wet sandy slurry from below had to be pumped out of the caisson. Miraculously they sank slowly into the river-bed, then a new section of concrete would be cast on top and the whole process was repeated until they were buried one hundred feet into the river-bed.

The project was very well-organised and accidents were rare. The Koreans were seriously hard-working with a never-say-die attitude. Getting stuff to the site was so difficult they made all the hardware for the caissons there in a yard using a range of huge machines. It would then be shipped over to the different sites using cranes, tugs and barges. On one occasion when they needed another boat they simply welded one together – job-done. Okay, it wouldn't have won a beauty contest, but it did the job.

As my time in Bangladesh came to an end, I could say that the four craft were in pretty good running order. This was mainly because we devoted a disproportionate amount of time to maintaining them. The running log for the four craft totalled only 72 hours in three months, less than 3 hours a week. Modern hovercraft, with their superior air and fuel filtration systems, will take these operating conditions in their stride.

After three months, it was time to start putting my stuff together ready to return home. It felt good to have survived in this alien place with hardly any contact from home, figuring everything out for myself. When I first arrived, doubts about whether I was up to the job had plagued me constantly but as time went on, I came to realise that expecting to be found out and exposed as a fraudster or an idiot is a common enough anxiety among self-reflective people; fraudsters and idiots, on the other hand, do not feel self-doubt, or at least never admit to it.

I had just come across the dog-eared Aeroflot ticket tucked inside my passport when Iain turned up. The prospect of another thirty-six-hour epic did not seem so bad now: I had endured nothing but dust and monotony for so long that I almost looked forward to a bit of misery, discomfort and deprivation.

'Aeroflot, eh?' said Iain.

'Yes, unfortunately.'

'I use 'em all the time,' he told me.

'Out of choice?' I asked.

'Yeah, sure. Fantastic safety record and can't beat them for price. But I always take a few of these with me.' He held up a packet of sleeping pills. 'Yep, these little boyos do the trick every time. Here...' He snipped two out of the foil wrapper. 'That'll make you right.'

Surprised, I shook his hand, thanked him and tried to dismiss from my mind the rather uncharitable thought that he might be trying to poison me.

The outward flight is never very enjoyable – you are stricken with wondering and worrying about the unknowns, burdened with the stress of finding your way in a strange country, never knowing what you will actually face. Equally, there is something sublime and uncomplicatedly wonderful about stepping on the plane home, in the knowledge you are heading back to the place you have been dreaming about every night since you left. Familiar faces, familiar food, time off, your own bed.

So, buoyed up with a couple of Heinekens in the airport bar, I was in good spirits as I eased myself into my cramped seat and remembered Iain's little gift tucked in my wallet. All that remains in my memory from that flight home is a prolonged, blurred impression of free-floating over the Atlas Mountains under the tender auspices of the genial Aeroflot cabin crew. I had been wrong about them, I realized, when I saw a poster which explained it all. 'If we're not smiling, it's because we are working hard to make you smile.'

If hovercraft can go anywhere, how did we end up here?

Sweden 2012

Despite our exhausting day off, another eight hours on the job for once saw us a little farther forward and with no steps backward, but we couldn't let this momentum drop if we wanted the job finished to make it back to our families by Christmas.

Because of this reasonable amount of progress, we found ourselves in the Bishop's Arms a little earlier than usual.

'Svävare,' I said, checking Google translate on my phone.

John lifted his pint. 'Svävare,' he responded.

'No, it's Swedish for 'hovercraft',' I said. 'I heard Micke use that word today.'

As I flicked through the other translations, it was interesting how the different names for hovercraft reflected traits of the national character. The French, aeroglisseur, *has a certain streamlined elegance, whereas* luftkissenfahrzeug *has a serious Germanic gravitas about it (but I must admit it also has a certain billowy, bosomy sound which I quite liked). The fact that a Spaniard has three names to choose from -* aerolliscador *(Catalan),* aerobarco *(Galician) or* aerodeslizador

(Spanish) – must show their proud spirit of identity. I like to think that the Philipino word hoberkrap *is not indicative of their sentiments although I can definitely see where they're coming from: it's a word I have reached for myself on many occasions.* Waka Topaki, *the Maori, has obviously either wandered out of a* Star Wars *script or is the name of a wind-throwing warrior, and the Albanian* atomjet *has a marvellous cold war, fifties feel about it, reminding me of a picture I once saw in* Boys' Own *where an enemy hovercraft, shaped like a flying saucer, is bearing down on some jolly nice chaps who, not surprisingly, look slightly alarmed.*

The name 'Hover Craft', a clumpy hybrid term for the first Saunders-Roe air-cushioned vehicle (SRN1), was just a trade name which stuck. Other brand names which could just as easily have been taken up include the Glide-Mobile, the Flying Saucer, the Aeromobile, Cushion-Craft or – my personal favourite – the Vertipod. A business card reading **'Russ Bagley, Vertipod Engineer'** *would be undeniably cool.*

Individual hovercraft also sometimes have names, as in the pretty Sandfly and Decibelle in Bangladesh; the Alaskan craft was pleasingly called Arctic Hawk. A craft I'd once commissioned for the Belgian Army was touchingly named Barbara after the CO's wife. I wonder if she was flattered as he commanded: 'OK, chaps, all jump into Barbara at the double!' And stooping to plain bad taste, I was once told of someone who had an idea to call his racing hovercraft Blowjob but this was vetoed by his wife.

'I towed an aeroglisseur *across France once,' I told John as our fish and chips arrived.*

Votre aeroglisseur est trop large

Chapter 7
Votre aéroglisseur est trop large

Russ: Europe 1986

JG, my boss, was doing what he liked best in the world – towing a large object with a Land Rover – and his cheery mood was infectious. Having crossed the Channel that morning, we were on the second leg of our journey to Rome where the hovercraft – a Griffon 1500TD 15-seater (see appx. 5) – was booked to make a cameo appearance as the 2200 AD equivalent of a postilion carriage in a futuristic Italian remake of *Treasure Island*.

Then in a way that sometimes happens, events took a sudden nose-dive.

'Uh oh,' murmured JG, breaking the long silence during which we had been trying to bring to mind the most notable acting triumphs of Ernest Borgnine, who was to play Billy Bones. As JG signalled and started to slow down, I could see that we were being directed into a lay-by by a liveried patrol car which definitely hadn't been there a moment ago. Police de Frontieres.

My French is not terrific. Travelling across the country by train some years before, I'd been keen to practise what I knew by attempting to talk to my fellow passengers, but like most non-native speakers I had trouble dealing with the verbal torrents which came tumbling out in response to my painstakingly constructed sentences. It was hard recognising where each word began and ended. Not one to give up, I managed to recall the French for 'please speak slowly' but time and again the request was met with a puzzled, if not slightly offended, reaction. An English-speaking French friend put me right.

'*Doucement?*' she repeated, when I told her. 'You've been saying – what? *Plus doucement, si vous plait?*' I nodded sheepishly, withering under her scornful gaze. 'Idiot. You mean *lentement. Lentement* is the French for slowly.'

'Then what....'

'...*doucement*? It means 'softly'. Speak more softly, please.'

'Oh, no.' I cast my mind back over the assortment of strange reactions the phrase had invoked: the nervous expressions, the sudden lowering of the voice to a whisper, the guarded looks, the flashes of conspiratorial sympathy as if I was suffering from a hangover. This also explained the mystifying term 'slow cheese' which I had often puzzled over in the supermarket. This time, to avoid such difficulties, I had already checked out some French words which might come in handy, such as '*aeroglisseur*'.

In the lay-by we jumped down from the cab and stood waiting a full minute, deafened by traffic noise and buffeted by blasts of hot dusty air, before two gendarmes emerged from the car. Wiping their brows, stretching, yawning, donning hats, they seemed in no hurry. Probably just intrigued to see what we were towing: hovercraft tend to be great ice-breakers (in both the metaphorical and the literal sense actually).

'*Papiers*,' demanded the shorter, broader guard, curling his fingers in a complacent, 'give it here' gesture while keeping his eyes fixed on the trailer. He looked mean and I decided to forget the line I'd been rehearsing in the hope of generating a little entente cordiale. (*Est-ce un oiseau? Est-ce un avion? Non, c'est un aéroglisseur!*) JG rummaged in the glove compartment and pulled out our crumpled paperwork, the carnet which gave all the statistics of the craft which our visitors were by now studying in a suspicious way as if it was a receipt for a dodgy second-hand car. They cupped their hands to peer through the tinted cockpit window and tugged experimentally at the various fittings and restraining strops.

The fact that the hovercraft was modified to look like a spaceship probably didn't help. The bullet-shaped fibre-glass dome we had specially fitted over the craft, designed to give it a sleek, space-age appearance, had been ingeniously and thriftily made from the mould of a large mooring buoy we'd found lying about in a local boatyard. The disguise wasn't terribly convincing but it was probably enough to confuse these two sweaty-faced officials – at least, references to *aeroglisseurs magnifiques* were notably absent although I did hear the somewhat derogatory term *rosbif* more than once.

They were carefully studying the carnet now and trying to peer through the fake windows. They asked: '*Nous voulons regarder à l'intérieur, si'l vous plait...*'

But looking inside was no simple undertaking. The only way into the craft was through a small access hole we had cut at the last minute into the roof and this could only be reached by climbing over the temporary and quite delicate superstructure. We gave both the guards a leg-up and with some difficulty, they squeezed inelegantly through the hole and disappeared, still clutching the now quite dog-eared carnet.

Once in, the burly officers spent an inordinate amount of time stumbling about the messy and cluttered interior which bore little resemblance to the outwardly sleek appearance. A few more minutes passed before the sweaty head of one of the officers appeared at the hatch, hastily straightening his cap and breathing heavily.

'*Qu'est-ce que ce... la grande boîte...*'

'Which? The big box? That one? Oh, it's just a spare propeller,' JG replied with studious nonchalance.

'*L'helice,*' I interpreted, giving JG a sideways look.

'It's not on the bloody carnet,' he murmured to me. 'The prop arrived just before we left, after the paperwork was issued.'

It had been one of those things done in the last-minute rush. We had ordered a new propeller for another craft which had arrived while we were preparing to leave. On the spur of the moment, we decided to take it along – after all if we damaged the craft's prop during the filming it would be a disaster. Nobody had given the carnet a thought.

A second head squeezed through the narrow hatch now, and the two officers studied the paperwork with a puzzled expression.

'It's part of the standard spares kit,' JG blustered in sudden inspiration.

The first officer jumped down. The second, being less athletic and portlier, took a little more time but with a bit of help and a few moments to get his breath, he was soon able to reassume his air of disapproving officiousness. There was more talk and remonstration with Gallic gestures. These two had all the time in the world but we were only too aware of our tight schedule. When charm and innocent protest failed, JG tried to adopt a confiding tone but this is less effective when you have to shout over the traffic.

'This hovercraft,' he began, 'has to be in Rome in two days to star in a movie. It is very important that we get there on time. The film is going to be very famous.'

Thinking I detected a vague flicker of interest at this information, I decided that a little judicious name-dropping might help swing the balance.

'The film stars Ernest Borgnine,' I said. There was a silence which could be heard above the traffic noise. The two men looked at me blankly. '*Poseidon Adventure?*' I prompted, doing my best impression of a big ship sinking.

At this point JG shot me a sharp sideways look. In difficult circumstances such as these, he automatically slipped on the mantle of his posh, authoritative alter-ego and I was beginning to cramp his style. Time to back off, I decided.

The continual whoosh whoosh whoosh of traffic almost drowned out the conversation so that I could hear only snatched fragments of Franglais. More discussion, more studying the carnet. As usual, JG had kept his good humour and was gesticulating in that extravagant way of his which was often a good sign. Good old JG. Perhaps we would now be free to go on our way. In the past, his suave demeanour had worked on arrogant sheiks, high government officials, grumpy harbour-masters and sceptical bank-managers. So why not on the Police de Frontieres?

At last some agreement seemed to have been reached. 'It appears we need to go along to the Gendarmerie,' JG said cheerfully. 'Sure we'll soon get it sorted.'

'Ok, when?' I asked, thinking we could amend the carnet ourselves at our convenience. After all, it was just a clerical error. But as JG was already climbing into the Land Rover, I guessed the answer to that must be 'now'. Soon we were just another whoosh on the road.

There is nothing more guaranteed to bring on despondency than heading in completely the opposite direction from the one in which you want to go and from where you have recently come. The Gendarmerie was back towards Calais and pretty soon we had undone half of the little progress we'd made since entering France. Once parked up in the Gendarmerie compound we began the interminable drawn-out business of checking in, checking passports, checking the paperwork, interspersed by long bouts of aimless waiting. JG disappeared to fill in yet more forms and, left to stew in a sweltering green corridor with only my own thoughts to distract me, my mind was soon at fever-pitch. I wondered how long it would be before the story got out and sparked off a *War of the Worlds* panic among the local population, a situation which would surely rapidly escalate to a diplomatic incident. Headlines swirled before my eyes:

'Brits in UFO Hovercraft Hoax; Ambassador Summoned over French Hover Bovver'.

Meanwhile, in my mind's eye, somewhere on a tense Roman film-set the atmosphere is suddenly rent with angry shouts from the distinguished and notoriously exacting director with the leonine hair as he harangues one of his Ray-Banned minions: Where is that fucking hovercraft? (or the Italian equivalent) he demands. Fifteen people with clipboards immediately scuttle off to track us down. Before the scenario could grow any worse, JG emerged from the small interview room, smiling and chatting amicably with the gendarmes as if they were old friends. At last. Now maybe we could get on with our journey and make up some lost time... we could drive through the night and still make the deadline.

'Problem solved,' said JG cheerily.

'Great. Can we go?' I asked.

'Very reasonable chaps,' said JG. 'Yes we can go, but first we have to leave the spare prop here.'

'Oh, could be worse I suppose'

'Should be on our way within the hour.'

And then it dawned on me. 'Do you remember, when we loaded all the spares in the cabin we didn't have the fairing fitted?'

'Yes. So?'

'The prop won't go through the hatch – we'll either have to take the fairing off or make the hatch bigger.'

And that's how JG and I found ourselves in a police compound somewhere outside Calais sawing a large, jagged hole in the roof of a hovercraft disguised as a spacecraft while being watched by the usual ill-assorted group including several mustachioed gendarmes, two sombre children, and a poodle dozing on the back seat of a Renault Espace. Once the hole was just about big enough, I risked personal injury by squeezing into the craft and claimed the propeller which I raised aloft through the makeshift hatch. The officers then took custody, solemnly locking it away in their bonded store so that it couldn't cause any more trouble. You'd think that the matter would be considered sorted at that point, but no, another eternity passed while receipts were stamped and issued, the carbon triplicate dockets duly completed and signed with a flourish, a caution given to be more careful in the future. Top copy for Police de Frontieres' records, second copy for us to wave at anyone who wanted to know, and the third to – who knows? – perhaps to be entered into a big dusty ledger by a sallow-faced official in the Ministry of Pedantry.

We were free to go on our way but the best part of a day late.

'Nice chaps,' reflected JG as we drew off. 'Better keep that piece of paper safe.'

As I picked it up from the dash board, the signature line caught my eye: 'Insp R Rosbif' it read, in loopy handwriting. For a moment, I was certain that we had been elaborately hoaxed – innocent victims of Camera Candide, perhaps?

'Inspector Rosbif?'

'Yes,' yawned JG. 'He was the short one.'

'But Rosbif? Come on. Sure it's not a joke?'

'It's not so strange. No more than if you or I were called Mr Frog.'

'You don't think it strange for someone to be called Mr Frog?'

'No, not at all. Hedgehog, maybe – that would be strange.'

Being unable to think of anything to say to this, I tucked the receipt in with the carnet, and enjoyed the sensation of being back on the open road and heading in the right direction. It wasn't until we stopped for coffee some time later that it began to dawn on us just how late we were. We took stock. The reality was, we needed to be in Rome in two days and we still had 1,000 miles to go.

'Realistically we have to allow at least 24 hours towing this lot,' JG calculated, tracing the route on the map. 'That's two 12-hour days of driving - assuming we don't get any more delays.'

'No, I think we've just had a bit of bad luck. We'll romp through now,' I said optimistically, and immediately wished I hadn't.

'It's a hell of a long drive,' said JG looking glum. 'Anyway, I think we should try to reach the Italian border by tonight - that's about halfway.'

And it did seem that our luck had changed. We fairly tanked along the French AutoRoute, heading for the Alps and the Mont Blanc tunnel, then slowed as we started climbing along the tortuous mountain roads near Chamonix. There was one tense moment at the Italian end of the tunnel when the Frontier Guards half-heartedly measured the width of the craft, but then waved us through with just a cursory scan of the carnet. After a few hours' sleep in the hovercraft cabin in the corner of a quiet car park, we wound our way down through the glorious alpine scenery in the first thin morning light. This felt like the home run, only a mere 500 miles between us and the start of our film careers. No more officious jobs-worths could get in our way now.

The moment we reached the Autostrada and JG put his foot down, an Alfa-Romeo overtook us. Traffic police. For the second time in two days, we were being pulled over. Out jumped a *Polizia Stradale* guard in a crisp white shirt and mirror shades.

'Now what?' muttered JG irritably. Another petty official about to do his damnedest to bring the wheels of industry to a halt.

'Dove stai andando?' he asked then, when we looked blank, 'Where you going?'

'Ah, to Rome,' said JG politely while shooting me a warning look in case I was thinking of trying out my very poor Italian. 'We're actually making a film with RAI Television, starring Ernest Borgnine.' I noticed the old name-dropping tactic came into play early this time and for once it seemed instantly to strike a note: Ernie did have Italian roots after all. The officer smiled. *'Si, si.* Ernest Borgnine,' he said, nodding vigorously. He proffered his hand to John for shaking. Then he returned to his duties, got out a tape measure and indicated that he needed to check the craft. Of course, we knew we had nothing to fear because the dimensions had already been taken at the border without any problem.

But this *politziotto* was much more thorough over his measurements. *'Troppo largo,'* he declared finally, *'È troppo ampia...* Too big – for the *autostrada.'* He explained the rules in broken English and we gradually pieced together the news that autostradas have a width restriction which is narrower than the regular roads. We could only speculate why the autostradas are more restricted – had they not made the toll booth lanes wide enough? Through a series of gestures and mispronounced English and Italian our policeman who turned out not to be the despot I had expected, but seemed to want to help, explained that we could either use the smaller roads, or if we went to their headquarters in Genoa, we could apply for a wide-load permit, a miraculous scrap of paper which would somehow circumvent the narrow parts of the route.

Studying our watches, we tried to calculate how long this unwanted detour would take. Could we still make it to Rome in time? With the trailer unhitched we could go faster and since it was early in the day we should easily arrive while the offices were open. We decided to go for it, leaving the hovercraft in a secure compound, and sped off to Genoa unburdened.

Another hot stuffy government office, another sheaf of forms. We set to work filling them out. How wide? How heavy? Type of fabrication? Purpose of vehicle? That was a tricky one, with only a well-thumbed English-Italian school dictionary to help us. Half an hour later we triumphantly presented the pretty clerk with the completed papers which were duly accepted and carefully placed in a folder, and a chit given as a receipt.

'And we need the permit please,' JG reminded her, 'to take the hovercraft on the autostrada?'

'Of course. No problem. It will be posted to you within 30 days,' she replied pleasantly. 'Oh, wait - possibly longer because it is a foreign vehicle.'

Thunderstruck, I thought of the time we had wasted, time we didn't have in the first place. JG started to remonstrate - 'What? We have to be in Rome by tomorrow! Can't you hurry it through for us and issue it now?' but he knew and I knew that it was really no use.

We walked out of the hot office into a hotter car-park, utterly deflated. A long and thoughtful silence filled the cab of the Land Rover as we drove back. It was only after several kilometres that JG said:

'You know what we have to do now, don't you?' I had already come to the same conclusion.

'Take the side-bodies off,' I sighed.

'In this heat,' he added.

'...right next to a busy motorway...'

'...and we haven't had any lunch... or hardly any sleep!'

So, brimming with enthusiasm we tore into the task. The Griffon 1500TD had side-bodies which could be folded up to reduce its width for transport. They were made in two sections each side and we stacked the four pieces on the Land Rover's roof rack. It was indeed hot, noisy and dusty but at least we felt that it was a solution and that we would soon be on the road again.

Just as we were strapping the craft back on to the trailer our friendly traffic cop returned and smilingly pronounced us *autostrada*-worthy. He then handed me a camera and indicated that he would like me to take a photo of him and JG. These were the days when photographs had to be taken away to be developed so you never saw the pictures until weeks later, when you discovered that they were overexposed/blurred/wonky and you couldn't remember why you had taken them in the first place. I wish I'd seen this one, however, as I am sure it would have perfectly illustrated the fundamental differences between Italians and the English: without a trace of self-consciousness, in automatic reflex to the lens, the Italian struck a macho pose giving him an air of confident authority; JG's expression stayed exactly the same, giving him the air of a man standing next to a hovercraft. The officer shook JG's hand.

'Very good,' he said. '*The Poseidon Adventure. Molto bene. Ernesto Borgnine – magnifico!*' I climbed back into the Land Rover leaving JG signing papers.

'Got the paperwork?' I asked as he climbed in empty-handed.

'Oh - no. He just wanted my autograph,' said JG, as if this was an everyday occurrence.

'Why would he want your autograph?'

'Well apparently, his mother's quite keen on old Ernie. I'm sort of Ernie once-removed.' Once again, I could think of no reply.

A few days later, in a tiny studio outside Rome crammed with the ever-present hangers-on who always seem to be there on a film-set (but not counting myself as one of them of course), I couldn't help agreeing that Ernest Borgnine was pretty magnificent. On the signal 'Action' he lit up like a fruit machine. From a genial, jokey, ordinary sort of bloke he became an edgy, glittery-eyed maniac feverishly raving on his sick-bed. This is what actors do. They become somebody else, not half-heartedly or timidly, or with one eye on people's reactions but actually become someone else then slip back into their own skins without missing a beat. It may have been a tinny, B-rated movie but to me, standing shoulder to shoulder with my fellow gawpers six feet from the action, it was a Shakespearean performance.

The film-set was a triumph of plywood which portrayed a time in The Future when the world, clearly down on its luck, had mysteriously become exactly like a grimy concrete multi-storey car-park in which people shouted and looked anxious and occasionally cooked blue jelly in a space-age device styled along the lines of a Morphy Richards microwave circa 1980. You have to remember that in 1986 mobile phones were the size of breeze-blocks, computer monitors were the size of rabbit hutches and everything electronic had big clunky oblong switches made of white plastic. The future high-tech world portrayed by the film mirrored its own time: boxy, lumpy, over-sized, analogue.

'Cut!'

A girl with a high pony tail and a clipboard pushed her way through the throng to adjust Ernest's dirty tabard, a garment which seemed, in various shapes and colours, to be the prevalent fashion in The Future. A make-up person mopped his brow; the hairdresser carefully arranged a stray lick of hair. I waited eagerly for the scene to continue but when after half an hour of milling about with the crowd, absolutely nothing had happened, I found a new place to mooch. I had learned two important principles of film-making. Firstly, it's two per cent interesting (which means it is ninety-eight per cent boring). Secondly, there are always three times as many people as necessary to make a film and nobody knows who they are. These two principles are self-supporting in a way because when your mind completely runs out of things to think about in the doldrums of wasted time, you can fill some of the hours idly trying to figure out the people, distinguishing between those who have a job to do from the vast army of hangers-on. What is that person doing here? Does he have to bring that dog? Are two vets really necessary? Is he wearing a wig? Is that the turkey trainer's wife, girlfriend, assistant, daughter or none of these? Isn't the girl who serves on the catering van also an extra in the angry down-trodden crowd scene? These questions are never answered, not that you care much about them anyway, and the day drags on.

It turned out that we needn't have hurried after all. The hovercraft had been on the set, primed in readiness for two days before it was eventually needed. In the deep shade of the huge fake buildings which we named Plywood City, we hastily stuck it back together thinking our call could come at any minute but then in the unexpected extra time at our disposal we were able to add a go-faster stripe. We carefully put the finishing touches to the craft, keenly aware that our work was being observed by the macho crew of a red rival hovercraft of unknown origin which had a slightly higher profile in the film but was garish and had the lines of a cheap sports car.

On the third day, there was a bit of added buzz around the craft: technicians and production assistants sketching out the route that we would have to make, discussing camera angles and other technical issues, talking over each other in a way that only Italians can. A pretend road had been built along the beach and behind Plywood City, but it was narrow and winding.

'All you have to do is come off the water and drive along the road. Yes?'

JG and I exchanged glances, picturing the tight turn that would be needed. To complicate matters, this beach was made up of deep sand which had been transported specially, and fake cacti studded the whole area. Space-age lights had been rigged at ground level and we knew these would be almost impossible to see when driving. But we were ready to give it a go.

Half an hour passed which is an awfully long time when two quite large people are squashed together in a sweltering airless cabin, like goldfish in a bowl left out in the noonday sun. Half a dozen people, clones of each other in designer sun-glasses, were thrashing out the finer details of the scene - at least, we presumed they were, although for all we knew they could have been discussing the importance of free speech or the cheapest place to buy flip-flops. Then just as we were finally about to melt there was a peremptory rapping on our plastic space-age cockpit dome.

'*Pranzo.* Ready to launch,' called a voice.

'Here we go,' I said.

But JG was already out of the cockpit and I could see the clones disappearing up the beach. He made to follow.

'What's going on?'

'You heard,' he said. '*Pranzo.* Lunch.'

I knew then how an astronaut feels when a mission is aborted at the final countdown.

'Lunch!' I said. 'That means another three hours hanging around.'

'Three hours of being paid to do nothing,' JG pointed out. 'Let's see what's to eat.'

After lunch, there was more mooching, a few minor crises and lots of time spent cooped up in the sweltering hovercraft, then everyone drifted away and it wasn't until the next day that we were at last called to do our scene.

As we fired up the engines, the usual bunch of hangers-on appeared, eager to see the stunt. We had to aim for a particular marker on the beach, a process which was made more difficult because of the blacked-out windows. There was a small letterbox of visibility, better positioned for the navigator (me) than the driver so I had to give precise step-by-step instructions. It was tense but we somehow managed to swoop up the beach and arrive at just the right spot, a feat which drew our audience closer, thinking we were about to stop. But we still had to cross the beach and get to the road. We had tried to explain the effect the hovercraft would have on a sandy beach and no doubt the film crew had passed on our warnings but Italians don't even have a word for 'hovercraft' so perhaps the message didn't get across or got lost in translation.

We swept on up the beach, setting off a spectacular sand-storm worthy of *Laurence of Arabia*. The onlookers were taken by surprise.

In an instant, carefully styled hair became a wild tangle, people hung on to their hats, sunglasses blew off of startled faces. Several plastic cacti shot across the fake desert terrain pursued by a beach umbrella cart-wheeling along at a leisurely pace.

In all the excitement, it's possible nobody noticed the skill with which we executed a text-book turn onto the road – a very tricky manoeuvre. Okay, so we lost a few of those carefully positioned lights and dislodged a fake rock or two but nobody asked us to do a second take, so it must have been good.

In fact, if you care enough to look on YouTube or manage to find a rare Betamax Videotape of the film on EBay, you will see the part the 1500 craft played in *L'Isla de Tresoro*. It wasn't a huge role – a

minute's footage for three weeks' work would be a fairly accurate ratio – but it held its own. Sleek and mysterious with its blacked-out cockpit windows, it pulls smoothly into view leaving an impression of hushed anonymity, and power held in reserve. It does its stuff in the British way: quietly, efficiently and with minimal fuss... and not a flying cactus in sight.

That's another thing I learnt about film-making – it's just amazing what editors can do.

If hovercraft can go anywhere, how did we end up here?

Sweden 2012

After a week in Luleå, it was now time to tackle the problem of the generator – another bloody awkward job. It had been rammed into a compartment at the back of the craft without an inch to spare. This was fine until any maintenance tasks were attempted. It is possible that over time, humans might evolve and mutate into creatures with three triple-jointed arms, x-ray vision and an ability to levitate but Micke said he couldn't wait that long. We needed to modify the mountings so it could slide out for routine maintenance.

Luckily for him, Olaf had managed to escape back to Kalix for Christmas so John and I set to forcing our protesting bodies into new and interesting Houdini-type sequences of contortions. John's slighter physique meant that he was the inevitable choice to do the work while I sort of choreographed his movements. 'Ok, left-hand down a bit and then you should just be able to squeeze through between the pipes to reach that flange. Now, right foot down, just by the red pipe.' The Coastguard station was pretty much deserted but to a stray passer-by it would have sounded as though were playing a giant game of Twister. With no chance of undoing the generator's existing fastenings, we had to grind them off so that they could be replaced with a well thought-through, practical and user-friendly system.

Seeing the toll all this was taking on us, Micke kindly invited us to his house, fed us and gave us a tour of his property. There is something very blokey about life in the tough climate of northern Sweden. When the ice forms, suddenly it's playtime. The winter months may be cold and dark but like many icy places, Luleå actually gains a fun dimension when it freezes: nature rolls out roads of ice, making short-cuts to places which are a long way away in the summer. Boats are hauled ashore, skis and snow-scooters come out of storage. Micke not only had a ride-on lawn-mower but his own personal snow-plough. Like many

Swedes, he also had a workshop of enviable proportions which housed the tools, weapons and other appliances essential to life in rugged places. Made by Saab and Husqvarna, they looked as if they could bore a hole to the centre of the earth: whether you need to grind, drill, cut, weld, lop or chop you will find the right machine tucked away somewhere behind the pines.

I was reminded vividly of another member of the Swedish Coastguard I had worked with in 1993. Like Micke, he had shown me great hospitality, taken me home to share a meal with his family and then proudly showed me round his land, ending the tour with a visit to his workshop. Pride of place was taken by a machine which stood as tall as a man. It was basically a big circular table-saw fitted with a giant, log-splitting screw which protruded from the side. It was not difficult to imagine the sort of punch it would pack. He confided that he had once had a terrible dream in which he'd caught his head in the machine and woken up with a terrible headache. It was a gruesome thought. Some years later, when the Coastguard contingent visited our premises in Southampton, I asked after my friend and was met with sad head-shaking from the others. 'He died,' I was told. 'A terrible accident with garden machinery.' I felt the hairs on the back of my neck stand up and asked no more.

We passed the afternoon pleasantly in Micke's kitchen, swapping stories and drinking coffee. Hunting and fishing are a big part of life in the north of Sweden, not just for sport or leisure but for the meat: apparently, each household has a quota so there is much swapping and sharing out of moose and reindeer parts. When Micke offered us some cured moose tongue, a sought-after delicacy, I was secretly glad I was vegetarian, but I hadn't always been.

'Have you ever eaten pelican?' I asked him.

Micke laughed. 'No pelicans in Sweden, only storks. Don't tell me you've eaten pelican?'

'Yes,' I said. 'And it wasn't bad. You see, I met this hunter in Pakistan...'

A Short Walk
in the
Rann of Kutch

Chapter 8
A Short Walk in the Rann of Kutch

Russ: Pakistan 1982

The first time I flew to Pakistan, it was on the back of rather a loose arrangement. A civil engineering project 'needed someone to drive a hovercraft somewhere near Karachi,' Mike explained. He was hurrying to go off to his Magic Circle meeting at the time and so was a bit vague about names and contact numbers.

'Someone will meet you at the airport,' he said when I asked for details.

He didn't sound too sure. 'And if they don't? Plan B?' I asked reasonably.

Mike finished checking the contents of his attaché case, clicked it shut and considered. 'Go to the Hotel Midway House and wait. Someone will get in touch.'

No-one met me in Karachi although I waited and waited until I was the last person in the arrivals hall apart from a tiny woman who was sweeping the same patch of vast floor over and over with a dainty feather broom, pausing only to glare at me from time to time. Reluctantly, I headed out from the safety of the building and instantly found myself surrounded by helpful people offering to carry my bags or sell me tea. There was no shortage of drivers either, offering to take

me to a very good hotel they knew of in town. Remembering Mike's advice, I was firm in my resolve that I should go to the Midway and agreed a price for the journey, even haggling it down a little. When I arrived, I found out why Mike had specified the Midway House Hotel – it was two minutes' walk from the airport but I discovered this only after I had parted with a substantial wad of Rupees in taxi fare. I fell into a jet-lagged sleep and was awakened by someone knocking loudly on my door. Someone called Malcolm.

In the jeep, on the way to Hyderabad, Malcolm explained what the project involved. Crops were failing in thousands of hectares of agricultural land in Sindh province in the south of Pakistan. The reason for this was an increase in salt concentration in the groundwater following years of irrigation without adequate drainage. Now there was a proposal for a massive project to remove this saline groundwater. The survey was concerned with extending an existing drain (Kadhan Pateji Outfall Drain - KPOD), 44 kilometres south-west, across the Rann of Kutch to discharge into the Arabian Sea.

After a few days of preparation and provisioning at the company house in Hyderabad we drove our convoy of jeeps and pick-ups 160 kilometres south to the town of Badin and then beyond, where a further 20 kilometres of rudimentary dirt track lead to the canal road, then that too petered out near a fishing village. KPOD, a 20m wide waterway very close to the Indian border, was to be our launch point for the two craft. There were five of us: myself and Malcolm; then Farooq the cook, Sameer the driver and Vijay the security guard. Vijay was an emaciated fellow with bloodshot eyes and red teeth from chewing *khat*. Rather worryingly, he was the one with a gun.

Wikipedia describes The Great Rann of Kutch as a salt marsh that spreads across the border between Pakistan and India. That's only half of the story. It's a wilderness, as barren as the moon – a grey-brown expanse sweeping away as far as the eye can see. Nearer the coast, there are at least a few tidal creeks to break up the monotony. The wet areas along the link alignment consist mainly of large, very shallow lakes called *dhands*. The dry sections are mud with a baked crust which, despite appearances, and as we later learned first-hand,

is not firm enough to support a vehicle. Hence the need for a hovercraft.

The two Skima 4 mk3s (see appx. 2) were carried dismantled in the back of a pick-up truck. Once we arrived at base camp, it was my job to assemble them and, for some masochistic reason, I chose the hottest part of the day to start. It was a job which required hard physical effort, especially pumping up the inflatable hull. Before long, a steady stream of locals, mainly fishermen, began to materialize out of nowhere. I wondered how word got around without any sort of phones available. However this news was transmitted, the system worked very well. The spectators assumed an easy squatting position, forming a rough semi-circle which kept widening to accommodate newcomers who watched my every move. To people so far removed from any organised entertainment, the spectacle of a sweaty irritable white man wrestling with a hovercraft probably made a nice change. The thought that I was the best show in town made me put a bit more effort into it all.

With the two hovercraft commissioned, work commenced. The alignment started at the end of KPOD and this spread out into a wide and very shallow lake, Pateji Dhand. Vast but barely more than an inch deep. We had to lay down the course of the new drain with a series of markers. During the first few days we set out these to a compass bearing, placing one approximately every 2 kilometres, or at the limit of sight. The marker was in fact a stake driven into the mud with a bamboo tripod flying a hi-vis flag above it. They were aligned in the morning on the outward trip, and the distance between them measured on the way back with an electronic measuring device.

Malcolm was an experienced hovercraft driver who had learned his skills in the UK. We operated as a pair simply because the very versatility of the hovercraft – its ability to traverse many terrains accessible to no other vehicle – means that if it breaks down, nothing else can come to its rescue. The prospect of walking tens of kilometres across snake-infested lake beds is not a welcoming one.

We had been warned about these poisonous water-snakes whose *modus operandi* is to produce venom that paralyzes the respiratory system, ultimately causing death. Needless to say, we were careful to carry out all the water work from the safety of the hovercraft, resisting the temptation to paddle.

All went well for the first week. Progress was easy in such perfect hovercraft territory: with water so shallow it was always calm, the craft travelled fast and easily over it. We marked out 10 or 15 kilometres per day.

But the honeymoon was soon over. As we moved further down the line where the area became more tidal and the surface changed to dry salty mudflats, I noticed an ominous drop-off in the performance of the craft. One might think that a hovering vehicle would be unaffected by the surface it hovers over but of course the skirt is in contact with the ground all the time. If the skirt begins to wear, a hovercraft will inevitably hover lower and lower - until it stops. Thus my first check was the skirt. A Skima 4 is light enough that it is possible to lift one side of the craft and prop it up with a paddle to inspect the underside. However, this is a risky operation in warm climates: the dark and humid conditions under a hovercraft attract all sorts of creepy crawlies. But what I found horrified me more than any snake or scorpion – peering through the fetid gloom, I stared in disbelief at a skirt which was hanging in tatters, as if it had been running for a year rather than a few days. A quick calculation told me that we had completed less than a quarter of the overland work. My immediate reaction was to get straight onto Gosport and have them send out more segments made from a heavier material, but I dismissed this pretty quickly, knowing this would slow the craft by increasing drag; also because the segments would be stiffer, they might wear even faster. When I thought about it still further, remembering that I would have to go to Hyderabad to get a message home, I realized that the job was scheduled to be finished before the new segments would even arrive. I decided to monitor the problem and hope that the spares we brought would see us through.

A note from my log book reveals a rather alarming preoccupation, not to say obsession, with the problem. Did I really get down on my knees and measure the height of worm-casts?

> *29th November, 1982*
> *There are five main types of surface here.*
> 1. *Water – no problem.*
> 2. *Wet mud in tidal areas – no problem*
> 3. *Wet, sticky mud. Very draggy. Has areas of large worm-casts… small mounds which are about 25-50mm high in dense patches. Pulls down bow of craft and reduces speed. Doesn't feel abrasive.*
> 4. *Dry crusty mud. Very abrasive. Possible to travel fast (too fast!) across this. Still has dense patches of mounds as above but dry.*
> 5. *Mud tracks. Some parts dry (probably the worst surface encountered), others sticky, providing painfully slow progress. Experience loss of lift, requires full power to cross.*

The skirt problem began to escalate when we neared the seaward end of the alignment and encountered the dreaded Lakhpat Road. This is an ancient camel trail stretching south along the coast from Pakistan and into India. It is made up of millions of camel footprints, each one a 20-30cm circular depression which has been repeatedly washed with sea-water and then baked hard, producing a salty crust as hard as concrete. Unless you're a camel, it is the most excruciatingly uncomfortable surface to walk on especially as it is covered with a granular coating of salt, giving the texture of coarse sandpaper which would strip your skin if you fell on it. We tried the only skirt-preserving tactics available – either reducing the payload as far as possible or trying to avoid the Lakhpat Road completely, but we had to cross it a few times to finish the job. There seemed nothing we could do to prevent the skirt shredding to tatters and reducing the hovercraft to a crawl. We were literally driving the craft into the ground.

Daily life consisted of a monotonous and unchanging routine and in the unoccupied hours, I worried incessantly about the craft. I made

sure I updated my mud-diary every night, dolefully recording the number of segments which had worn out that day. Every week, I wrote home dutifully and although The Great Rann of Kutch sounded like a very exotic address, it is possible that these were the most boring letters ever written, full of minutiae about mud and technical jargon which must have been quite baffling to the folks at home.

Eat, work, eat, work, eat, sleep went around and around in endless rotation. In my case sleep was fitful, not helped by the running battles with insects which always preceded it. The mosquitoes seemed to view my mosquito net as an interesting challenge, a bit like an obstacle course: they would ease their way through the netting, whine across my bed (stopping for a bite to eat on the way), do a few aerobatics and squeeze out again on the other side to reach the light of my flickering paraffin lamp. No amount of mending, folding or re-hanging of the nets could keep them out.

Now and again the monotony was punctuated by a minor excitement which distinguished one day from all the other identical days. On one occasion as we were crossing the *dhand* in the hovercraft, I noticed that Malcolm was lagging a long way behind me. He appeared to have stopped suddenly and was bent over the side of the craft. Had he been taken ill? Attacked by a poisonous sea-snake? As I closed in, I realised that he was actually scooping water with his hat and splashing it over the stern. Only then did I notice the smoke: the back of the craft was burning! The exhaust had come loose and set fire to the fibreglass. Malcolm's quick thinking (and his very serviceable hat) saved the craft from much damage. Back at camp, after an enjoyable session of bush engineering, we had the exhaust pipe inelegantly re-routed, out of harm's way.

The smallest diversion seemed disproportionately exciting. One night an unidentified furry creature shot through the main tent, whizzed under the camp-beds and out the other side, pursued by a large rat and then finally a barking dog. There was a tense pause as we all waited for a goat or possibly a camel... but that was the end of

151

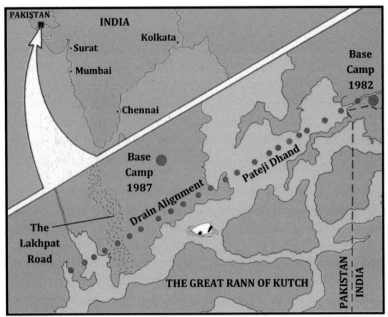

it. The darkness swallowed them up. That night I dreamt of an endless parade of animals running to the soundtrack of *Good Morning* by the Beatles with its barking dogs and crowing roosters; the tent caught fire and melted, causing the camel footprints to blossom into huge floury *chappatis*.

Forget sand. A desert is a place devoid of stuff. A non-place. Somewhere so empty of features or interest that you have to resort to amusing yourself the best you can with what's inside your head. I found this to be a disappointing experience. Far away from familiar people and things, there is nothing to confirm your identity; your frame of reference disappears, just as every sound is swallowed by the emptiness, leaving no echo.

Some evenings just after sunset, driving the hovercraft back to camp, a slight mist made the horizon disappear and the sky, land and sea became seamless. A creeping sense of panic would set in. Losing all sense of perspective, I was suddenly unsure of what was level, what was up and what was down. Worse still, I found myself disbelieving the compass. The mirror-calm water offered no clues to our attitude or direction. Then a flock of birds would appear, with a corresponding reflection, and everything would jerk back into place – you could believe your eyes again, but it was a disconcerting experience. The first time this happened, I glanced back at the hovercraft wake and realised that I'd been driving in a huge curve. After that I always followed the compass, however counter-intuitive it felt.

I had heard stories of the voices out of nowhere and other delusions which tortured lone long-distance sailors: Chichester had been beset with a growing conviction that there was a man living in his sail locker. Once on a night-watch a friend of mine had become so convinced that there was a rabbit running around the foredeck of his yacht, he duly noted it down in the log-book. Driving through the surreal calm one evening on the way back to the camp, fighting that dizzying sensation of being adrift in space, I noticed a smudge to starboard. We did very occasionally see small local craft on the *dhands*, but I had never seen one like this, in which the sole occupant appeared to be a large white bird. Nothing about it moved. The boat and the bird shimmered as one thing, suspended in the atmosphere, sabre-like beak folded against a serpentine neck, encased in bone-white feathers, the jaunty tuft on its skeletal head belying the penetrating primeval stare of its ancient beady eye. I slowed the craft, closing the distance between us but the creature showed no sign of alarm, no flicker of interest, just remained perfectly still in its attitude of sorrowful contemplation.

The other Skima was some way ahead of me by now, and I knew I should follow. I was in the customary end-of-day state: tired and hungry, my salt-encrusted skin sore and sun-burnt. I started to steer away towards Malcolm's wake, when the giant bird suddenly shivered, heaved itself upwards and literally grew arms and legs until a figure stood before me, half-man, half-creature, a sinister pantomime character crossed with an Egyptian god. This is it, I thought. I have flipped, gone over to the twilight zone where just as sky is indistinguishable from sea, reality is interchangeable with imagination, man has become beast. Standing before me was a man... a man with the head of a pelican. Then the arms reached up to the bird which fell lifelessly forward and toppled, making him just a man holding a dead pelican.

We made eye-contact. I raised my hand and he raised his, the meeting of two worlds far enough apart to be on separate planets. As I pulled away I looked back and only then did I see that there was also a little boy in the boat; he had scrambled eagerly into the prow and was waving and waving. His excitement broke the spell and brought

a welcome normality to the encounter, a little boy like any other, watching a hovercraft, now disappearing into the mist.

I asked Farooq about the pelican man and gathered he was a hunter with a remarkable technique. He would paddle his boat to the middle of the *dhand* and lie down with the hollow pelican on his head. To demonstrate what happened next, Farooq flapped his arms, becoming the unwitting bird flying overhead, which sees the boat, the kindred pelican, swoops down on ragged wings, lands... Farooq's outstretched arm changed from a wing to a gun. BLAM! He licked his lips and nodded emphatically.

Farooq's repertoire of meals was small. Every morning we ate hot *chapatti dahl*; packed lunch consisted of cold *chapatti dahl* and in the evening, back to hot again. There was one exception, however when one day we were surprised to be offered meat rather than the usual fare. Malcolm rather naively asked the cook if it was chicken:

'No Sah,' he replied, 'pelican.'

Malcolm pushed his plate away with an expression of disgust. I said nothing but I thought it was rather tasty!

We eventually reached the day when we could say for sure that the dwindling supply of spares wouldn't be enough for us to finish the job. It was time to put into action a plan I had been considering during the long days and sleepless nights – I would set up our own skirt shop in a separate tent solely for the purpose of repairing worn-out segments.

In order to stock up, Malcolm and I made the bone-shattering three-hour journey to Hyderabad with a shopping-list of glue, rubber fabric, a bench grinder, a sewing machine and other sundry tools. There could hardly be a bigger contrast between the teeming traffic-snarled streets of Hyderabad and the eerie emptiness of the salt-flats. Moribund and in a state of long-term suspension from underuse, my senses were suddenly uncomfortably saturated. We wandered round the market in a daze, unused to close proximity to thousands of strangers. Keen to head back as soon as possible, we managed to find everything on our list within an hour.

Thereafter, we spent one day in three repairing and replacing skirt segments and managed to keep the craft in running order for the remainder of the survey.

Maybe everyone should spend their forty days in the wilderness. It made me realise the worth of the ordinary things in my own life – places, people and events which kept me looking outward and suited me better than being lost in gloomy introspection. When I left, I did not expect ever to return to the Great Rann of Kutch, but it hadn't finished with me yet.

Russ: Pakistan 1987

Five years later, I found myself back on a different phase of the same project: the job was now to mark the alignment of the drain permanently and more accurately to give a course to the dredgers which would be excavating the new canal. There were differences: second time around, I was working for a Dutch company and this time we had a single (bigger and better) hovercraft which was assigned to two surveyors, Daan and Dick, who worked for the dredging contractors.

The Skimas had proved the case for the hovercraft in civil engineering projects such as these, which were hampered by difficult conditions in marshy terrain. More survey equipment was needed for this part of the project so the company had invested in a new craft, a Griffon 1000TD (see appx. 4), a 30-foot, one-ton, robust, diesel-powered hovercraft, as different from the Skima as a rubber dinghy is from a work-boat. This was a clear endorsement of the company's faith in the role of the hovercraft. It was supplied to the customer complete with a road trailer fitted with low-ground-pressure tyres to cope with the soft terrain south of Jati. We towed it by Land Rover from Hyderabad to base camp, a route made up of some metalled roads but mainly dirt-track. Our driver was Parvez, a quick-thinking, well-educated man from the Punjab who spoke excellent English and cursed in Urdu at the ox-carts straying in our path.

We provisioned up in Hyderabad, spending the subsistence money given to us by the project manager. Remembering the endless *chapatti dahl* dinners, lunches, packed lunches and suppers we had endured last time, I decided to buy some luxuries, like tinned baked beans and vegetables to add some variety to the diet. We trailed the craft up to where the road ran out in Jati then stopped to stretch our legs and buy tea at a street stall. A couple of senior surveyors from The Water and Power Development Authority (who owned the craft) preceded us for the last 30km, following an Aveling Barford grader to prepare the road. Some narrow parts of the dirt track crossed filled-in ditches which needed planks across to prevent the vehicles sliding

off sideways; the odd pot-hole had to be filled but these were small delays in a seemingly uneventful journey. Not entirely uneventful though: when we came to unpack, we found the box of food was missing, probably stolen when we stopped for our tea-break. All my carefully chosen delicacies gone! I consoled myself with the thought that whoever stole them probably needed them more than I did; but there were times when I had less charitable thoughts as I faced my fourth meal of *chapatti dahl* in one day.

The old Great Rann of Kutch looked just the same; probably the same, in fact, as it had looked for the last ten thousand years. The camp too was a similar arrangement to last time: a group of tents in a semicircle, one for the Europeans, one for the Pakistanis, and a cook-house. An earth latrine a hundred metres from the tents completed our facilities. We began work straight away armed with an array of state-of-the-art 'modern' devices which would now probably only be found in a museum. They were part of that pre-digital transitional technology which lasted for a few brief years, along with videos, faxes, banda-machines and tape-recorders. Many of our measurements were gathered using a device called a Topofil. This was a mechanical counter, the size of a desk-top pencil-sharpener, to which was attached a reel of nylon line. To measure the distance across a creek, for instance, we needed to hammer a peg into the bank and tie the end of the reel to it, set the counter to zero then drive the craft to the opposite side and make a reading. To prevent the flimsy line from blowing around and getting hooked up round the craft, we learnt to make high-speed dashes, belting across at full-speed to keep the line taut. We then needed to measure depth of water, going slowly back to the stake, taking soundings all the way. With this information, a profile of the creek could later be drawn up. A compass was not accurate enough to measure our heading or establish the direction of our 26-mile alignment, where even a minute compass error would become magnified to an unacceptable extent. Instead, we used a sextant to take sightings from the ever-present sun.

The two Dutch surveyors did in fact have a new and very expensive first-generation GPS set which they treated with great reverence. They insisted (quite wrongly) that the antenna must be mounted high above the craft, to which end they fashioned an enormous 10m edifice from sticks and string, lashing it to the stubby mast which held the navigation light. It looked ridiculous and made handling the hovercraft very unwieldy in anything but the calmest conditions. We persevered for 2 days until, in a fresh breeze, the windage from the mast caused the craft to violently plough-in sideways on some sticky mud. I insisted they took it down there and then, and erected a modest stick for the antenna. The GPS worked just as well.

This time, planning more logically, we'd sited the camp near the middle of the alignment to reduce the amount of travel required to reach either end of the line. But the nearest point we could get a vehicle was still several kilometres away – several kilometres of dry, salty mud that had to be crossed twice daily before we could even begin working. We had been careful to bring plenty of spare skirt

segments with us in the light of our previous experience; however, within a few days it became obvious that the different operating practices were wearing the skirt even faster than before.

Parvez was turning out to be a great asset. He had a cheerful disposition and was a good engineer. Never rushed but taking time to think things through, he proved himself to be sensible and versatile, able to improvise and increasingly inventive. At every opportunity I had been training him up to drive the craft and he had learnt quickly. Indeed, he would often reprimand me, if he thought I was going too fast, with the disapproving comment: 'We are speedy!'

When the skirt-shift winch cable broke, we worked together to mend it with bulldog grips, standing back proudly from our low-tech practical solution. One day, I decided to show Parvez how to do a routine oil change. Having seen some of the oil which passed as refined, and the problems it caused, we drove to Jati to buy some highly expensive, high-performance oil. Step by step, I showed Parvez how the oil change should be done, and he paid careful attention. If he wondered why I did not put the drain plug back, he didn't say. But as the precious oil ran straight out of the open sump and disappeared into the bilges, Parvez showed me just how much I had taught him.

'Shit!' he said.

This, his first curse in English, was well-picked and just right for the occasion: the very one I would have used myself in such circumstances. I felt proud. And nor did he offer another word of reproach as we drove to Jati for the second time that day to buy some more highly expensive, high-performance oil.

We decided to see if we could relocate base camp closer to the alignment. We fitted the low-ground-pressure tyres from the trailer onto the Land Rover and set off to find a better site. We followed the track west for several miles before deciding to leave the road and head south across what looked like solid ground. Within 50 metres of the track the 'all-terrain' tyres were up to their axles in liquid mud. In the dying heat of the day, we spent several hours using whatever was

to hand – canes, sticks, shovels – trying to provide enough grip to spin free but nothing worked. By the time we finally gave up, we looked like proto-mud-beings newly-formed from the ground beneath our feet: the liquid mud which covered us set hard in the heat and cracked as we moved. There was nothing for it but to set off and walk the 15 km back to camp, arriving after dark. Next morning, we made a round trip into Jati, bouncing and juddering along 30 kilometres of dirt track there and 30 kilometres back, to engage a man with a tractor and planks. The whole day was taken up with retrieving the Land Rover – although with the right equipment getting the vehicle unstuck took only about half an hour, while waiting for the said man to turn up took most of the day. We handed over a modest fee and thereafter abandoned the search for a new camp.

In the tidal areas at the seaward end of the line we encountered some very deep gulleys at low water. The thing that made them particularly treacherous was that they were almost impossible to see until the craft was actually upon them. But even when we did get it wrong and found ourselves straddled across the gulley there was no

damage – it just meant we had to spend several hours waiting for the tide to fill the trench enough for the craft to hover out again. At such times we would tune into the cricket and although I knew nothing about the game, I found its words and phrases redolent of home as they floated out poetically into the silent emptiness. In my ignorance, I did not even know that I was listening to a match which would go down in cricketing history as one of the most exciting ever.

It's a hundred and five for five, now everything depends on Botham.

Far ahead of me, a donkey moves across the horizon led by a figure in black.

The substitute's running round, he's caught it.

A flock of white birds rises to the air, instantly mirrored in the smooth water creeping towards us.

And that's Botham out!

Judging the water high enough for us to hover out we started the engine and carried on with our working day.

We had often seen men on camel-back in the vicinity of our camp – fierce-faced bearded men, dressed in spotless *shalwar kameez*, ancient rifles slung loosely over their shoulder. They were frontier guards, patrolling the much-disputed border between India and Pakistan. Their camp was near ours but they seemed remote and haughty characters and we had never approached them. Then one evening during dinner, instead of swaying on past as they usually did, two of the soldiers steered their camels in our direction. They presented us with an invitation from their Commanding Officer to come for tea the following evening.

Compared with our shabby tents their camp was a haven of order. We were escorted to a small wooden building which served as the CO's office. Before our eyes adjusted to the gloom, it appeared that our host was sitting in solitary splendour behind a grand polished wooden desk but as we drew further in, I could see half a dozen or so soldiers squatting around the edges of the room. They were of a type I was later to notice in mothballed military bases, remote border crossings and dusty offices all over the world. I came to think of them as the Extras – men employed by the government, presumably to fulfil some official quota. I saw them hanging about in corridors or loitering in stairwells, leaning against walls and smoking, with nothing to do except wait for their superiors to bark out an order or send them packing on some spurious errand.

The CO was tall and commanding with an air of calm nobility which made me feel very aware of my own unwashed scruffiness. After a period of smiling and friendly gesturing one of the men was sent to organise tea, a welcome fussy ritual which filled some time. By now it was apparent that our host spoke no English whatsoever. There were several false starts at conversation, more smiling and nodding until that too petered out into an excruciating silence broken only by the occasional hawking and spitting of the men in the shadows. When the silence in the room had stretched way too far, the Commander suddenly rose to his feet and stood before us at his full impressive height, as if about to make some sort of declaration – a formal welcome speech, perhaps, or an exhortation to convert to Islam. Instead, he fixed his eyes on a point somewhere above our heads and with perfect enunciation he began to intone the words of *Twinkle, Twinkle Little Star*, word perfect, all the way through. His grave and careful recitation seemed to imbue the words with a significance I had never noticed before. We listened respectfully, bemused, but also rather moved, and clapped politely at the end, and thanked him, then walked back to our own camp in the soft darkness, under our own mass of twinkling stars.

The Dutchmen got their data and despite the skirt wear, nothing could rival the hovercraft as the undisputed king of the *dhands*. No other vehicle could have coped with the extreme unpredictability of the terrain in the Great Rann of Kutch. Without doubt, the hovercraft was tested to the limit and I was tested too – by the heat, the mud, the daily monotony… The lasting lesson, however, is discovering what truly matters. In my case, I felt an unwavering line, like a tangible cord, which started with me and rose out of the brown wilderness, past the ancient trails, the salt-pans and their rows of patient donkeys, floating high over the Atlas Mountains and ending with home.

The desert strips everything away and then shows you what is left.

Sweden 2012

John and I left the warmth of Micke's house to head back through the darkness to the Comfort Hotel, both feeling rather homesick. Even when the almanac told us that it should be daylight, it never was, not really. A sulky dawn slunk unwillingly into a long-drawn-out dusk with very little in between, and then night swallowed it all up again.

'Living in the twilight zone,' I grumbled.

But John was thinking of something else. 'You know, I think I must have been very close to the Great Rann of Kutch when I was in India,' he said.

'I don't remember seeing you.'

'In Bhavnagar,' said John. 'Even did a bit of lion-hunting there.'

'Small world,' I reflected, feeling rather miffed that it made the Rann of Kutch sound a bit touristy.

'I went out to Mumbai to rescue a craft which had been stuck in the docks for months, tied up in red tape.'

Don't Panic!

This is a drill

Chapter 9
Don't Panic! This is a Drill

John Mumbai, India 1992

As names go, Addison Silk had a dependable ring about it.

I was hanging onto this thought in an effort to reassure myself that, after twenty hours of moving very fast and two hours of standing still in the immigration line at Mumbai airport, the offices of our agent would be an oasis of post-colonial order and calm. The altercation I had been watching through the taxi window was between a man on a bicycle, who appeared to be the owner of a bundle of rubber pipes which were scattered haphazardly over the dirt road, and an old man who was laying out a hundred yards of rope down the side of the said road. Bicycle Man ranted at Rope Man while a crowd of children looked on, now and again trying to take one of the pipes when no-one was looking. A skinny brown dog sped by, stopping briefly but purposefully to pee against the back wheel of the bicycle before rushing on. Then Bicycle Man shooed away the dog and went to rescue his bicycle, Rope Man went back to rope-laying and the children started bashing each other with the unattended floppy black pipes.

Jet-lag and heat are a potent combination. When I closed my eyes, I was still flying. Hours and hours earlier I had strained to catch my first glimpse of India, looking out from the descending plane expecting to see the glittering illuminations of the modern metropolis of Mumbai; instead, I had seen a million muted yellow puddles of light, the sort of light that might emanate from a tassel-shaded standard lamp in a room full of heavy furniture, making the gloom gloomier and accentuating the darkness. Now, to stop myself falling asleep in the taxi, I looked again at the notes I had hastily scribbled about the location and operating conditions of the hovercraft I had come to India to commission for a passenger route from Bhavnagar to Surat. Vast tidal range, shifting sandbanks, strong currents. Largely uncharted. In other words, foolhardy and impossible for a boat, perfect for a hovercraft.

For over eight weeks, the twin-engine Griffon 4000TD 50-seater (see appx. 11) had been slowly cooking on Quay 409, held by customs, until the 'correct paperwork' was produced. Being the first passenger-carrying hovercraft in India, there was no precedent for what constituted 'correct paperwork': it seemed that there just had to be lots of it, far more than the final certificate which showed that the craft had met the stringent criteria specified by Lloyds, thereby proving its total sea-worthiness.

Among their numerous business interests, the customers, Modern India Enterprises (MIE), ran a transport company in Gujarat. Their assurances that they were connected to the right people and had the right insider knowledge to get the craft quickly through the red tape so that we could commission it was beginning to seem like wishful thinking. So far, MIE's string-pulling had merely resulted in a terrible tangle.

During that time, we had sent out engineers to assemble the craft but, hampered by bureaucracy, they had run out of time, leaving it only partly assembled. Now, at last, we'd had confirmation the craft was ready to be released which is why I was inching my way through the streets in a stifling taxi, towards the offices of Addison Silk, our Mumbai agents.

Every time we slowed or stopped, people crowded at the window, some with hands outstretched simply asking for money, but most of them trying to sell an astonishing range of goods. To keep myself awake, I'd been jotting down each item I'd refused and now had a sizeable list. Had I not been feeling rather queasy from the flight, I might have succumbed to buying some refreshment, choosing from milky tea in ceramic cups, *chapattis*, coconuts, peanuts, lurid sweets, hot-mix, bananas, halva or sandwiches. Once fortified, I could then have indulged in even more retail therapy with a choice of saris, 'Sony' Walkmans, disposable cameras, adhesive hooks (white or pink), screwdriver sets, hankies, bed-sheets, trainers, socks, chains, key-rings, padlocks, nail clippers, bottle openers, light-pens, combs, batteries, shoe-shine service, scissors and rechargeable torches. Should you suddenly develop a pressing need for a novelty inflatable hammer, you would also be catered for.

But no matter how I tried, I simply couldn't stay awake. I kept sinking into those shifting sandbanks... they were nothing to worry about after all... I felt pleasantly surprised by their softness as I lay waiting for the vast tide to cover me. Only when the taxi stopped and the driver cut the engine did I surface from their pillowy depths. For a moment, we seemed to be in just another anonymous dingy side-street filled to bursting with the generous tumult of human life but in one of those Indian miracles when one realises that there is order among the chaos, I happened to glance upwards and there, in a grimy second-floor window, a plastic sign read 'Addison Silk, Shipping Agents'.

Undoubtedly lack of sleep was contributing to my sense of disassociation from reality but as I climbed up two flights of rickety stairs I swear the world turned black and white. I found myself in a room full of whirling fans and young men and women typing steadily on rattling mechanical typewriters next to toppling piles of paper held down with paperweights. Unbelievably, it seemed I was expected but the very chap I needed to see had just popped out. In the meantime, I was given my first glass of Indian tea. By my third, just as I was again losing the fight to keep awake, Mr Roy finally arrived, breathless and sweaty. There were pleasantries, although it became obvious that he was not completely clear who I was or where I had come from.

'So you have flown from America, no?'

'No, no. The UK.'

'Very nice. And what is your good name, please?'

'Er, John. John Barker. From Griffon Hovercraft in Southampton?'

'Ah, Southampton, very nice. How are your children?'

'I don't have any, I'm afraid. Just two cats.'

'Ah, you have two cats. Very nice.' More tea arrived.

'The craft...' I began.

'Basically, it is very, very good. Very fine.'

'Thank you. We need to get it out of the docks. You have clearance now?'

'Ah yes.' My heart leapt at this good news. 'This is what we need to talk about.' My heart dropped. Mr Roy sighed and rummaged in his drawer to extract a manila folder. For some time, he flicked through the documents inside. Among the unfamiliar papers, many of them hand-written, I felt relieved to see the all-important certificate of seaworthiness which Lloyd's had issued several months ago.

'That's the one. That certificate is the essential thing.'

'But this is all you sent, no?' said Mr Roy, his voice rising a little. 'We are needing the rest of it since some time.'

'That's all that is needed,' I replied confidently. I picked up the certificate, actually a rather handsome document with an embossed border, some gold-leafing and a symbol of a Lion and Unicorn in one corner. 'The certificate shows that the craft has passed all the necessary trials and is in line with all the regulations, set by your government, for carrying passengers.' I remembered with a little stab of alarm the long passage we had yet to make, the craft's maiden voyage in effect, from Mumbai Docks to its operating base in Bhavnagar through the 'largely uncharted' waters along the Maharashtra coast. I couldn't help reflecting that this was quite enough to have on my plate without missing bits of paper.

Mr Roy nodded. 'But where is the rest of it?' he repeated. 'Have you sent all of it? What about the details of the trials and so on? What is the name of the person who has authorised the craft? Also, one needs everything in triplicate.'

'I'll look into it,' I hedged. 'But there is nothing else I can give you at the moment.'

Mr Roy looked downcast. 'Then I must contact my superiors,' he said sadly, then brightened up. 'No matter. All will be well.' He seemed eager to move away from the subject. 'You have a good hotel, no? Where are you staying? I will call a cab and you come back early tomorrow.'

Overslept. Got to Addison Silk at 11.30. Little sign of activity. Mr Roy not available. Waited in small office. 3 cups of chai, read Times of India. Mr Roy returned 1pm; sat in his office while he made about six phone calls. Result: someone will contact him tomorrow.

This entry from my diary illustrates the pattern of my days for the next week and a half. Until we obtained the 'correct papers', I couldn't see the craft. I felt fragile with jet-lag, unequal to the mighty opponent of Indian bureaucracy. My only rather unimaginative strategy was to turn up every day and wait, wait, wait. In doing so, I was forced to begin to adjust to the perplexing pace of Indian life. It is not just that time goes slowly; sometimes it seems to go backwards, then sideways. For every move forward, there is a falling back. Evasion is a great Indian tactic: yes means no, no means maybe. Plans change confusingly without explanation until you doubt your own grasp on reality and even begin to suspect a conspiracy. Misinformation is rife, although it is delivered with such charm that you are never sure whether it is due to malice, incompetence or a genuine desire never to disappoint.

But with dogged persistence, the Southampton Office did manage to track down each separate element of the paper trail which had culminated in the certificate. Then each one of these pieces of paper, each trial report and smudged checklist, was copied in triplicate and sent out by courier to MIE, who sent it to Lloyds of India to be inspected and stamped. As you might expect, this was a long process, so much so that I became all too familiar with the routine of the Addison Silk working day. Every day Mr Roy would give a little start when he encountered me, then regain his composure and ask politely about my cats. To while away the time, I had taken to buying a newspaper which I read in the cluttered foyer. I was particularly fascinated by the headlines written in old-fashioned, gangster-ish idioms.

Maybe it was as I raised a wry smile over 'Cops fire to chase away dacoits in campus heist' or 'Goons hijack bus' that in a dusty office somewhere else in the city, some small occurrence took place: a piece of paper uncovered in an in-tray, a rubber stamp inked and wielded, a signature scrawled. In the same way that a tiny movement in a cog-wheel, nothing in itself, moves a larger wheel and sets a whole process in motion, there must have been a sudden coming together of events, resulting in a phone call which brought good news. Tomorrow, it seemed, I would see the craft and actually begin what I had been sent out to do.

Since arriving in India I had been forced to rely on my own wits, and my emotional resilience was beginning to dwindle. Now it was all-systems-go, I found myself with almost too much help. First I was introduced to the newly appointed Operations Manager known as Capt R. I could tell by his air of confident authority that he would be a great asset. He appeared to know the right people and quickly organised some extra pairs of hands – young men from outlying rural places, incredibly keen but trying not to let this show too much. There were seven of them, all of the same height, age and demeanour and of course wearing the same uniform of shades and immaculate white shirts. It took a little while before their individual characteristics materialised sufficiently for me to fit the right name to the right face. In the interim, I made helpful notes.

Rahul (moustache)

Kabir (hat)

Dhruv (young, straight hair)

Vijay (young, wavy hair)

Ayaan (eyebrows)

Sanjay (shirt)

Ajay

Exactly what was so distinctive about Ayaan's eyebrows or Sanjay's shirt slipped my mind long ago, but it evidently meant something at the time. Ajay, for whom I had no comments, must have been the basic model.

All seven were waiting for me early next morning with a couple of nifty little Maruti Suzuki jeeps supplied by MIE. Despite this early start, it was 10.30 by the time Capt R arrived with a chit which he told us would get us into the docks. After some discussion about who should drive the jeep, we all piled in for the usual hair-raising, ear-splitting, kaleidoscopic whirl, bombing down the crowded side-streets and screeching to a halt outside many places thought to be the right Dock gate, but weren't. We did somehow eventually arrive at the correct gate and in the fullness of time we were even standing in front of the right desk. To my amazement, the chit worked! It only took another hour before we were in and being escorted through the docks to Quay 409.

I was cautious about what condition the craft would be in but for once, things were better than expected: a first. Our previous engineers had done well and the craft was more than half-assembled: the side-bodies were on and so were the ducts, props and rudders. I also knew what my first job needed to be: during last-minute trials our calculations suggested that the skirt shift bolts were undersized and bigger ones were needed. Back in Southampton, this job would have taken about an hour. It simply required the holes to be drilled out from 10mm to 12mm and the larger bolts fitted. There was no time to do this before the craft was shipped so I packed the new bolts in the craft ready to fit in India.

Capt R – living up to his reputation as a man who got things done – had already booked a crane to lift up the front of the craft to allow this simple job to be done.

As soon as we began work, I felt better: back in control, once again dealing with the tricky but ultimately predictable problems of inanimate objects. Our 'keen but green' apprentices were a mixed blessing as I seemed to spend half my time explaining things over and over again. But they were eager to learn, good company and had an infectious enthusiasm which many times saved me from despair. After some experimentation with the positions of the spreader bars, we got the craft lifted and the starboard skirt-shift lever arm removed and, although the port arm was less straightforward, we were soon ready to fit the new bolts. I felt pleased with myself that I had even thought to bring the right sized drill-bit.

If only I had also packed a drill!

At this point, an official car carrying three men arrived. They spoke gravely and importantly to Capt R for a full minute, standing in the oblong of deep shade cast by the container. I worked on, pretending not to notice the frowns and the amount of paper they were shuffling around on their clipboards.

'We must stop,' announced the Captain finally. 'The papers are apparently not in order.'

I shrugged, not bothering to ask for the finer details. I knew it would get me nowhere. 'Lunch, then?' I suggested. 'We can talk about getting these holes drilled.' At a sedate pace for once, we left in the jeep, trailed closely by the official car just to ensure, I suppose, that we really left the docks. The three men watched us go, presumably satisfied that they had successfully prevented any work taking place.

While Capt R attended to sorting out the situation with the papers, over curry and *dahl* in a local restaurant the rest of us talked about the whereabouts of drills. The others were full of helpful suggestions: somebody's brother-in-law actually had one, but he lived way outside the city. Somebody knew someone who used to have one until it had been stolen. The debate and discussion continued for an hour. In the end, we had to face reality: no-one had a drill or knew where we could get one.

Capt R arrived. Mercifully, he knew of a nearby engineering outfit where we might borrow a drill. So it was back in the jeep, Kabir driving at a crazy pace, going out of his way to hoot at every pedestrian in sight. The 'nearby' workshop transpired to be nearby only in the Indian sense. Like a ball-bearing in a pinball-machine, we drove through the maze of streets for about twenty minutes until we arrived at Yogi Engineering Services (YES) hidden away in a tiny side-street and housed in one of the ubiquitous 'go-downs'. The owner, Cyrus, welcomed us with effusive greetings. Entering the sweltering premises heavy with the smell of oil, sweat and grime, I had some sense of what it must feel like to be basted in an oven. There was a busy feel about the place, wiry men soldering and angle-grinding in the gloom, spasmodically illuminated by the blue flare of welding arcs. I caught sight of a shadowy figure gas-axing a metal plate which he held steady with his bare foot. All wore shorts and shirts perforated with round burn holes, not a pair of goggles or a steel-capped boot in sight.

We accepted the offer of *chai* and only after the second cup, served by men with blackened, oily fingers, could we begin to discuss the drill. There followed a long period of, for me, unintelligible noisy chatter. Just how much was there to say about borrowing a tool? Only last month, Barry, my next-door neighbour, had borrowed my drill. There'd been a knock on the back door and there he'd stood in his baggy jeans and Southampton shirt. 'Can I borrow your drill, mate?' he said. 'No problem,' I replied. 'Ta, won't be long.' He'd returned it within the hour. We hadn't felt the need to share four cups of tea before the request was even made, nor ask about each other's distant relatives or swap lengthy views on the economy. At last, after many false finishes, Capt R stood up; there were effusive expressions of thanks and long goodbyes.

But no drill.

I looked questioningly at the Captain. 'Did we…?'

'The drill will be ready tomorrow,' he assured me. I nodded. Understandably, we couldn't take it now. Such a dizzying rush of events would not be appropriate: like a widow in mourning, a seemly amount of time had to pass before the next phase of drill-borrowing could be entered into. Negotiations had now run the correct course, the deal had been brokered, but, steady on! That's enough for one day.

Banished from the Docks and prevented from working, I found myself at a loose end. Dhruv suggested a trip to Elephanta Island. It was a nice little place, green and high. With Ajay tagging along, the three of us punted across the river, helped ashore by two ladies (for money, I discovered). We climbed the green slopes to a cave-temple then on to Cannon Hill, the highest point. There amongst the tourists, the monkeys and sedan-chairs, we drank Fanta and mooched around the gift-stalls which were full of onyx deities and carved sandalwood elephants. From our high viewpoint we could see buffaloes strolling along the muddy causeway and white and grey egrets lining the shore. I had brought the GPS from the craft with us to test it out. It worked! It was a good afternoon, like bunking off school on a summer's day.

On the way back, Dhruv persuaded me that we should hire a security guard to keep watch over the craft when we weren't there. When I'd pointed out the impassable 10-foot high, 6-foot thick perimeter walls which were patrolled by soldiers, not to mention the matter of the impenetrable red-tape, Dhruv assured me that this did not mean the craft were safe from those who were inside the walls. He could recommend someone, Mr Sai, a distant relative and a very honest man, who would come at 4 o'clock every afternoon and sleep in the craft.

Back at the Diplomat Hotel, I dozed off, waking at 7.30 in time for dinner at the Taj. There is something unforgettable about walking through a tropical city at night, something that stays vivid in the memory. Pockets of decaying splendour – pitted plaster, worn pink balustrades flanked by palms – gave way to glimpses of squalor – craters in the broken pavement, beggars with babies, dollops of human excrement. Down a backstreet, I could see a group of boys playing cricket in gathering darkness.

When a heavy downpour sent me running back to the hotel, I thought of the woman into whose hand I had just dropped a few rupees; she'd held out her baby to me like an offering, wrapped in a grimy cloth, so small and still it could have been a doll.

Sure enough, back at YES the next day, a drill was waiting for us, packed in a wooden crate. It looked robust enough for the job. Things moved at a rollicking pace. We were in and out of the workshop in just over an hour, then half an hour driving to the Docks. Even then, I somehow expected that we would be admitted without question as we had passed security the day before. What was I thinking? The issue of missing paperwork from yesterday cropped up again and was eventually solved when I pulled out a rather crumpled carbon-copy from the pocket of my overalls, drawing smiles of relief all round. After that, we went through the same routine as the day before: questions, signatures, entries in ledgers, colour-coded dockets and flimsy chits with carbon copies. All set to go? A security officer had been checking the contents of the vehicle; now he walked past us, carrying the drill in its wooden crate. There was an air of restrained triumph in his expression as he drew it to the attention of his colleagues. Consternation. Where had the drill come from? What was its background? Capt R tried to vouch for its good character, but that wasn't enough. The drill would only be admitted if it had its own permit: make, model and serial number were painstakingly noted on separate pages of a yellow form and each piece of paper then had to be stamped by someone who wasn't there and had to be tracked down in some far-flung hangar the other side of the complex.

Numbed with boredom, faint with lack of food, the day had built up a stifling heat by the time we were finally escorted to our designated area. It took a while to get galvanised into action, then there was a problem with finding a power supply, but before too long, we were ready to use the drill. The bit fitted, measurements were double-checked, the borrowed drill was poised.

At that moment Dhruv arrived with an old man, puny even by usual standards. His head and neck were swathed in a threadbare piece of blue cloth – scarf would be too grand a word – over which he wore thick glasses which made his eyes look huge. He held a cardboard roll under one arm and a shopping bag in the other. Our new guard, Mr Sai.

Just as we were about to get acquainted, the long mournful cry of a dying whale broke over my head.

'What the hell's that?' I asked.

No-one else seemed perturbed, not even Mr Sai. The others were packing up. 'End of day,' they announced. I recognised the sound then, a factory siren, signalling home-time. On cue, people began streaming out of buildings.

'Not for us, surely? We've only just got here,' I pointed out.

But our escorts had appeared and it was clear that we too were expected to go, no question. It seemed that I was the only one to feel a whiff of the surreal. I comforted myself with the thought that tomorrow – tomorrow – we would be able to begin work straightaway. Everything was set up. I placed the drill carefully inside the craft and covered it with a pair of overalls before taking my place in the back of the jeep. As we left, Mr Sai was arranging his few meagre possessions inside the plastic-swathed cabin. I just hope that he would not be called on to thwart any dacoits in one of their attempted heists.

Next day, after the usual red tape and hanging about, we were inside ready to work before eleven – a record. The sight of the craft jogged my memory about a dream I'd had in which we had lifted the concealing overalls to find the drill had gone.

I lifted the overalls. The drill had gone.

It might have been a known drill, an officially recognised, fully-paid up member of the Mumbai Docks with its very own passport, but it wasn't there. Had it been kidnapped? And if so, why were we paying a bloody guard? Once the others caught wind of the missing drill, Dhruv spoke angrily to Mr Sai who listened calmly and pointed across the docks to the offices.

No-one had heard of the drill. They seemed defensive. A long telephone call was made. Reassuring smiles. The drill had not been stolen but taken away to a place of safety as its day permit had expired. Besides, it had been left unattended which was against regulations. But it would of course be returned. We just needed to complete some paperwork...

A weary despair flowed through me as I thought of the forms and the signatures, and all that rigmarole. The part that needed drilling was not large. If we couldn't take the drill to the part, then we could take the part to the drill: we needed to return the drill at some point, why not take the part along too? Very pleased with myself, I suggested this to Capt R who immediately phoned YES and struck a deal; even better, they would come and pick up the part and the drill. Ayaan and Kabir set about removing the second arm; collection would be at 1pm. At 12.30 I was pleased to see the YES jeep arrive. For half an hour, as the lads worked, the driver lounged about watching and smoking. I helped the others to bring the arm over safely then looked around for the jeep. There was no sight of the vehicle or the driver. But not to worry – he'd told Vijay he'd only be gone for ten minutes. After half an hour, we decided to go for lunch.

Capt R made another of his phone calls and the upshot was that the jeep would come to pick me up after collecting the drill and part. By three o'clock no-one had arrived. We walked back to the Docks and phoned YES once more. No reply.

The next morning we were in the Docks by 9.00am. Capt R phoned YES again and was quickly in deep discussion. No, they hadn't picked up the part. Why not? Because the part was too big to be taken out of the Docks – paperwork would be required. Capt R asked to talk to Cyrus; I could hear their voices rising little by little, cutting over each other. There was a long spell where Capt R just grunted occasionally, in response to long tirades from the other end. Whatever was said seemed to mollify him because soon their exchanges were back to normal volume. By the time the call had finished, everything was agreed: a YES truck which was already unloading from a ship in the docks this afternoon, would also pick up the part and drill. This handover would take place at noon. We drove to the craft, leaving some of the lads to do a few routine jobs, made sure everything was packed up ready to go, then we drove to the agent's office to check for faxes and collect some other bits and pieces for the job. The narrow street was teeming: there was no choice but to double-park outside.

My day seemed plagued with vanishing objects. When we came out, the van had gone. Ajay was sent to investigate.

When he hadn't returned after half an hour we called a cab but just as it was pulling away a smiling Ajay turned up with the recovered van. It had been towed away. We swapped vehicles and drove straight to YES. There was no sign of the stuff from the docks... still going through the system. Perhaps the drill was being interrogated, or de-briefed; then the permit would have to be revoked, probably a lengthy process. We decided to have lunch instead of waiting in the fumy atmosphere of the workshop, but we were back by four. Still nothing. At 5pm a call came to say that the part and drill had been taken directly to the machine shop, so we made a dash with a YES mechanic and driver and were finally reunited with the part and the drill.

Everything was taking place on the pavement: cars rebuilt, bicycles mended, scrap sorted piece by piece. Only inches away, trucks rumbled by piled high with stuff, each with a security man or two on top. As soon as a vehicle stopped, it was immediately surrounded by people, like ants round a sugar-slick, but the tough guys on top were ready: leaping off the lorry, they faced the crowd, wielding long sticks to beat back potential robbers (*ie* everyone in the vicinity). Amongst all this violent activity, I spent an hour squatting with one of the mechanics explaining the job and marking the positions of the holes to the attentive listeners who nodded much too readily, making me feel instantly uneasy. The drilling needed to be accurate to a millimetre; four holes were needed but I emphasised the importance of drilling one first so that I could check it before the other three were done. I tore out a page of my notebook and drew a diagram. Yes, yes, yes. The holes needed to be drilled at a certain angle. No problem. I found a pencil and marked the metal to show the exact position. Who will do the job? I asked. After a lot of discussion, the bare-foot gas-axer was pushed forward and introduced. A very good man, the best man for the job. We shook hands. It would be ready tomorrow. My heart sank. Another day wasted, another day longer before I could go home.

I did not feel good about things as I returned to the hotel. Detached from the rest of the group who were in various scattered places, I started to eat alone but half-way through received a concerned visit from Dhruv and Ajay: a possibility of water in the turbo-charger. With dinner unfinished, I sent a fax to the Southampton Office and phoned ABEX, the manufacturer's agent, to get permission to strip it down. After that I phoned Capt R to arrange a crane for the next day. Bed.

At 9.30 the next morning, I was looking at the rust-stained water which had poured out of the right turbo on the port engine – quite a quantity of it, but less than the 4-6 pints that I had been told. Enough, though, to warrant removing and inspecting the turbo. A phone call to YES at least established that the part had been drilled and was ready to collect. I got a ride out to the workshop only to find that despite my warnings, sure enough all four holes had been drilled.

Wrongly.

Once again I went through what I wanted, explaining the angle that was needed. Again, the mechanic listened attentively and nodded and nodded. I was told to come back at 4 o'clock.

Back at the hovercraft, the turbo was off and looked ok, just two studs sheared off during the removal process. My heart sank as I realised that this part also should now be taken to the workshop for the amount of play to be checked. Off I went. My daily routine seemed to now consist of incessant to-ing and fro-ing, cadging lifts where I could, or cadging calls in the various offices to track down someone who could come and give me a ride.

I made sure that I arrived back at the workshop before four and, as I had hoped, was in time to personally supervise the drilling. By 5.30, the part was ready. Four holes drilled in a piece of metal. It had taken six days, or one and a half days per hole. I tried to summon up some sense of triumph but found myself only thinking how we could now make good the wrongly drilled assembly. I walked back to the hotel to find that Ajay was waiting for me. The turbo, he assured me, was ok now. Yes, they had run the engine. Did it get hot? A little. From the look on his face, I knew he was using 'a little' in the Indian sense. Wearily, I sent faxes to Southampton and one to ABEX enquiring about the acceptable range of oil temperature and pressure. Dinner. Despondency. Bed.

The reply from ABEX was waiting for me the next morning, all positive regarding my queries about the oil temperature and pressure. Considerably buoyed up by this good news, I was determined that at whatever cost, this would be the last day of the drill saga. At YES, with just the basic social preliminaries and one cup of tea, I got them going on repairing the wrongly drilled assembly and arranged its delivery to the docks. At the craft, I checked the prop taper locks, no problem with loosening. By the time I had finished this pleasant routine job, the part turned up and was fitted before lunch.

I experienced a brief spell of relief that this interminable episode was finally sorted. Dare I hope that my stars had shifted into a new phase? Maybe everything would start to come together at last. What I didn't know was that if my horoscope for the past week had read: You will be beset with mechanical problems which will see you running from one place to another like a blue-arsed fly, it would now read: Mechanical problems will take a back seat, eclipsed by alarming muddles of red-tape and mindless bureaucracy.

I was dismayed to discover that an unexpected meeting had been called at AS at 3pm the next afternoon. Half a dozen people squashed into a small room: me, Mr Shah of AS, Capt R and an unsmiling man called Mr Ramon from the Indian Government, plus the usual clerical minions. The Government of India, said Mr Ramon, were still not satisfied with the paperwork. We had to realise that this vessel was a first for India: every detail had to be absolutely water-tight, and in apple-pie order so that the right precedents could be set. I nodded my agreement, knowing that we had covered all this, and began to say so but the self-important Mr Ramon raised his hand to cut me off.

'Quite simply, until we have the letter of contract regarding the plans, calculations and all the relevant data, correctly stamped and signed off by the Civil Aviation Authority and the Department of Transport, you cannot launch the craft, you cannot even run the craft!'

I was still digesting this uncharacteristically direct statement as Capt R and Mr Shah waded in, voices raised, expressing disbelief that the government was still coming up with these pedantic requests long after they had been sorted. Then everyone switched to Hindi which made it easier for an outright slanging match to take place. Only when Capt R reprimanded them, not for shouting but for not talking in English, did their voices return to a chilly conversational level with each blaming the other for unpaid harbour dues, something else that I did not know about.

The meeting finally came to an end well after 7pm, only after we had given repeated assurances that we would communicate with the UK straightaway and clear up any confusion, although no-one could actually tell us which pieces of paper were missing.

A word here about the hybrid nature of the hovercraft which has always caused problems because it falls under two distinct jurisdictions but is never fully in either. It goes without saying that boats and planes are very different. In the early days, hovercraft travel acquired and cultivated a similar image to flying; one took a 'flight' in a hovercraft; drivers were 'pilots' and there were even hostesses. In the 70s the CAA drew up a set of regulations governing hovercraft design and construction, but these were written around large passenger hovercraft. Wherever possible we complied with these, but since our hovercraft were a fraction of the size, some of the rules were plain daft. Later on, the International Maritime Organisation (IMO) published an International Code of Safety for High-Speed Craft. Again, many of the rules which were relevant for larger vessels did not apply to small hovercraft: for instance, sprinkler systems would be impossible on a hovercraft because it hovers above the water.

We always built hovercraft as high-flying boats rather than low-flying aircraft. We used marine equipment and materials. Whereas aircraft manufacturing utilises light materials which are highly engineered to be failsafe, marine technology is about having redundancy built in. In other words, aircraft are built never to go wrong as the consequences are too dire, while even if ships go a bit wrong they still continue to act as a buoyant shelter for the passengers. The biggest compromise is that hovercraft have to be light – a characteristic which tends to be less important in ships.

True to my word, I tried to phone Southampton but there was no reply.

I slept fitfully.

The next morning, I tried to put these new bureaucratic worries out of my mind and be single-minded about the preparations we needed to make for the voyage. It was no small thing to drive the craft 150 miles up the unfamiliar coast to Bhavnagar. There was no shortage of other preparations to make: we decanted lube oil from a 45-gallon drum into 5-gallon jerricans, then had a meeting to organise the launch, which meant lining up cranes, clearance from the docks, pilot services and so on. It was good to be purposeful and busy. We even got as far as checking the charts and seriously looking at the possibility of going the next day but the pace was too much to sustain: at 4pm everybody melted away without any firm arrangements in place.

The paperwork issue, like many big black clouds, did not in the end result in a cracking storm but simply broke up bit by bit. Over the following days, the office sent more stuff through, I talked to Mr Shah and seemed to get him to understand the CAA certification. By now we had acquired an impressively large folder of documents which he asked me to organise into a logical order. I felt sure that the Indian Government would be impressed with the sheer quantity of paperwork which now amounted to quite a pile. I neatly clipped them in separate triplicate bundles, just how they liked it. For a while, it felt we were getting somewhere but over the next few days, a meeting was scheduled and cancelled; another scheduled but forgotten or ignored.

Having sorted the mechanical problems and started to make progress through the red tape we came next upon a new opponent: the weather. Our new obsession.

Capt R knew the captain of a container ship who provided us with a weather forecast print-out. He told us that there had been squalls in the night, blowing up to Force 10, causing the ship to drag anchor. There were still some off-shore squalls blowing out of the harbour and localised thunder storms.

To get firmer (and hopefully more positive) information, we decided to drive out to the Met Office at Colata Point to talk to the 'lady director' there. Sure enough, Dr Amala turned out to be helpful, friendly and sympathetic but the forecast she gave us was no better: a deepening depression out in the Arabian Sea moving north. Only in two days' time would we know whether it would go NW or NE. It was the end of the monsoon season and the weather had not yet settled.

Phoning or visiting Dr Amala for the latest forecast became a regular daily event, part of a new routine which emerged over the next two weeks. Basically, there was always some small, often inconsequential reason why we couldn't launch: if the weather was OK, we had a mechanical blip; once that was fixed, there would be a query from the authorities – money needed to be paid, permission for such-and-such sought. It was as if the problems were queuing politely, stepping forward one at a time. And every time a new one took the stand, we would bat it away.

A trawl through the diary shows the varied nature of the obstacles. Here they are, in chronological order. Each one lost us another day.

- Unpaid harbour dues
- No officials available to sign papers
- Storm over Oman
- No dock passes
- Fork-lift required elsewhere
- Trials. Air-speed not working. Port belt running hard against rear flange
- Have to fit new belt
- Large party of AS directors and families come for an outing
- Exhaust stub breaks and new one required
- Exhaust stub unobtainable locally – try to organise welding (oh no!)
- Customs clearance documents questioned

- Surveyors
- Low pressure arrives, 1.5 m waves, 20+ kt winds
- Weather report delayed/unobtainable
- 2-3m seas and 40+ kt winds

Then one day a meeting was suddenly called with the Chief Surveyor. He handed me back all the papers from the CAA, duly stamped. Everything was in order. Tickety-boo. All systems go.

It was a strange sensation: suddenly there was nothing to stop us from launching that afternoon. Before the situation could change we hastily threw everything in the craft, hovered it up so it could be towed by two fork-lifts – both there, both working – to another part of the huge dock complex where a crane awaited to lower it into the water. We started the engines and within two minutes flat, a great crowd of people had appeared from nowhere. They swarmed towards us, mostly attracted by the propellers at the aft end. As the turgid afternoon air was whipped into a monsoon wind, excitable children ran backwards and forwards and even tried to climb up on the side-bodies to better enjoy the novelty. With the craft now in the water, we were relieved to cast off from our crowd of clamouring but (so far) bodily intact admirers and make the trip over to our new quarters, which was a basin just the other side of the harbour. It may have been one of the shortest trips we ever did, but we had a wild and raucous send-off.

Two days later I learned a lesson. To my surprise, Mr Sai turned up at our new location, looking as serene as ever but even more bedraggled than usual. I spoke to Dhruv: did Mr Sai not know that his services were no longer needed? Had he not been paid? Dhruv spoke to Mr Sai; the two of them went into the craft and emerged again. More talking. Mr Sai sat cross-legged on the quay with the patient air of a man who had all the time in the world while Dhruv consulted with the others. I worked on, faintly irritated by all the fuss. I couldn't imagine what the old man wanted.

'Dhruv!' I called at last. 'We've got masses to do. Stop wasting time.'

Dhruv looked shifty and embarrassed.

'Mr Sai is looking for his bed,' he explained.

'His bed?'

'Yes.'

'But he was sleeping on an old piece of cardboard.'

'His bed, yes.'

A horrible realisation crept over me. To me, it had been not a bed but a piece of rubbish. I had thrown it away.

'But surely... I mean, can't he find another piece?'

Dhruv looked at his feet. 'Mr Sai has travelled a considerable distance to find us here, two buses, yes? Across the city. And a long walk, many enquiries.'

Shame made me hot. I hadn't given it a thought. This poor old man, uncomplainingly working for a few rupees, sleeping every night on a piece of cardboard.

'There must be an old box or something somewhere,' I blustered. 'Go and find him something.' Dhruv looked miserable and took his discomfiture out on Mr Sai, still sitting quietly, by talking as harshly to the old man as I had spoken to him.

I put down the jerrican I had been about to fill with fuel for the trip to Bhavnagar. I had thrown away a man's bed, a precious possession. I had to make amends. Waving the stuttering Dhruv away, I managed to get Mr Sai to follow me into the small shed where some odd stores were kept. We found a few large boxes which seemed to meet with his approval so I took a Stanley knife to one until it was the right size. I gestured to the other stuff – duct tape, packets of screws, a few pairs of gloves. But the only thing Mr Sai wanted was his bed, and he seemed pleased with the replacement which had the word Sūtrak emblazoned on it in red letters. As an afterthought, I picked up a roll of bubble wrap and held out a length of it for his approval. He regarded it with the expert eye of a connoisseur, feeling it between finger and thumb. 'Waterproof,' I said, gesturing rain. I popped one of the bubbles and we both laughed inanely. Taking a generous length with him – although whether for protection or amusement, I couldn't say – Mr Sai went on his way. I don't suppose he even thought about bearing a grudge – when you're bumping along the bottom, it's just another one of those things that happen.

I went back to my jerricans. For the rest of the afternoon, nobody said a word.

The next day, the wind obligingly dropped from 20 knots to 10 and, with our port clearance still valid until midnight, it was time to go.

The Bicycle Repair Shop

The voyage was going well: miles and miles of hazy, featureless coast slipping by as we made blissfully uneventful progress towards Bhavnagar. I found myself almost daring to enjoy the experience. I actually had time to talk to Capt R as I drove and found him to be an interesting and clever man. In the quiet hours, I took time to go over the logistics and background of the project.

The Gulf of Khambhat's trumpet-shape and orientation in relation to the southwest monsoon winds account for its high tidal range (40 feet [12 metres]) and the high velocity of the entering tides. Shoals and sandbanks are treacherous to navigation, and all the gulf ports have suffered from silting caused by tides and flood torrents from the rivers.

Hovercraft territory.

There is no doubt that the setting up of a hovercraft service from Bhavnagar to Surat was a sound idea. Bhavnagar is a remote but commercially successful city which has a lucrative diamond-polishing industry and a flourishing textile trade. The main market for these commodities, Mumbai, could in those days only be reached by plane or a gruelling train journey, the first third of this through remote bandit country – not a cheering prospect if you are carrying a bag full of diamonds. When (MIE) got together to address the problem, they came up with the idea of setting up a hovercraft ferry service to Surat, thus avoiding the most dangerous and isolated part of the road and railroad through the desert. From Surat to Mumbai is half the distance and would cut journey time to a third.

The company was owned by a powerful family who ran the town. The elderly patriarch was an important man in the area, a 'deified' person – local people would kneel in front of him and touch the hem of his robes. He clearly wanted to take credit for solving the town's transport difficulties but had no maritime knowledge whatsoever. It is true that a passenger hovercraft may have some things in common with buses and trains, but the sea is far less predictable than a road.

The water turned brown and muddy as we approached the Gulf of Khambhat where small, silted up tributaries branched off either side of the main waterway. We decided to head up one of these backwaters and land on the mud to refuel rather than to attempt it stooging about on the water. Again, a crowd quickly arrived from nowhere. Experience should have told us to avoid the little village on the banks rather than head straight for it, but who could have known that it was inhabited by a cast of thousands (okay, hundreds) like extras from an epic film who suddenly appear when the director shouts 'Action!'? The engine noise had barely died away when we were beset by a large and astonished audience who surrounded the craft in a great circle, like that scene from *Close Encounters of the Third Kind*. I knew then the exact expression on the faces of human beings if ever an alien space-craft lands in Chipping Norton or Basildon. It was evident that these people had never seen a white person before, let alone a hovercraft. At least half were children, who quickly overcame their initial awe and were soon on a dedicated quest to climb in, on or under the craft at any cost. The crew were totally taken up with the task of keeping them at bay. There was a lot of shouting, arm-waving and the judicious utilisation of long sticks while I set about scurrying round emptying diesel from the jerricans into the fuel tank. I was so intent on getting this done without injury or spillage that I was unaware of the arrival of a deputation until the crowd (apart from the children) suddenly grew quiet. I turned then to see a sinewy man flanked by minders. Presumably this was the village head-man. A long conversation began which one of the crew interpreted as best as he could.

'He says he is sorry that we are in this very bad trouble,' he explained. 'Other boats have run aground here and he offers his

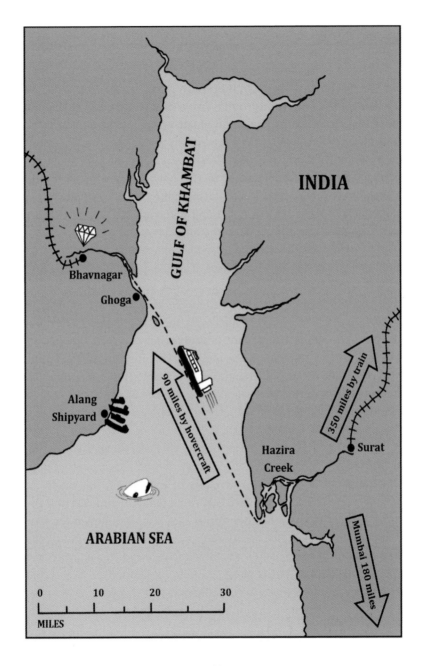

assistance. The people here are all fisher-folk who have a good knowledge of the water. They will help.'

Touched by these sentiments but impatient to carry on, I asked our interpreter to assure him that we were OK, were meant to be on the mud and had not run aground. This took a long time in itself, then there was more explaining to do about where we had come from, where we were headed, how a hovercraft works and, for all I knew, the price of fish (which would be a pretty relevant topic, come to think of it). Apart from a few of the older boys who were still determined to get past the crew and on to the craft, every pair of eyes had become locked on me, observing with rapt interest as I rather self-consciously continued the refuelling.

It was time to leave. Unlike *Close Encounters* where the great ship makes its farewell in an atmosphere of rhapsodic calm and respectful dignity, the departure of our little craft was accompanied by a lot of shouting and frenetic waving as excitable kids clung tenaciously to the side-bodies. After several attempts to clear the decks (literally) and force the hangers-on (again, literally) back to a safe distance, we had to resort to starting up the engines. This did the trick – as one body, the children shrieked and ran in the other direction, then fell about laughing and as we headed into the water ran back to try to catch up with us, banging the inflated skirt with sticks, waving and shouting until we were out of sight.

Late in the day, we arrived at the tiny village of Ghoga, just outside of Bhavnagar. The low, low tide had uncovered a vast plain of mud which rippled in the heat and stank of excrement, but made an otherwise perfect landing place. We came thankfully to rest and the stonking heat of the afternoon hit us like a cosh. I longed for four things: ice-cold beer, air-conditioning, a shower and sleep. But Ghoga was in a state of excitement – a voluble group of children who seemed identical to the last batch were climbing on lampposts, fences and each other so there was a lot of telling off and shrieking. One of the crew drew my attention to another deputation who awaited us on the road above the beach, their smart shirts and spotless whites contrasting embarrassingly with my sweat- and diesel-soaked clothes. In short, the town was out in force to greet us. A wave of utter weariness came over me; I felt unequal to the challenge of dealing with another invasion of the craft. This time, however, uniformed security kept the kids at a distance while the big-wigs came aboard and were introduced. There were the usual longwinded formalities and endless talk. Then the businessman who had funded the operation announced that we would make the journey to Surat in the craft tomorrow as a kind of dry-run to test the route. We would leave very early - 9 o'clock prompt.

'The craft will need refuelling,' I reminded him, knowing the tanks were now near to empty again.

This seemed to generate an inordinate amount of discussion until it began to dawn on me that they had not even considered the need for fuel.

'Can we not do it in the terminal building?' I asked. I had been vaguely looking around for this and now my heart sank into my boots as our hosts pointed to a structure I had overlooked, thinking it was a derelict ruin. 'But it's nowhere near finished,' I said although secretly I wondered (possibly due to the vegetation growing inside it) if it had once been finished and was now falling down again – it was difficult to tell.

'It will be a very good building,' assured one of the suited men. 'It will soon be completed.'

'But right now, it's not even built. How will we get fuel to the craft?'

There was a lot of dissembling, fudging and back-tracking from the group which I took to mean 'haven't got a clue'.

'Just a few details to attend,' I was assured. 'We will do the needful without further ado and all will be well.'

I shrugged: the choice was pretty simple: 'If we don't refuel tomorrow morning we can't go to Surat,' I said. With smiles and reassurances, the meeting ended and my spirits rose a little at the thought of that cold beer, then dropped as I remembered that we were in Gujarat, a dry state. Although we had taken the precaution of packing a generous emergency beer supply, it was hard to get at and I was beginning to think that a stiff whisky would suit me better in any case. Fat chance.

We set off in search of a hotel.

In the morning we were ready at eight for a nine o'clock departure. Nothing happened. I repeatedly asked about the fuel but no-one seemed to have any answers. Then finally, after a long unexplained wait, in the early afternoon a decrepit fuel tanker creaked up-river and tied up to the quay. I stood and watched as a questionable liquid ('the best diesel we can buy') was decanted into the craft's tanks. By three o'clock we were ready. Almost full to capacity in calm conditions, the craft took off with our destination obscured by the haze.

A mile off-shore conditions were rough and unpleasant with steep little standing waves whipped up by a strengthening wind. The choppy water was criss-crossed with currents and pitted with eddies. More worryingly, I began to realise that the route to Surat must actually be nearer to sixty miles, and not the forty we had been told.

I knew the client's reasoning was that at a cruising speed of 30 knots, the journey would take two hours, but of course due to the conditions we were making much less than 30 knots. Several hours later we had barely crossed the Gulf and it was very late in the afternoon when we started our approach to Hazira Creek where the river began its ten mile stretch inland to Surat. It was low tide and the broad entrance was like nothing I had seen before, a maze of narrow channels made up of steep gulleys between high sand banks and mangroves. Due to the silting and because these waters were uncharted, it was impossible to tell which one was the main channel – we simply had to rely on a mixture of gut-feeling and trial and error. Progress was very slow. Three attempts resulted in dead ends which meant we had to back-track on ourselves, keenly aware of time ticking away and the sun sliding towards the horizon. Once in the main channel, we made better progress. It seemed that Surat was a really big town, a city, with numerous large bridges spanning the river. Then I heard what I had been secretly dreading: the engines started to surge and lose power, a sure sign of blocked fuel filters.

I thought back to the tarry gloop which had passed for diesel.

At least by then we were in sight of our final destination. 'In there!' pointed the crew when the smart new 3-storey terminal building, freshly painted in red and cream, appeared on the right bank. A sign optimistically proclaimed: Hover Craft Ferry Station. Okay, it wasn't finished but it looked a bit less unfinished than its Bhavnagar sister. With the tide low, we could see the soft mud river-banks sloped gently upwards – perfect for landing the craft... except for the steep four-foot-high mud cliff between us and it. Even with engines running at full power, there would be no way that a hovercraft could cross it. With our engines now struggling to keep running at all, we turned instead for the opposite bank which sloped gently onto a large area of tidal marsh, thankfully no step in sight. A town stood beyond, silhouetted raggedly against the streaky sky. In spite of the loss of

197

power, we negotiated the slight slope, all the time on full alert, scanning our surroundings for a potential landing-place, heading across the marsh which was dotted with deep inky pools.

As I approached the first of these, it erupted into something large and bulky which took me a moment to identify as an indignant bovine animal. There was a second when our eyes met in mutual surprise. It looked panicky which is probably a dangerous state for a cow – its horns alone were bigger than a welsh dresser... I'm sure it could easily have killed me, but that's probably how the startled animal felt about the hovercraft. Luckily, although big, it didn't seem to want a confrontation but clambered out of the pool and headed into the night. Water buffalo. We could now see in every pool at least one ruminating head sticking out just above the surface. In the gloom, their sweeping horns looked like fancy hair-dos which they were determined to keep dry by holding their heads primly out of the water. They reminded me of a group of elaborately coiffed genteel ladies whose aquarobics class had just been gate-crashed by a rugby team. As most didn't seem inclined to move, the only way to avoid running them over was to perform a careful slalom round the pools as we headed towards the natural shoreline, some way distant.

We finally parked up near some stilted wooden huts just as the light faded completely. The entire population of the town came streaming out to greet us. People gathered nearby on the city bridge to get a look, clambering up on railings and parapets. The traffic was at a standstill. Despite all the commotion, my immediate priority was the filters. I wasn't at all surprised to find they were completely black and needed a thorough cleaning to shift the layer of sticky, tarry muck which now clogged them. Draining would clearly not do much good and stupidly we had packed no spares. Someone came up with the suggestion of finding a bicycle repair shop. It seemed crazy – where would we find a bicycle repair shop in this place at this time of night? The crew pointed towards the crazy skyline of a ramshackle town crammed with makeshift buildings, toppling towers with flat corrugated roofs, criss-crossed with ropes and teetering masts. Here was a town where you could find anything and everything, and no such thing as closing time. Leaving Capt R and some of the stalwart crew to stand guard, we found a route across the mud and stepped into the town where we immediately acquired an entourage of people all trying to be helpful. Yes, I was assured, there was a bicycle repair shop, a very good one, and it was open.

As our kind guides led us unfalteringly through an intricate maze of alleys, I sensed no threat, only warmth. I had seen poor places in Mumbai and in other parts of the world but what stretched before us, illuminated with flickering open fires, was a vision of poverty unlike anything I had seen before. The overall impression was a higgledy-piggledy stack of cock-eyed buildings, the colour of earth as if they had been moulded out of the ground. Crumbling red earth trodden smooth and littered with decaying objects: bones, pottery shards and rusty spikes. A spent stream ran through the centre of town, ten parts pollution to one part water and in it people were washing a number of things: goats, clothes, babies, themselves. Tin shacks lined the mud thoroughfare and in between them teetered cardboard lean-tos with corrugated iron roofs, filigreed by rust. The air itself clung like a damp mulch, sweetly fetid and foul, clogging the nostrils and turning the stomach. Anyone able-bodied seemed busy and active, those less lucky bedded down in doorways, or scooted around on haunches, holding out their hands with little expectation. Evidence of disease was everywhere: in blank, unseeing eyes white with cataracts, in goitres dangling like turkey crops. But life churned away in the streets, full of purpose and activity. It was impossible not to wonder at the energy and resilience of these people.

Eventually, we arrived at the Bicycle Repair Shop. The owner leapt up and greeted us with alacrity, anxious to help. In the absence of new filters, driving compressed air through them was the best way to clear the muck and within the hour we did indeed have clean filters. One problem solved. Suddenly, I found myself with time to draw breath and take stock. Two issues were pressing: a) where to safely leave the craft? and b) what to do about the barricade between us and the terminal building?

In the case of a), we knew of nowhere else to leave the craft. It was by now very dark and if we set off in search of somewhere more secure to leave it overnight, chances are we would only end up somewhere worse. We decided to leave it where it was and Capt R, who knew everybody, hired a local to stand guard: there was no shortage of volunteers.

As for b), the Great Step of Surat, we decided that it had to go but just how we were going to get rid of it was a decision for the morning.

The next day, Capt R was up and about early and things moved with surprising speed: first a bulldozer arrived. We watched as it worked through the day, slowly and steadily eroding the barrier until it was about half its original size. For India, this was a breakneck pace! Another day should do it. But the next morning I was surprised to see the digger had been replaced by a dozen people with baskets on their heads, directed by Capt R, grubbing up the mud with their bare hands and carrying the full loads up the bank to dump them on an ever-growing spoil heap.

'So what happened to the digger?' I asked him.

'Last night, when the tide was out, the digger could not get back up the slope. Mechanical trouble. The tide comes in...' Here he demonstrated the sweeping tide with his hand. '...and when the tide goes, guess what? No digger.' He sighed deeply.

One thing India is not short of is people. As more and more came to help, the barrier was soon cleared, probably in no more time than it would have taken a machine.

Then came the tank incident. In answer to my questions about refuelling, I'd been confidently shown a huge metal tank lying as if abandoned on an area of flattened foreshore. It was just a tank, unconnected to anything but I was assured it would soon be sunk into the ground and once a pump was fitted it would be a state-of-the-art

refuelling station. I'm sure it would have been too, if the tide had not come up and carried it out to sea to join the digger. It was this mishap which led me to seriously doubt that the project was ever going to work.

In between events and mishaps such as these, we set about recruiting some locals to drive the craft. Typically, the Indian authorities went way over the top by insisting that any applicant for the post must be a fully-qualified ocean-going sea captain. Such exalted people were hard enough to come by but the odds were even steeper against finding one with time on his hands and with the desire and aptitude to drive a hovercraft. In the end, only one came forward: Captain Banerjee, a charming and urbane gentleman who had spent his life at sea in command of big ships but now wanted a life on land. I have no doubt that he was an excellent sea captain but this did not make him even a tolerable hovercraft pilot. He was quite elderly and sadly, his ocean-going experience did not really help him in his new role as the pilot of a relatively small passenger hovercraft. He had been used to walking the bridge giving instructions to his large crew, including a helmsman who steered the ship. In fact, he did not even drive a car, which was a relief to anyone who saw him wrestle ineptly with the controls of the hovercraft. Everyone, including Captain Banerjee, agreed he was hopeless and so another solution was sought.

Capt R had the bright idea of approaching the two pilots from Bhavnagar Port. Yamir and Gadin were the direct opposite of Captain Banerjee: young, confident, quick to learn and decidedly cool in their crisp white shirts, jeans and shades. They were experienced boat-handlers and Gadin was also trained as a helicopter pilot.

This time the training went smoothly. The two pilots were good company and one weekend, Yamir suggested we go on a sort of safari trip. He happened to have a family farm near a protected wildlife reserve containing the last few of the fast diminishing population of Indian lions. I readily agreed. In my mind's eye I saw myself lounging under a shady canopy in the back of a stationary Land Rover, looking through binoculars (from a safe distance) at a dozing family of lions where cubs frolicked and mum and dad lazed around swiping away the odd fly with their tails as they digested a gazelle.

The reality was less idyllic. First we drove a very long way in Yamir's Mahindra jeep to a modest building in the middle of the countryside where we were welcomed by his family. The following day we drove into the national park to look for lions, bumping through long, long grass in the beating sun, unable to see more than a metre ahead. We met a ranger who told us that lions were definitely in the vicinity. To prove this, he jumped into the jeep to better direct us to the mauled carcass of a sheep he had noticed that morning a little way away. After bouncing around for nearly an hour looking for the spot, we managed to locate this evidence of lion activity mainly through the flies and the birds which had found it ahead of us. It was indeed a dead sheep: bloody and chewed. Quite a mess, actually. The ranger knew of another carcass we might like to see. Oh, good. This one was older and an even more horrendous sight than the first. I began to question just how much I wanted to see a lion after all, pointing out that anything could be lurking unseen in this grass which grew higher than the vehicle. I certainly hoped I saw him before he saw me so that I didn't end up as just another mauled piece of meat to be pointed out to the next group of visitors.

'Yes, to date this lion has killed four sheep, an antelope and a rather skinny hovercraft engineer. Here's his hat.'

After a couple of hours in which we failed to see an actual lion, it was decided that we should visit a local village to get their take on lion activity. The villagers were sheep farmers by tradition, and although it seemed like the last place anyone would choose to keep sheep, they had permission to live in the park in a sort of unhappy symbiosis with the lions and other predators. These people were nomadic and here, as in any other place they settled for a while, they had built a stockade from pieces of wood and flattened out oil drums, to keep out the big cats. After some forward negotiation by the ranger while we waited in the jeep, a gate in the structure creaked open and we were allowed into an enclosure full of tents, goats and sheep, rather like the set of an *Indiana Jones* film. The inhabitants seemed tolerably pleased to see us. A sheep was summoned, and milk was ceremoniously extracted for our refreshment. Quashing my misgivings about hygiene, bacterial infections of the stomach and a general dislike of milk, I took a sip from the wooden bowl as it was passed around. It was warm and smelled strongly of sheep. Our hosts knew only a few words of English and we knew rather less of their language, except for the ranger who purported to know a bit, although not that much judging by the puzzled looks on their faces.

I think the conversation went something like this:

'So, what are you doing in these parts?'

'We have brought a hovercraft from far away.' (Here, much miming of a boat becoming a plane.)

'Very good.'

'Have you seen any lions lately?'

Here, there was a long interchange of ideas and a lot of hand gestures. 'No. Would you like some more milk?'

On the other hand, as we were relying so heavily on sign language, the villagers might have had a completely different view of the encounter.

'What did that lot want?'

'They're trying to fix up a hovercraft.'

'Those things still going then?'

'Apparently. Oh, and they asked if we'd seen any lions.'

'How do they expect us to see lions over the top of this great big fence?'

'That's what I said. Anyway, they loved the milk. Friendly lot. I'm sure they have a fascinating culture.'

We still needed permission from the Gujarat Transport Authority before the hovercraft service could operate at all. When I heard that we would be taking the Transport Inspector on a run back to Bhavnagar with us, the first thing I did was to high-tail it down to the Bicycle Repair Shop and have the filters re-blasted, once again receiving cheerful and efficient service. Our gleaming filters held up for nearly the whole mercifully uneventful 4-hour journey, then the engines started to surge. The inspector, who was an elderly man and probably rather tired by this time, did not seem to notice: by the end of the day we had been given permission to run the first passenger-carrying hovercraft service in India. And I could finally start the long journey home.

Sweden 2012

The modification on the generator was done. At one point, we'd had to summon Olaf all the way back from Kalix for help with a manoeuvre involving a particularly inaccessible bolt. He'd seemed pleased to oblige, maybe thinking that it was his special engineering expertise we were seeking. In fact, when we said we needed 'another pair of hands' we meant it literally – another pair of hands, that is, on the end of a pair of long, thin arms.

The news that we would take the craft for a trial spin the following day brought a rare smile to his face. From our point of view, it was the best sort of trial because there would be no-one there for us to worry about or impress. Most demos are pre-scheduled and often arranged for a VIP – some high-up general or an important customer – and have to take place even when weather conditions are tricky.

As we cleared up in the workshop, I told John and Olaf about my visit to the Finnish Frontier Guard. They became one of our customers after the Swedish Coastguard had proved what a valuable tool the hovercraft could be in the Gulf of Bothnia. By 1995 the Finns owned three craft and very sensibly deployed one in the north, one in the south and one in the middle. I made several visits to Finland, always in the depths of winter, to commission the new craft and train the crews to drive and maintain them.

If hovercraft can go anywhere, how did we end up here?

I had spent a long time with the Swedes and in my naivety reasoned that since Sweden and Finland are less than 100 miles apart across the Gulf of Bothnia, and geographically similar, with a similar climate, you would expect the Swedes and Finns to be similar too. Not a bit of it. To begin with, Finnish is an entirely different language, more closely related to Hungarian than Swedish. And the Finns have a dourer disposition than the Swedes. Rather surprisingly, Swedish is more widely spoken in the south of Finland where the Gulf is wider.

The first trip to Turku began rather unconventionally. I flew to Helsinki where I was met by one of the Coastguard's senior engineering consultants, a man called Viktor. The first thing I noticed about him was that he wore the most extraordinarily powerful glasses which made his eyes appear huge when he looked directly at me. An affable giant of a man, he led me through the snow not to some chunky four-wheel drive, as I had expected, but to a purple Nissan Micra. It is a challenge to get two large men, both wearing heavy winter coats, into the front of a Nissan Micra but once we were firmly wedged, we set off towards Turku. We bombed along for the first fifty miles or so, making the best of what limited conversation we could manage between us. In his hesitant, and not very fluent English, Viktor's sentences would tail-off with phrases like '... so we shall see...' or '... and that is how it is...' while he shot you an unsettling glance with those fish-bowl eyes.

When we reached the outskirts of Helsinki, Viktor somewhat apologetically announced, 'I must visit someone here... so we shall see...' We pulled into a residential area. 'Just for a short time... yes, that is how it is.'

As Viktor made no sign that I should go with him, I sat and waited as he disappeared into the lobby of a concrete block of flats which stood among many other concrete blocks of flats. All sorts of scenarios started up in my head. Who knows what he was up to? After all, I didn't know him very well. Drugs? Contraband? Guns? Was he really from the Finnish Frontier Guard at all? Ten minutes later, some of my more imaginative suspicions were reinforced and some new ones aroused when Viktor emerged from the lobby into the car-park with something obviously stuffed under his coat. Opening the car door, he plonked a bundle into my lap – a striped towel out of which emerged the head of a tiny quivering Chihuahua.

'Isn't he sweet? My mother has asked me to bring this to my aunt in Turku.'

I was lost for words. I had never owned a dog and I didn't much care for them. This might have been apparent in my body language as I instinctively recoiled, alarmed as much as anything by the creature's bulbous eyes which gave it an uncanny resemblance to Viktor. The dog must have sensed my ambivalence and so made up its mind to win me round with friendly gestures. The rest of the long journey was spent fending off the determined advances of this amorous creature, by turns trying to lick my face and satisfy itself by making trembling advances on my leg, interspersed with bouts of deafening yappy barking. If Viktor hadn't been a customer, I would have put a stop to its behaviour – after all, I had three whole hours to ponder on the various methods of doing this.

The demo also turned out to be awkward. It took place on a windless day in relentless, heavy rain. Even in a tropical monsoon, I have rarely seen heavier rain, and certainly none straighter. We were expecting a high-ranking official, so half a dozen crewmen had been lined up in his honour to salute the car as it arrived. Unfortunately, the party was running late and the men had already been standing in the downpour for half an hour before the official car swept through the gates. The General emerged followed by his aide, a severe and efficient-looking blonde woman. Keen to stave off imminent hypothermia, the frozen crew then piled hastily on board, followed by Viktor and me.

Two things then went wrong. Due to the dripping crew, the floor was soon covered in puddles and the moment we closed the doors, every window on board steamed up. The General homed in on this as a contractual shortfall, which was annoying because we had spent a lot of time and effort on the heating and ventilation system, especially its

If hovercraft can go anywhere, how did we end up here?

demisting facilities including heated windows. However, once the fault was identified, the General was happy he'd done his job so the pressure was off. Thankfully the windows cleared themselves after a few minutes and it was the only fault he could find.

The stern woman wrote copious details of the defect in her notebook then both she and the General sat back to enjoy the ride. Unfortunately, the mirror-calm conditions were perfect for setting off a phenomenon known as skirt-bounce. This is practically only ever experienced in new craft, where the seal between the surface and the skirt is actually too good, preventing the lift-air from escaping quickly enough; the skirt lifts momentarily to let pressure out and then drops again sharply to reseal itself. In inexperienced hands (such as the trainee now at the controls) this can develop into an alarming cyclic bouncing and the craft begins to jump up and down with increasing severity.

It soon became clear that the General's aide was fighting her own personal battle within the oscillating craft. She clamped her folded arms firmly over her chest, trying to keep nonchalant and maintain her dignity while her wayward bosom took on a life of its own. The line of dripping crewmen sitting directly opposite really had nowhere else to look and it took a prolonged and valiant effort for them to keep their eyes off the mesmerising breasts. It was Viktor who inadvertently came to the rescue. At the moment of highest tension, an especially fierce bounce caused his glasses to fly off his face, jettisoning one of their bottle-bottom lenses in the process so that it ricocheted against the bulk-head with an audible ping. Viktor immediately fell to his knees with a cry, blindly fumbling on the floor between everyone's feet for bits of his glasses, thus diverting attention away from the other spectacle (and towards his spectacles). This could have been seen as a well-staged act of chivalry. I personally think this is unlikely but we were nevertheless given a thankful excuse to stop the craft for a few moments, re-establishing normal gravity while we groped around in the puddles and under the seats until we found the last tiny missing screw Viktor needed to repair his glasses. While the crew were busy on their hands and knees, with a few judicious twists and tugs our female passenger calmly put everything back in order. Any surreptitious glances upward from the crew were instantly quelled with a look as sharp as a laser beam leaving no-one in any doubt that she was not a woman to mess with.

In spite of my efforts at miming some of the story, Olaf did not crack a smile. He just looked deeply puzzled.

'I had an interesting demo in Nigeria once,' said John. 'It was when I was working with Dev. We had a load of oil company big-wigs to impress.'

'Oh yes,' I sympathised. 'What went wrong?'

John looked surprised. 'Nothing. It was just – you know – interesting.'

'What even when nothing went wrong?'

'Things don't have to go wrong to be interesting.'

I was in no position to argue; I couldn't think of a demo which hadn't been terrifying, although they usually seemed to turn out alright in the end.

'Who are you, what are you asking me, and why do you need to know?'

Chapter 10
'Who are you, what are you asking me and why do you need to know?'

John: Nigeria 1995

Dev was a charming, immaculately turned-out Indian who had made Nigeria his home. He had worked for many years for a firm that chartered crew boats to the numerous oil companies working in the Niger Delta. He claimed to have made the company millions with a combination of good management and good accounting although apparently, his efforts had gone unappreciated by his superiors.

'Crooks! Thieves! Bastards!' he would curse whenever their name was mentioned. Crew boats were the main form of transport in the Delta, an area with thousands of rivers but few roads. These rough and ready vessels are the buses and trucks of the whole oil operation, carrying equipment and people over a huge area. Except executives, who went by helicopter. After an increasing number of fatal helicopter accidents, an alternative transport needed to be found. Dev had chucked in his safe but unappreciated job and bought a hovercraft to fill this void. He was a one-man band in a sea of multinational corporations.

Dev's way of dealing with people, I'm sure learned by long, hard experience, was to use a combination of being very demanding and very confrontational. With people he knew and liked this was toned down to an amiable verbal sparring.

He would always finish a conversation with a question. 'And what else?' Questions from an unknown or minion would immediately be met with 'Who are you, what are you asking me, and why do you need to know?' This worked particularly well with the menacing groups of armed police who would regularly stop the car whenever we were out and about to demand money. They would saunter up and lean on the side of the car tapping the windows with the barrels of their guns to indicate they wanted to talk. Although heavily armed and therefore used to getting their own way, they were completely unprepared for the verbal assault that ensued.

'Give me your name. What is your rank? Which station are you from and who is your commanding officer?' This was just the opening salvo. 'Do you know who this car belongs to? No? Well I'll tell you, it belongs to General ******. And he will be very displeased when I tell him you stopped us.' Totally outgunned they would back down and let us pass.

However, this approach had its drawbacks in less intimidating situations.

One evening a group of us went out to a well-reputed local restaurant. It was busy and we hadn't booked. 'I want your best table,' Dev demanded. The waiter took us to the only available table over in a corner. 'Is this the best table you have?' Dev questioned. The waiter mumbled some apologies. 'OK but bring me the menu now, we are hungry.' Menus quickly appeared. 'Is this your normal menu? Bring me your best menu and some hot towels.' This latter referred to a nice hospitable custom in Nigerian restaurants - a hot towel to freshen your face and hands before a meal. 'But make sure they are really hot,' continued Dev. 'I'll send them back if they're not.' The towels duly arrived. 'Are they really hot?' Yes agreed the waiter, handing one to

Dev, who impatiently tore off the foil wrapper then dropped the towel like a stone. 'Fuck! that's really hot!' he cursed. The waiter's face showed not the slightest flicker of a smile.

Dev had given me lots of advice about what to do when arriving in Lagos.

Keep smiling, don't get into arguments. Don't trust anyone. Don't get into a car with anyone I don't know personally. I will send a driver to collect you. Check his ID.

With all this to remember, I felt very nervous but told myself that things often aren't as bad as you expect. I was soon to learn that in Nigeria the opposite rule applies: things are always worse than expected. As soon as I got off the plane it began. People came up and demanded to see my passport, or offered to help me, or came up begging for money. The arrivals hall was bedlam, jammed with queues and people jumping queues. Shouting, arguing and not much movement. It took ages, but finally I reached a desk with lots of unfriendly men behind it. Some were in uniform, others in traditional dress. It was impossible to tell who was who. I handed over my passport to a man in robes who studied it closely. He beckoned over someone in uniform who took his time studying it then handed it around to his colleagues. There was a lot of discussion and head shaking; questions were fired.

'What are you doing here?'

'Where are you staying?'

'Who do you work for?'

Doing my best to follow Dev's advice, I kept smiling and tried not to look rattled. Finally, I think they got bored: as instructed, I hadn't brought any cash, no American dollars, and once it became apparent that I didn't have any money they tossed my passport back. Relieved, I went on to tackle the baggage claim. I fought my way to the carousel in time to see a bag that looked like mine and reached for it. Several hands reached out too. It wasn't mine so I retracted my hand. All the other hands retracted too. I realised I was surrounded by people who

214

wanted to 'help' me with my bags. So I had to play a game, take my time to identify my bags then stay still, keep nonchalant, grabbing them at the last minute, before any of the 'helpers'.

When I had finally gathered all my stuff, I made my way to the exit. The doors opened ahead of me, I was almost out, almost standing in the hot Nigerian sun, when two armed soldiers stepped in front of me. Like many Nigerians, these men were huge; their towering physique gave them an intimidating presence, as if they could squash you with one fist if they felt so inclined.

'Let me see your passport,' said one. I handed it over. 'Who is meeting you?' I had a name written on a piece of paper, given to me by Dev. I handed it over. 'Wait here, we'll go and find him.' Before I had a chance to respond, they went off out the door, still holding my passport. Shit. I felt foolish and afraid. What would happen now? After what seemed an eternity, the two of them returned with a scruffy, downcast looking bloke. Not what I was expecting. Surely this person wasn't an employee of Dev? He must be a plant, just someone they have found outside and commandeered into the scam.

'Hello, I'm John Barker,' I said as cheerfully as I could, 'You must be Mr ****?' He was surly-faced, barely acknowledging me. 'Thanks for meeting me,' I continued with hearty forced confidence. Please say something... 'How is Dev?' I pressed.

Still nothing.

The soldiers asked, 'Do you have something for us?' They took the news that I had no cash with remarkably good grace. After a bit of hanging about, at last they returned my passport and wandered off – there are many more fish in the sea. I was left alone with my scruffy mute.

'We go to the Hotel,' he said, suddenly breaking his silence, and headed for the door. I grabbed my bags and stumbled after him. We stepped outside straight into a wall of heat and noise. He led me to the kerb and said, 'Wait here, I'll be back in ten minutes,' and disappeared. I stood out like a glowing beacon, a pale, naive, affronted

Englishman abroad. People started gathering around me like vultures, eyeing my bags and clothes.

Where was I from? Where was I going? Did I have anything for them? I was feeling increasingly panicky. My ability to maintain a shit-eating grin was beginning to waver. I was tired, hungry and stuck in hell. Then a red pick-up truck pulled up. I couldn't believe it – Dev's man had, true to his word, come back.

But was he Dev's man? Could this be a scam? I got in the truck and, at his command, obediently locked the door. Then we drove off through narrow streets, crowded with people and traffic, surely not a district where one would find an airport hotel? We were soon deep in the back streets of the town. Panic resurfaced. I was being abducted, for sure. After fifteen increasingly fraught minutes, we pulled up at some tall gates, which opened and in we went.

Incredibly, it was a hotel! At the reception, sat a big grumpy man in robes with a fly swish. 'I made a reservation.' Our man was finally saying the right things. He seemed as relieved as me, talking confidently. It didn't last long.

'But he's a foreigner,' Mr Grumpy pointed out. 'He must pay in advance. American dollar.'

My man looked crestfallen. 'Have you got dollar?'

'Sorry, no. Only Sterling travellers' cheques.' We showed them to Grumpy who sneered.

'For him only dollar!' To his credit, my man promised to sort things out and went off to make some calls while I slumped in a chair surrounded by my bags, disoriented. What time was it? My watch was still on UK time. My clothes smelt and I was thirsty as well as hungry now. I felt shattered, but at the same time pumped up with adrenalin.

After an age, my friend returned with a brown paper bag. With a flourish he tipped the contents onto the desk in front of Mr Grumpy. A mountain of money. At the time, there were 120 Nigerian Naira to the pound and the largest note was a 100. This looked like a lot for a night in a hotel. Mr Grumpy didn't hesitate: he scooped up the money and tossed a key onto the counter. I was in! A porter took us up in a rickety lift and along a lot of corridors to a scruffy room. My man was more communicative now. Was I hungry? Very.

'Use room service and don't open the door until you have looked through the peephole and made sure. After that, lock the door and don't open it until we come for you tomorrow morning. I'll be there at 6.30.'

That time came around very quickly. A club sandwich and a beer, some fitful dozing and there was a knock on the door. Sure enough, there was my friend, this time with a man who kindly explained I now had to pay the check-out fee. What? My man didn't seem too fazed. Maybe this was normal? We paid what appeared to be, if not another mountain, then at least a significant hill of Naira, and in no time I was back at the airport for the short internal flight to Port Harcourt. The only white face in the whole place. When we landed, there were no terminal facilities. The plane just stopped on the tarmac, the passengers filed off ready to go to the open cargo bay for a free-for-all scrum to get our baggage, as usual with lots of 'helpers' hanging around.

Port Harcourt was the city at the centre of the Nigerian oil industry and Dev wanted to show off the craft to all the various oil companies in town to drum up some business. He had a contract with one oil company, but was counting on getting more. Surprisingly, the unloading and assembly of the craft went smoothly, except there was no slipway so the craft had to be craned in and out of the water each day. On the first day a group of oil company officials arrived and we did a trip up and down the river. When we were nearly back I was alarmed to hear a sudden ear-splitting volley of gunfire which seemed unnervingly close by. It's funny – there are many situations when what I have thought to be gunfire has turned out to be fire-crackers or a bird-scarer; but when you hear the real thing, there is no mistaking it.

I ducked instinctively. 'What was that?' But none of the Nigerians seemed even slightly concerned. I felt tense as we went alongside to let off our passengers. A beaming security guard came to assist.

'I thought I'd give you a gun salute with my rifle,' he explained, 'to welcome you back.'

It was the rainy season, so it rained every day. Sometimes it rained all day and sometimes it rained part of the day, but every day it rained. The soil was red and so there were puddles of red water everywhere. In a matter of minutes I was hot, sweaty, wet and muddy. But as we drove around, splashing through the puddles in the rain, smartly dressed Nigerians could be seen emerging from modest little houses by the roadside to go about their business, walking or waiting for buses, sheltering under small umbrellas, but always looking immaculate. How did they do it?

Ken Saro-Wiwa, a poet and activist for the Ogoni people who are indigenous to this area, had recently been executed. He had been campaigning for the rights of his people to have a fair share of the oil revenue taken from their land. The city was on high alert and the oil companies were all under suspicion. As we drove around we were regularly stopped and searched by gangs of armed police. Dev dealt with these in his usual confrontational style and we got away untroubled. There were long queues at all the petrol stations because fuel was in short supply. Most of our evenings were spent in Dev's big, echoing, austere house, eating a meal cooked by his housekeeper, usually in candle-light due to the regular power-cuts.

Then one evening, on his housekeeper's day off and for a change, Dev took me to a restaurant in Port Harcourt. On the way home we were bumping gently along the potholed road when a young lad on a moped, deftly weaving around the puddles, overtook Dev's huge Peugeot saloon on the inside.

Seeing this Dev exploded.

'These fucking monkeys!' he screamed, gesticulating at the motor cyclist.

He put his foot to the floor and accelerated, the whole car bouncing violently along the rutted road.

'I'll show you, bloody monkey!'

Only when we had finally out-run the little moped did Dev visibly relax. Then like a man suddenly awoken from a disturbing dream, he looked around with a troubled expression.

'What's the matter?' I asked.

'I've just driven past my house,' he admitted. He turned the car round. We drove back very slowly and the incident was not mentioned again.

Once all our demonstrations were done the craft was packed up and put on a truck for the 100 kilometre journey to Warri, another big oil town to the north-west. From here it was to run a ferry service to Opumami, an oil installation out in the jungle. Now 100 kilometres isn't very far, so I was surprised when I was told we would stop overnight along the way – two days to do 60 miles? As soon as we got on the road in Dev's car, I understood. It was a single lane road, full of potholes, jammed with traffic. After a few hours of slow progress, things just ground to a halt. We got out to stretch our legs. I was hungry and there was a small open stall across the track selling food.

'What is it?' I asked Jonathan, our driver.

'Goat's head soup,' he replied. There were quite a few customers. For every new serving, the cook gave the murky liquid a vigorous stir so you could clearly hear the horns clunking against the side of the metal pot. I peered inside, waving away the persistent flies. It was the sight of tufts of wiry hair floating on the top which finally finished off any appetite I might have had.

After a long tedious wait, the reason for the delay became clear. For several hundred metres the potholed road had been completely washed away and the result was a quagmire, full of stranded vehicles, overturned trucks and abandoned cars nearly blocking any route through. Everything was red brown: the mud, the huge puddles and the vehicles. The scene extended all along the road as far as we could see and into the dense jungle at either side, where abandoned vehicles could be glimpsed through the vegetation. A gang of mud-spattered local blokes hung around the edge, demanding money to push vehicles through. If you didn't pay, you caused more of a hold-up as negotiations got heated and tense. If you did pay, there was no guarantee of getting through. After a while there was a lot of commotion from behind: an army jeep was making its way past the queue by angrily commanding people to pull over to let them through. Ah, a bit of authority is all that's needed to sort this mess out, I thought naively, as they forced their way past. But rather than stop and bring order to the chaos, they just continued on their way, their four-wheel drive jeep ploughing through the muddy sea and disappearing the other side leaving the travellers to fend for themselves.

Eventually it was our turn. We stood at the edge of the crumbling tarmac, facing the brown morass, surrounded by threatening, impatient men. Jonathan, our driver, had the window down and appeared to be negotiating genially with them. After a short while, an agreement appeared to have been reached and the gang started drifting around the back of the car, ready to push. Suddenly, without

warning, Jonathan floored it. The big, stately Peugeot shot forward, over the edge of the road and down the muddy slope. There were angry shouts behind us as the gang of men made chase, desperate to touch the car to be able to say they had pushed. If we stopped this would get nasty. To his credit, Jonathan kept the car going. We slalomed through the littered vehicles and big muddy puddles, somehow managing to find traction where so many others had failed, leaving a truck battlefield. Finally, we reached the opposite slope and without hesitation started up it. We were going to make it! At last, the gang started to drop back and give up. But there was no escape. As soon as we had climbed to the tarmac on the other side, we were held up by impatient drivers blocking both lanes, jockeying to get in position to make their dash across. The most determined of the gang caught us up, but a combination of Jonathan's determination and Dev's tongue-lashing convinced them that we had not needed their help and we owed them nothing.

Soon after, we cleared the jam and began to make progress, but it was growing dark by then and this was obviously not a road to travel at night. We made our planned stop for the night at a motel which loomed out of the darkness at the roadside, a sort of half way staging post between Port Harcourt and Warri. The next morning, we started early and arrived at the base just as the place was starting work for the day. We drove through guarded gates into a compound littered with oil industry hardware and buzzing with activity. After the harshness of the journey everyone seemed overwhelmingly friendly, many stopping to say hello. In the melée, I inadvertently failed to acknowledge one man and he came back to correct me. 'Sir I am greeting you.' I apologised and he asked after my family's health and shook my hand.

We spent the morning meeting people and were shown around the site. It was full of pipes, heavy machinery and drilling rigs. The compound was surrounded by thick jungle and a wide brown river flowed through it. Beyond the dock bristling with cranes and barges there were dug-out canoes, fishing boats and wooden huts on the opposite bank. All around, in the near and far distance, oil flares burned above the trees. A gentle rain was falling.

After an hour or so, the hovercraft, a Griffon 2000TD (see appx. 7), arrived on the back of a mud-spattered truck. God knows how it got through the quagmire. We were shown the place where it was to be unloaded, at the head of a steep, narrow ramp into the river, and we were given a choice of cranes to lift the craft off the truck. I took the big one.

As we prepared to connect the craft to the crane, I noticed that there was a problem – the wire was jammed in the hook. Once I pointed this out, the big crane was grudgingly replaced with the small one. The rain was falling ever harder and not wanting to get wet, my fair-weather helpers drifted off until there was just me and the crane driver – him in his little cab, and me standing out in the rain, holding a rope to steady the craft. I gave the signal and the craft lifted with a sharp jerk, swinging on the end of the wire. I signalled to swing to one side. In the lashing rain I glanced down and noticed my arms and chest were black. Black rain? I looked over at the crane. A spray of hydraulic fluid was spouting from a burst pipe. After some frantic signalling, the craft was dumped on the ground. Not in an ideal place, but safe. We started work on getting it operative while the crane was taken away for repair.

In the meantime, the big crane that I had rejected had gone down to the dock. I was impressed that they had fixed it so quickly – perhaps things were more efficient around here than they looked. Now the rain had stopped, the buzz of activity restarted. My helpers reappeared and we began unfolding the craft. As we worked, I could see barges coming and going on the river, loaded with pipes and equipment. Suddenly there was an almighty crash. The big crane had toppled over! It was now lying on its side with its jib across a barge and the cab balancing on the steel safety rail along the edge of the dock. The pipes it had been lifting had fallen into the water and their weight was holding the jib down. Amazingly, no-one was hurt.

There was a shocked silence, quickly followed by intense debate. How could the crane be set upright again? We went cautiously back to work on our own task, observing from a safe distance. The discussion about what to do seemed to be getting nowhere when I saw someone go over to the crane and reach into the cab. Horrified, I realised that he was going to release the brake on the winch drum and thus allow the heavy pipes to fall into the water. I saw him jump back. The jib flew up like a medieval catapult and the huge crane crashed back up onto its tracks. For a second, it looked as if the momentum of this would make it fall the other way but after a tense few seconds of rocking, it settled in an upright position.

Again, miraculously, no-one was hurt. Luckily everyone was wearing hard hats, steel toe-capped boots and life-jackets for health and safety reasons. If only common-sense could be issued as easily!

With that drama over, the hovercraft was ready to go. My job now was to train the two pilots Dev had employed to drive the craft. Indra and Hakesh were both Indian but there the similarity ended. The chief pilot would be Hakesh, who had spent his life as a fishing boat captain in Southern India. The second pilot would be Indra, an electrical engineer from the north, with no marine experience at all.

We practised the route to Opumami with a local guide. The river twisted and turned through the dense jungle. Other rivers joined and branched off. After every turn it would either widen and straighten or narrow and twist through a maze of brown water and green vegetation where everything looked the same. It took an hour and a half of winding and twisting to get there with only the occasional straight bit to be able to build up any speed. It was clear that the first thing everybody needed to learn was the route. Opumami turned out to be a remote outpost at the head of a narrow creek in a clearing - little more there than tanks, valves and pipes.

Occasionally, we come across someone incapable of piloting a hovercraft. They are unable to understand the principal of how it

works and can't cope with the peculiarities of the controls. Often this is no great problem, particularly if the craft is operated in open water with few hazards, but here on these winding rivers there was no room for error. Make a mistake and we were in the trees. Hakesh turned out to be one of these hopeless cases. A bundle of nerves who froze every time we approached a tight bend, unsure if he would be able to get the craft round. Fortunately, Indra soon got the hang of it and was a careful and confident driver.

It was a nerve-wracking two weeks. The more Indra's confidence grew, the more Hakesh's ebbed away. Along with him, I became a bundle of nerves, frustrated by his resistance to my best efforts to teach him. We all finally learned the route by memorising the small signs: a few huts here, a fallen tree there. Then came the day we started the ferry service. With Indra driving, the trip was quick, smooth and the passengers arrived happy. By contrast, Hakesh's runs were slow and uncomfortable with lots of complaints. But my time was up and it wasn't my place to hire and fire. A few weeks later, I heard Hakesh had resigned, replaced by Timothy, another Indian who was successfully trained by Indra. Sadly, some time later, I heard that Indra was killed in a plane crash caused by a bungled hijacking. He was flying home at the time, to see the family he had so often talked about.

Before I left, Dev kindly offered to help me buy some gifts to take home. I hadn't seen anything in Port Harcourt that resembled a gift-shop but Dev assured me that he knew an excellent place. After what seemed like hours, we arrived at a ramshackle hut in amongst the acres of other ramshackle huts that make up the city suburbs. We were already running late so I kept my eye on the clock, anxious that I might miss my plane. A proud looking man stood outside; Dev greeted him like an old friend. We ducked inside to find a dimly-lit interior, much bigger than it looked from outside. As my eyes adjusted to the light, I could see it was a treasure trove – carvings, metalwork, ivory. Exotic looking artefacts lined every wall and much of the floor. Enchanted but aware of my limits of space and weight, and still mindful of the passing time, I chose a selection of delicate smallish wooden carvings, rejecting any with ivory on them. These collected on the counter until I was sure I had something for everyone at home. Dev stepped in to negotiate the deal. I didn't understand the price quoted but predictably Dev was outraged.

'We came here in good faith, and you try and rob us! I thought you were my friend.'

'How much is it?' I asked innocently. Translated into Sterling, it seemed to me a very reasonable price and well within my budget. But with Dev, haggling was a matter of honour and he didn't expect to lose. I backed away as the negotiations became increasingly heated. Why couldn't I just pay the man and go? In a final outburst, Dev announced, 'No, I'm not going to pay!' He swept up the items and headed for the door. With so many fiddly objects to hold, after a couple of steps he began to drop them. The first to go was a beautiful, delicately carved bowl which fell from his hands and chipped on the hard dirt floor; other items then began to escape his grasp – a carved flower, a tiny soapstone elephant – rolling on the floor at our feet. As he stooped to pick them up, he dropped others. Finally a metal bangle fell with a clang, the vibrations gradually dying away to nothing. There was a stunned silence and then Dev quietly set about regathering all the pieces. Some were OK, others a little worse for wear. I paid the original asking price and we left.

On my own again in Lagos airport, the atmosphere was as tense and intimidating as before but this time I was more worldly-wise. I kept myself to myself and tried to look confident and aloof. I'd hated my time in Nigeria. It seemed like the most dangerous place I had been. I waited nervously to board the plane, checking the departures again and again. My flight was marked 'on time' but I was still convinced that at the very last minute something would happen: I would be detained, or the plane would be prevented from taking off. It was while I was in this state of rising anxiety that I decided never to return: the probability of something bad happening would increase every time I went back. I am glad I trusted my instincts on this and declined the next trip to Nigeria. The man who went instead of me was a bit of a legend, I was told, the sort who would go anywhere for the right price. I felt like a wimp until I heard that he had been kidnapped, along with another ex-pat. I hate to think how I would have responded in such a situation, but The Legend apparently escaped. (The other expat didn't do so well. He was taken out into the jungle and thrown into a hole. When the ransom demand was met two days later he wasn't in good shape.)

In spite of my fears, there was no last-minute disaster to prevent me from leaving and when I finally boarded the plane, I felt an overwhelming sense of relief. People were laughing and chatting, something I hadn't seen for a long time. With the plane finally full, a man stood up and announced in a loud American voice:

'First thing I'm gonna do when I get home – I'm going to get a T-shirt made that reads: When I die I know I'm going to heaven, because I've already been to Nigeria.'

People actually applauded, me included.

Sweden 2012

We took the craft out the next day and everything worked well. Our job was done, which meant we could at last think about going home.

Olaf took the controls and, at last, his face lit up! I'd had the same feeling when I'd first driven on ice decades ago. I remember when I took the craft out from its hangar in Luleå airport where we'd assembled it, and hovered onto the perimeter road to deliver it to the Swedish coastguard base in Svarton. We hadn't gone far when I glanced in the rear-view mirror and noticed a Saab Viggen jet-fighter right behind me. My nervousness quotient, already high, rocketed instantly. Keeping up one hundred per cent concentration, I headed for the bank at the end of the runway, knowing that the frozen sea was just beyond. My nerves melted away as the hovercraft drifted seamlessly onto the new surface. Wow! It was like a home-coming, as if the hovercraft had been built for, and I had been born for, that very moment. Even at low engine speeds progress was completely effortless. The very thought of it still makes me smile.

Without deliberately planning our trips this way, in the past I had usually ended up in the coldest, darkest places on the planet while John basked in the tropics. Travelling to these icy wildernesses can bring many rewards: endless daylight and extraordinary landscapes. But ice and snow did not always equate with beauty. One of the remotest jobs I had taken on was in Alaska. In fact, it wasn't really a place at all, just an empty icy space under which there happened to be oil, and above which all the paraphernalia for getting it out.

Final Destination: Deadhorse

Chapter 11
Final Destination: Deadhorse

Russ: Alaska, 2003

There is a point in every trip when you are through passport control and baggage-reclaim and find yourself at that stomach-churning moment when at last it's just you, alone in a strange place. As you step into a sudden wall of heat or turn up your collar against the unexpected cold, every nerve strains to make sense of thousands of new, possibly threatening, sights, sounds and smells – vibrant, colourful, puzzling – and you stand a moment taking it all in as you try to get your bearings. It's never what you expect, and never typical of where you end up: after all, airports are just places that everyone is trying to get away from. Trying to look relaxed, you scan the scene before you, searching for your name, however mis-spelt, among the forest of cardboard placards held up by waiting drivers. If you're lucky someone has turned up to meet you.

At Deadhorse there was none of that uncertainty. The airport was nothing more than a metal clad building outside which stood a yellow pick-up truck the size of a bungalow. It was two feet away and difficult to miss, being the only thing which wasn't grey in a cold, flat and distinctly un-vibrant landscape. The driver seemed friendly under his mirror shades, hi-vis jacket and hard hat. Obviously not taking any chances. He was clearly used to picking up rookies like me. Once in the car he proceeded to give me a well-rehearsed spiel as he drove. As the town was really no more than a collection of boxes and shipping containers, there were no landmarks to point out but he did tell me that the place was permanently frozen in winter and in fact there were only six ice-free weeks in each year. 'Now, over there, that's the Deadhorse General Store,' he said pointing to a rectangular box which bore a sign with the words 'Deadhorse General Store' above a cartoon of a horse lying with its legs in the air. It occurred to me that this was the least equine town I had ever come across. I had heard of one-horse towns but here was a no-horse town. I had just flown from Anchorage over hundreds of miles of icy barren tundra and had not seen any trace of a horse, even a dead one. Another sign pronounced: 'Deadhorse. End of the Dalton Highway'. It struck me that there was a bit of a negative theme going on here – horses, not only dead but non-existent, the end of the road and now another sign I had seen quite a few times already proudly drawing attention to the absence of something else: All this Far and Still No Bar.

'See that. No alcohol here,' he said. 'This is a dry town. You get caught with any then it's window or aisle.'

'Right.'

'Window or aisle. Yep. Straight on the plane. And there's not a lot of night life. Know why?'

'Er...' I looked around at the big windy nothingness which surrounded us. Because there's fuck-all here? I wondered. 'Well, you tell me.'

''Cause there's no night. Twenty-four hour daylight. No difference, day or night.'

'Uh-huh. Must take some getting used to.'

'What you need is aloomin'um foil.'

'Really?'

'For the windows. So no light can get through. You're welcome to borrow some if you haven't thought to bring any.'

I hadn't. 'Thanks that would be good.'

He went on to fill me in on the geographical details: the Dalton Highway mentioned on the sign is the only year-round Alaskan road which goes all the way to the Arctic Ocean. It's a dirt track and is the very last leg of the Pan American Highway which runs through practically every American country, south, central and north, until it arrives at the final destination of Deadhorse. But the ultimate anti-climax awaits anyone travelling north along this route: fifteen miles before the point where the road finally reaches the Arctic Ocean, there is a check-point beyond which no-one but authorised personnel can travel. Instead of a rewarding glimpse of the sea, the road ends at a metal barrier manned by a grumpy guard.

It was at this barrier that we drew to a halt. Beyond the fence were more rectangular buildings from which emerged a security guard

kitted out identically to my driver. 'PPE-ZONE BEYOND THIS POINT', screeched a large sign; 'NO PPE? NO ENTRY!' proclaimed another. It may seem hard to believe today, but these initials, although clearly important here, meant nothing to me and I was anxious not to show my ignorance about something that was obviously so vital. Had I brought any PPE with me, I wondered. Was it something to do with the aluminium foil? Personal hygiene? It must have been the culture shock making my mind work slowly. In the end it was the pictures of boots, goggles, hard hats and gloves that gave me a clue. Personal Protective Equipment.

My passport was studied without much interest but my woeful lack of PPE, even while in the safety of the car, was instantly flagged up. I was clearly under-dressed. My flimsy glasses in particular were found wanting – they lacked side-shields to protect my eyes. Sure enough, as soon as I was through the gate, I was issued with overalls, waterproofs, goggles, rigger boots, hard hat and a hi-vis jacket. This at least gave me the feeling of fitting in. The last thing I wanted to do in this macho environment was to stand out in the crowd or be thought of as a nerdy wimp. Cocooned in my PPE and happily indistinguishable from all of the old hands, I set off to familiarise myself with The Arctic Hawk, the hovercraft which only a few weeks ago I had helped to commission at a small boat-building company based in Seattle. In the United States the Jones Act restricts the import of vessels which could have been built in the US. Hence, this hovercraft was licence-built in the States to provide a crew transport service here in Alaska.

The Griffon 2000TD (see appx. 7) was needed to bridge the seasonal gap between truck and boat. In the winter the oil company would build an 'ice-road' to the site by pumping water onto the ice until it froze and was sufficiently thick to support a vehicle. They could use this for most of the year, and for a few months in the summer they could operate boats, but in the transitional periods at spring and fall, both forms of transport carried serious risks. The hovercraft was brought in to be used for general transport to the offshore oil production sites in these in-between periods, a job which until then had been carried out by a helicopter, chartered at great cost. As usual, the hovercraft was a much cheaper option: the cost of one hundred helicopter trips would buy the hovercraft.

The question of drilling for oil in the Arctic is said to be a 'political football', a metaphor which can be endlessly extended. It has certainly been booted around for decades: always hotly pursued, periodically kicked into touch, subject to fouls, tough penalties, thrills and – unfortunately – spills. Ever since large oil deposits were discovered at Prudhoe Bay in 1968, the issue has been under constant debate. The discovery of the Prudhoe Bay oil field was huge – not just any oil field, but over twice the size of the next biggest, East Texan oil field. It's 'Middle East sized', worth $300 billion, has over 1000 active wells and has accounted for up to 25% of the USA's domestic oil production. In the 1973 Oil Crisis, when an embargo was placed on America and other nations by the Organization of Petroleum Exporting Countries (OPEC), the cost of oil in the US quadrupled, immediately making the pipeline project financially feasible. Legislation cleared the way and between 1974 and 1976, 800 miles of Trans-Alaskan Pipeline were built, stretching from Deadhorse to the ice-free port of Valdez, and the first Alaskan crude oil was shipped through the pipeline in 1977. The oil takes about eleven days on average to make the trip all the way down the pipeline. When it reaches Valdez, it is loaded onto super-tankers for transport to either West Coast refineries, or since 1998, for possible export to Asian markets.

Not surprisingly, Alaska's anti-pollution laws are the toughest in the USA. When the Arctic National Wildlife Refuge (ANWR) was set up by congress in 1980, it became the largest protected wilderness in the United States. But the decision whether to develop the oil resources of one and a half million specific acres in the coastal plain was deferred. This subsection of ANWR, known as the '1002 Area', is the hot potato of Arctic oil exploration. Given this context, it was not surprising to see what extraordinary lengths the oil companies were required, and prepared, to adopt to prevent pollution. With the political and economic situation constantly fluctuating, the oil companies' presence in Alaska was always on a knife-edge. Nothing could be allowed to go wrong; there could be no more accidents or spills. In fact, to leave no mark or trace on the environment is the ultimate goal here: all the buildings are temporary and can be dismantled and removed whenever necessary. Even human waste is pumped out and taken away in tankers; I didn't enquire where to.

After carrying out a few checks, I went back to the accommodation block and made it as homely and orderly as possible, thankful that I did not have to share it. No matter how stressful a day, or how difficult the circumstances, having your own space to retire to and think things over always made life easier. As the driver had told me earlier, Alaskan old-hands always pack a roll of cooking foil and duct-tape in their bags to black out the windows and make a dark room anywhere

they stay, so I spent some time doing this with a black-out kit which, true to his word, the driver had kindly loaned me.

With the first Safety Meeting due to take place at six o'clock sharp, my first day of work began, as subsequently did every other, at 5.30am. It was warm and toasty in my cabin and my Bacofoiled windows allowed no glimpse of the outside: it was hard to believe that we were in extreme climes but I obeyed regulations and got kitted up in my gear, then stepped outside to find a perishing 10 knot east wind and drifting fog. Throughout my stay, I found it hard to get used to the startling difference when stepping out of the cocooned warmth of the pre-fab rooms, which could have been anywhere, into the raw cold of a vast wilderness.

In 2003 the USA was way ahead of us in matters of Health and Safety. At home in the UK, we were still at the stage where we complained about step-ladder training courses and moaned about having to use ear defenders. My first Alaskan H&S briefing left me incredulous that nobody else showed any sign of irritation at this waste of time and nobody laughed. When I was a boy, my mum would urge me to be careful: 'Don't go falling over now!' 'Mind the road!' 'Watch you don't slip!' 'Don't choke on that!' Delivered at moments of potential danger, I guess these exhortations were intended to save me from all sorts of nasty injuries, bringing me to my senses as I romped towards the edge of a cliff or attempted to eat a bag of gobstoppers in one go. The 6am Health and Safety meetings ran along these same lines – that is to say, a trotting out of statements of the Bloody Obvious, except that it's not your mum, it's the Operations Manager. After a few identical meetings, you just stop hearing it, in the same way it never occurred to you to take any notice of your mum. Old hands, many with over twenty years of experience, would sit through it all without comment as we were told to watch out for the snow, that it's very cold out there so wear plenty of warm clothes, be careful with machinery, don't get frostbite, ice is slippery and make sure you have a clean hanky at all times. (Okay, not the last one.)

There then came a point when the assembled workers were asked if they had issues to raise but only a very brave man would have done so - the daily litany of advice was one thing you couldn't escape but prolonging it by questioning or commenting was an unspoken crime. Anyway, it wasn't a very life-affirming process, this gloomy contemplation of all the terrible things which might befall one in the day ahead. The meeting closed with the real reason we were all there. 'Everyone present please sign the minutes to say you have attended and understood the briefing' (which in mum-speak is 'I told you to be careful - don't expect any sympathy from me'). With the paper duly signed, we set off to confront or avoid the numerous dangers that lay in wait for us, hopeful that we would somehow survive the day.

Within a short time of meeting up with a few of the trainee drivers and taking Arctic Hawk out for a first spin that morning, I was feeling much better. I could see straight away they were an amenable bunch. It is not always the case that the people you come to train actually want a hovercraft for various reasons – say, company politics or pay – nor are some crews necessarily disposed to become good drivers, but not only were these guys thoroughly in favour of the craft, they also had a perfect mix of seamanship, experience, and enthusiasm, as well as a sanguine approach, taking the view that everything was doable, fixable and all would be fine. Rick and Larry in particular stood out as promising drivers. By late morning, dazzling sunlight had replaced the fog. We set out cones and practised decreasing figures of eight – quite tricky in the wind but the men kept steadily raising their game. Doughnuts and coffee came next.

The hovercraft was there to carry crew and supplies out to North Star Island, a man-made off-shore oil platform, and it was part of the training schedule to make a dozen round trips. It was a fairly easy run and the first one passed with no problem, after which we decided to go up on an old ice road near the beach, raised a couple of feet above the rest of the ice, where we had a lot of fun trying to get on and stay on the road. By then it was time for lunch.

You may have started to notice the frequent references to food. I soon discovered that it was high priority in this place – what else was there for three thousand tough men to do for enjoyment? Instead of a bar, there was a 'help-yourself' fridge full of ice-cream. I was a vegetarian – or more accurately The Vegetarian. I confessed this to Rick in the dinner queue. My heart sank when he frowned as if he was undertaking some huge mental effort, such as trying to hold a complicated series of numbers in his head.

'So you don't eat... steak?'

'No,' I admitted.

'Hamburger? Hot dog?'

'No. No meat.'

He gave a low whistle.

'Man. You better tell Clarence.'

'Who?'

Rick nodded through the open door of the kitchen where a black guy was looming over a griddle. I have never seen a man of such fearsome appearance. He looked like a human pile-driver, with enough suppressed power, just in the hand that held the spatula, to poleaxe a cow.

'That's Clarence,' said Rick. 'He'll take care of ya.' I checked Rick's face for some sign of irony but there honestly wasn't any. 'Hey, Clarence!' he called. The din in the cafeteria died down a little as people turned to see who was calling Clarence and then to watch him walk slowly over to us wiping his hands on a cloth. 'This here's Russ. And he don't eat meat.' Clarence's huge eyes swivelled in my direction. 'He's from England,' added Rick, by way of explanation. Clarence put both hands flat on the counter that he towered over and leaned towards me.

'You eat fish, Russ?' he asked in a low voice.

'Yes,' I squeaked.

'No problem. You got any health condition? Allergies?'

I thought briefly about mentioning my hay-fever but decided this was probably not going to be a problem as I hadn't noticed any plants; also that a canteen full of attentive oil riggers was not really the right forum. 'Oh, no, no.'

'Well, I'll tell ya, that's no problem here, buddy. Don't you worry. You just see me for whatever you want. I got gluten-free too.'

The roomful of riggers looked pleased and reassured as if the thought of anyone being left hungry gave them actual pain. The lunchtime babble rose again. 'Good old Clarence.' 'He'll be ok if he eats fish. One thing we're not short of.' 'I've got an aunt who's veg'tarian. She don't eat nothing but fruit pies and pecan nuts.' A young lad behind me in the queue tapped my shoulder. 'Hey, man, we got ice-cream here like you wouldn't believe. You eat ice-cream?' I admitted that I did. 'You gotta try the peanut-butter. Ain't ever tasted anything as good.'

'Thanks, I will,' I assured him, wondering why any utterance that left my lips here sounded so stuck-up and hoity-toity in comparison with the drawling vowels and cool slang of the Americans. There were men here from all over the States which meant that they sometimes had more trouble understanding one another than understanding me. We had come up against the language barrier as we'd been getting fuel that morning. The pump operator was a grizzled oil veteran who I later found out was from the Ozark Mountains in Missouri. He had such a pronounced drawl that it was almost impossible to understand what he was saying, a problem which was exacerbated by the fact that he took snuff so was always making guttural noises which were difficult to distinguish from words.

'Need any ol at all?'

Rick and Larry looked perplexed. 'Huh?'

'Ol?'

'Huh?'

The old guy's already ruddy face flushed further. 'OL! OL! ENJUN OL!' he enunciated, revealing black, snuff-stained teeth.

'Oil,' I interpreted, as the mists cleared. 'No thank you, not today. Just diesel.'

'What?'

'Just some diesel, please.'

'What's that? Speak up.'

What else would I be asking for, I wondered, at a fuel station? A weasel? An easel? I pointed to the diesel pump and he nodded. 'You Australian?' he asked, as if that would explain a lot. I was about to tell him that no, I was English but the thought of the effort I would need to expend in order to establish this left me feeling weak. I took the easy way. 'Uh huh.'

'Thought so.'

That afternoon it was blowing 15 knots. Fuelled with salmon and chips, we did some high speed turns on the slushy ice to get in some practice for the open water and made several upwind turns at first, starting with wind on the beam and followed up with one downwind turn. This brought us back to the start point and just to bring things full circle, the fog came down again. I headed back to my cosy quarters, bumping into Clarence along the way.

'Got something for you, buddy,' he said as he caught sight of me. He reached over to the grill and pulled out a bubbling toasted cheese sandwich on which he swirled ketchup. 'You don't eat meat, you gotta keep your strength up, man.' It looked right then like the most delicious thing I had ever seen.

'So – it's all meat tonight then, is it?' I asked, thinking this was my dinner.

Clarence looked incredulous. 'No, man. I cooked you up an individual fish pie with extra cheese. That there's just to keep you goin'.'

I thanked him and tucked the delicacy, carefully wrapped in a napkin, in my pocket, feeling a little self-conscious about this favouritism. I was in a good mood when I arrived back at my room. Everything was working out fine. The sandwich was warm against me and smelt delicious. I would eat it while catching up on some paperwork. It's funny how quickly a very good moment can go bad:

as I approached my door, I spotted a man knocking on it. There was nothing overtly unpleasant about him: trim physique, huge seventies-style glasses, neat beard; nevertheless, I took an instant dislike which was due to more than the fact that he had gate-crashed a small simple pleasure I'd been looking forward to. It is a habit of Americans to state their name and occupation as an opening conversational gambit, as if giving their number and rank to a sergeant major. This is just one of the many minor but telling differences I have observed between the two races: Brits mumble something inconclusive about the weather and their winsome remarks fade away uncertainly, as if lacking the force of conviction to stand up on their own. This is because, at heart, most Brits do not really believe that anyone cares who they are or what they think. Such self-doubt had clearly never troubled Spike.

'Spike Marlon. US Coastguard Approved Hover Pilot and Trainer from Anchorage,' he announced, grabbing my hand and pumping it up and down. The next thing he said was more chilling. 'I hear you're a hover-freak too, so I asked if we could bunk up together. We'll have lots to talk about.'

'Russ,' I said lamely. A rather unwelcome recollection had entered my head, of a half-forgotten conversation from my last day in Seattle. It was all coming back to me. We had discussed the fact that we would need a qualified US pilot to sign off the training here, as a formality. It would appear, by some fluke or twist of fate, that Spike happened not only to fit this profile but actually lived in Anchorage, which in Alaskan terms is 'just down the road'. Despite the fact he may as well have TWAT tattooed across his forehead, it was evidently all too convenient an arrangement to forego.

'Roomies!' he prompted, as if my lack of enthusiasm at him foisting his way into my personal space was the result of some misunderstanding, as if I hadn't grasped the wonderful possibilities that awaited me, stuck in a hermetically-sealed Portacabin 300 miles inside the Arctic Circle with a self-described Hover Freak.

'Great,' I said, frantically trying to think how to get out of this. 'Yes.' He looked puzzled, probably because my face did not really match the optimism of my words.

'Thought we might take a look at the craft?' he said, breaking the silence.

'Er, well it's a bit foggy now and I was just going to have a sandwich...'

I don't think he was capable of processing the thought that anyone might pass up the chance of looking at a hovercraft.

'That's great then! Hover on – show me the way!'

The days acquired an unvarying pattern which basically consisted of training sessions punctuated by food. There were no days off at Prudhoe: there wasn't anything to do and no-one wanted to prolong their stint. Weekends were virtually indistinguishable from weekdays. Each day's work brought you closer to getting home for a generous few weeks' rest. It was June, so any thoughts of night were a long way off. From the 14th May to 28th July, the almanac, referring to the sun, just said 'up all day'. If for any reason it was necessary to go out in the evening from the artificially imposed night-time environment it was a shock to find oneself in broad daylight. I began to realise how much we need the night and darkness as an antidote to the demands of the day. Evening signals down-time, retreat and relaxation. Without these rhythms, I found the only way to achieve a good night's sleep was to stay in the blacked-out mess-room after work for a few hours, to fool myself into believing it was dark, and then head straight to bed.

Going to bed early became particularly necessary since I had been sharing with Spike. One of his excruciatingly annoying habits was to add the prefix 'hover' to any verb, and his favourite pastime was 'Hover Talk'. In my desperation to avoid this activity, I stumbled upon an effective strategy. By chance, I had bought a computer game called Myst at the airport. I soon realised that whenever I played it, Spike would reverentially leave me alone, tip-toeing around me as if I was engaged in some sacred activity, a respect that he certainly lacked for reading as I had tried that, or probably even praying, which I had considered. Once I had assured him that it was a Game for One Player, apart from the odd wistful remark such as 'Why that looks like a great game'/'That sure does look like a lot of fun' he left me alone. The strategy became even more successful when I found some headphones. This is the reason why I am more familiar with the topography of seven levels of a pretend country called Myst than that of Prudhoe Bay.

I was starting to feel suspicious about the level of Spike's experience with hovercraft, even wondering whether he had ever actually driven one – the more he said, the more glaring holes appeared in his knowledge. He had to accompany us on virtually every trip and would repeatedly pick up the other drivers on minor things, as if he felt he had to exert his authority over them somehow, but lacked the technical know-how to contribute anything useful. He would bellow out unnecessary advice ('Watch your hover-speed!')

until I had to pull him aside and ask him to stop interrupting me. Luckily, the crew were shaping up really well despite his interventions. Larry was a natural. There is sometimes a moment when learning to drive a hovercraft (or ride a horse, or row a boat) when everything falls into place. There is no going back from this point. Brain and body suddenly work seamlessly together and the machine/horse/boat becomes an extension of your hands and your mind. As we were picking our way across some hummocky snow late one morning, I saw that moment in Larry's face – suddenly, he really understood what he was doing. Spike had no such sense of the sublime: he chose this moment to shout 'Stick ahead!' to draw our attention to a twig protruding out of the ice. The politeness and patience of the crew never seemed to waver in his presence – after all he would be responsible for signing them off – but behind his back they mimicked him mercilessly and had his finest phrases off to a tee.

'We should close the hover-door before we start the hover-engine.'

'Fasten your hover-seat belt before hovering the hovercraft.'

'Be careful not to damage the hover-skirt while we hover away from the hover-pontoon!'

This soon escalated. 'Hey, Larry, pass the hover-ketchup.' 'Don't forget your hover-helmet, Russ,' or 'Well, I'm off to my little hover-bed, boys, to hover down for the night.

Spike was keen to tell me, quite often, that he was a 'Hover man through and through' and was interested when I told him that in England such a person is called 'an anorak'. The crew called him 'All the gear and no idea' but only when he wasn't there.

Look at any calendar, tea-tray or coffee-table book in the gift shop at Anchorage Airport and you will see how stunningly beautiful Alaska is. Not all of Alaska, though. Here, on North Slope, the landscape was windswept, grey and empty – an especially depressing sight on dull days (and nights). But places don't need to be aesthetic to be important or worth preserving – these remaining areas of

Alaskan wilderness provide food and clean water on which the last remaining indigenous people depend. Pieces of wilderness help to clean our air and filter our water but these untouched areas are most vital for wildlife: here this meant niche animals like the Eskimo curlew, the porcupine caribou and the short-tailed albatross as well as more common ones too – black and grizzly bears, whales, walruses and polar bears. (Sometimes at the H&S briefing there would be warnings of polar bear sightings and the excitement of this was almost enough to make me open my eyes. On North Star Island, metal fences around the compound kept them out; the request to 'please shut this gate' was probably never meant more earnestly). Conservation groups were continually fighting on all fronts – to uphold the Roadless Rule, for instance, which stipulates that permanent roads cannot be built. They also regularly petitioned against logging, mining and off-road exploration as well as oil production.

While I was helping one of the engineers to put fuel in the craft's tanks I was surprised to see him spreading out a bund (a huge inflatable apron) on the ground for several metres around the front of the craft where the filler is. Any spills, he said, and it would be the old 'aisle or window'. Many routines and practices which were simple anywhere else really needed thinking about in this conservation area. For instance, air filters could be vacuumed clean but not blown out as this would spray the contaminant around. But while I was there the unthinkable happened. On the shore of North Star Island, a fork-lift truck burst a hose and spilled gallons of hydraulic oil on the paved beach. The clean-up operation was impressive and thorough. First the oil was mopped up with absorbent wadding which was put into sealed bags ready to be shipped out. Next all the paving stones were lifted and shipped out in a container, and finally a huge hole was dug under the paving to remove any tiny traces of oil that might have seeped into the ground before the beach could be rebuilt.

On March 2, 2006, three years after my visit, there was a serious spillage from the pipeline. Back in the 70s, this vast construction project had posed huge challenges due to the nature of the terrain which is a permafrost wilderness. Because digging into this would be so difficult and costly, the pipe runs 5 foot above ground (high enough to allow wildlife to pass underneath) and therefore visible and vulnerable. The March 2006 leak was certainly not the first. Over the years there have been others caused by maintenance failures and sabotage, including bullet-holes. Initial estimates of the five-day leak said that up to 267,000 US gallons were spilled over 1.9 acres making it the largest oil spill on Alaska's North Slope. The spill originated from a quarter inch hole in the pipeline. Eventually, this pipeline was decommissioned and replaced with a 20-inch diameter line with its own Pipeline Inspection Gauge (PIG), basically a little machine with a camera which works its way through the pipes like a mechanical endoscopy and sends back pictures of anything that might be amiss.

As the days passed, everyone seemed more and more upbeat about the craft and keen to put in place the kind of infrastructure it needed to make it successful. A generously sized fabric hangar was erected to house the craft. It was a swanky affair, well heated and with electric shutter doors at both ends so that the craft could hover in one end and out the other without turning or backing out. The ground here was dry and dusty and the biggest problem that emerged was the dirt floor which, whenever the craft hovered, stirred up such a storm that the craft, along with all the tools and spare parts stored inside the hangar, were soon covered with a thick layer of gritty dust. It became obvious that some kind of floor-covering was needed. No sooner had the decision been made than a team of guys turned up to prepare the ground. With a great deal of hard work raking and levelling it was finished in no time and a new plywood floor was laid. Pretty impressive work and soon we had a nice clean hangar again.

Another consideration was to find a decent landing-place on North Star Island. The concrete paving blocks around it were in a bad way after the previous year's storms and it would have been impossible to land the craft here without major re-levelling. We decided to land on a couple of flat areas of ice at each side of the island (to be used for different wind directions) and to construct a temporary ramp from the flat ice onto the concrete, thus spanning the uneven ice at the shore. The trouble with working in the Arctic is that there are different sets of conditions as the ice comes and goes with the seasons: someone had the idea to build a 50ft by 40ft hover-on pontoon when the ice melted, with one end floating and the other tethered to the island. This was a risky proposal because as soon as the thaw begins, great rafts of ice weighing thousands of tons drift about with the wind and carry away anything in their path. Eventually they decided to re-profile the concrete beach to make a permanent landing that could be used for most of the year.

We took some oil company consultants and engineers out to North Star. They were receptive to our ideas about the type of ramp needed and we evolved a plan which was pretty well exactly what we wanted – encouraging. The best thing was that they were keen to get the craft in service without delay. After that, there was a daily call to check on progress, in a helpful way, and make sure things were going smoothly.

Training continued with some 'get you home' lessons for two of the engineers, who did pretty well. We also went out with a full load of 18 passengers. I was a bit worried that the craft felt overloaded but when I did a tot up I realised I hadn't allowed for the fact that these were Americans and on the burly side at that. One person is meant to be 175lbs and although I couldn't really ask, I'm sure that most of these guys looked more than 250lbs which would be the same as if we had squeezed another seven average-sized people into the craft.

Then came our first 'paying' trip to North Star. I set my alarm for 4.30, the dead of night and broad daylight. It was blowing 25 knots in the east which called for a thoroughly unhealthy breakfast of tea and a brownie. A crew turned up on time to get the craft really up together, warmed up and windows cleaned. The eight passengers had lots of baggage which we had to carry in the cabin making it pretty crowded but the craft trimmed OK. There were nine to bring back and this lot had all their worldly possessions with them too so Rick and I ended up sitting on the steps. Larry always liked to drive with the window open, and the forward heater was on the blink so we were really chilled by the time we got back but not to worry – this was

249

supposed to be our last scheduled trip of the day so we had food and warmth to look forward to.

As we dropped off our passengers, we were surprised to find an

unexpected group of hopefuls waiting for a ride. The fact that one of them was a woman, an attractive photographer hired by the company to take some promotional shots, may have helped in persuading us to skip the coffee/brownie break in the warmth of the mess-room. Like everyone else, she was encased in safety gear, but she managed to wear it differently somehow, as if to draw direct attention to what might, or might not, be underneath. Back in the mess-room after the shoot there seemed quite a crowd of men who had a keen interest in photography but up until now had kept this to themselves. They were eager to see her pictures. When she picked one out which showed the craft framed closely by the picture border and announced, 'I like this one, I like it in tight...' a tense silence followed, broken only by the sound of twenty men quietly gulping.

It was nearing the end of my time in Prudhoe and yet I had hardly been outside the base, so when the time came for Spike to head back home to Anchorage, I felt I just had to go to give him a proper hover send-off. I knew I had to see him board the plane with my own eyes and actually watch it rise into the air. How else would I know he had really, really gone? Besides, I was hoping to find a souvenir or two to take back for the folks and the only shop I had seen was the General Store in Deadhorse. Also Larry and Rick had invited me to a meal up at the hotel – it was going to be a day of unprecedented excitement for me after the monotonous routine of the past weeks.

Even the morning Health and Safety briefing was a bit out of the ordinary. We were told that the aim of the company was to get the accident level down to one per man every four hundred years. I found this an interesting idea. As anyone who worked here for 400 years would undoubtedly be having accidents all the time anyway, or would probably have already died of boredom or staged an accident just to get out, I found it easier to think in the terms of 'one accident a year for one man in every 400 men'. So for instance, out of a workforce of 2000, there would be 5 accidents in a year, hopefully not all on the same day or to the same man (or an even worst case scenario in which all 5 of these accidents happened to the same man on the same day). I was so busy day-dreaming about how this might happen, I hadn't realised that we were nearly at the end of the meeting.

'Has anybody got any health and safety concerns to raise today?' asked the Operations Manager, gathering up his papers.

'Yep. I got something to say about the johns.' Everyone turned in surprise to a broad, bearded, barrel-chested bloke at the back of the room full of other broad, bearded, barrel-chested blokes. I couldn't see how he could complain about the toilets. I had been particularly impressed by the rather clever system which was devised to avoid the use of polluting chemicals: instead of Flash or Ajax to clean the bowl, good old Alaskan grit was available for a little extra friction to tackle those stubborn areas. It's surprising how effective a handful of grit and a stiff brush can be. (I mean for cleaning toilets – I can't vouch for its efficacy in other roles although I am sure there are some on which we might be wise not to dwell).

'Now I'm not finicky or pernickety,' continued the BBBCB, 'but this morning at 6 o'clock someone had had a naccident in the facilities. I can tell you it was everywhere, and not a pretty sight. What I'm saying is, ok we all have days like that, maybe the stomach's not quite right for certain reasons like bad food or homesickness, or too much ice-cream, then there's a little too much pressure brought to bear and bam – there you go. Best thing is, take it easy in the first place, but if push comes to shove, it don't have to be left all over the place for other folks to look at.'

There was an uneasy silence, a noticeable lack of eye-contact and some visible squirming particularly at the phrase 'push comes to shove'. Everybody had an inward look about them as they thought back to their morning routine.

The Ops Manager cleared his throat. 'Thank you. So, folks, there we go. Anyone got anything to say about that?' he asked, looking around at the studiously neutral faces as if he expected someone to raise their hand and say 'Oh, yes, that was me!' When it became clear that no-one was about to claim responsibility, he said, 'Okay, duly noted. Have a safe day,' and we all went quickly on our way, eager to erase the various unwanted images from our minds.

I saw Spike off on his flight southwards across the state of Alaska to Anchorage and wished him well. It was easier to be friendly in the knowledge that I would probably never see him again after that day. So far my luck has held out. Then it was off for some retail therapy at Deadhorse General Store. There was more to it than I had expected – an upstairs which I hadn't known was there revealed an impressive line in fluffy toys (yes, polar bears and moose but also cats, mice, leopards and a few hybrids who were clearly going through some sort of identity crisis). There was also every kind of thermal garment you could possibly want, high calorie snacks – because no-one wants to eat celery in the Arctic – and a huge range of knives and guns. I dithered over choosing a wedding anniversary present for my wife but eventually ruled out all of the above as being unsuitable. This was the correct decision, my wife assured me afterwards. The postcards were slightly amusing so I bought one each for the kids and then that was the Deadhorse General Store all done. Unfortunately, I still had an hour and a half to kill, so I took a second look at everything, just to be sure I didn't like any of it. By then it would have started to look suspicious if I had stayed any longer so I went for a walk around the outskirts of town, which could be found five minutes from the centre and stretched for several hundred miles. I thought about how nice it would be to see a tree or a flower. A lone caribou grazed on some scrubby vegetation. Not surprisingly, I had no further inspiration about the anniversary gift; my brain was numbed by boredom and cold. I waited in the designated place by the store until the hour came round at last and it was time to meet up with Larry and Rick.

We drove to The Prudhoe Hotel. Like all the buildings it was basically made up of multiple trailers; this one was configured in a T shape. Outside were lines of dirty pick-ups. Despite its roughneck feel, it was fairly quiet inside, everyone was courteous and friendly and the food was hearty. Larry told me that they had two unexpected guests staying: the latest victims of the Great Pan-American Highway Disappointment. A couple had turned up in their Winnebago, having driven all the way from Cape Horn, a distance of 30,000 miles through about 20 countries only to be stopped at the Deadhorse Barrier, 15 miles before their goal. How stupid of them not to have sent notification (including photo ID) to the authorities, in advance, of the day and time of their expected arrival. It was probably the same security guard who had reprimanded me for not wearing safety goggles inside the car.

On my last full day, I went to the hangar at 5am to help the guys get ready, but ended up being not much more than a beach boy really: it was gratifying to see that they coped fine without me. A new trainee, Josh, did some driving around the cones while Rick sat next to him for a good while and when we were both saying 'Skirt shift!' or 'Trim level!' in unison, I knew then that my job there was done.

Packing up that evening I went into the laundry to retrieve some of my clothes, thinking how strange it would be not to be encased in orange polypropylene, and how nice it would be to wake up one morning and decide to dress entirely in beige if one felt so inclined. I bumped into Clarence there and thanked him for all the brownies, the toasted sandwiches and extra snacks he had provided which had very successfully prevented me from shrivelling away to nothing. We had a chat about general things including, surprisingly, the best fabric conditioner. He showed me some vast garments he had just taken out of the dryer to demonstrate their softness. 'Good as store-bought,' he said, and I had to agree. He gave me a friendly pat on the arm and once I had regained my balance, we said our goodbyes.

Slipping outside to look at the white Arctic night sky one more time I picked up one of the millions of flat grey pebbles which lay around everywhere here. It felt smooth in my hand. Whenever we went on holiday, it was a habit of ours to bring one stone back from a special place. Here was the answer to my lack of anniversary gift. With the date and place written on it in black marker, the stone still has pride of place on our desk at home. It seemed to symbolise more enduring qualities than a cuddly moose.

But why Deadhorse? How did the name originate? You can take your pick. One story says it comes out of a local entrepreneur's description of what it was like to make a living there – flogging a dead horse. Or you might prefer the over-embellished tale about a horse falling in love with a caribou. I would guess the one closest to the truth is this: that the runway was built by an aggregate haulage company called Deadhorse Haulers who got their name from a regular summer contract they had won to haul away dead horses from Fairbanks.

Another puzzle answered.

But wait - how did the horses get there? And how did they die?

Who knows?

The mystery is still far from solved.

If hovercraft can go anywhere, how did we end up here?

Sweden 2012

With the job in Luleå complete, it was time to check out of our hotel. Apart from being a fair walk from the Bishop's Arms it had served us well for the little time we had spent there. We were in the lobby checking out when the call came to say our flight to Stockholm had been cancelled. I was dumbfounded.

'There must be another flight,' I blustered desperately. 'Or a coach... or something. Or we could drive.'

But it was hopeless. We simply had to resign ourselves to another night in Luleå and get away in the morning. There is nothing as deflating as phoning home to say you won't be coming after all, cancelling taxis, and knowing you will be marking time, wasting precious hours hanging about in a place you have mentally left.

But there was worse to come: when we returned to the desk to book another night in the hotel, the desk clerk we had come to know so well looked sorrowful.

'It's a busy time of year,' he pointed out. 'A lot of people are arriving to see Father Christmas.' He frowned and scrolled down his bookings. 'Really sorry, guys, but we're full. There's simply no room.'

It was snowing when we shuffled out of the warm lobby into the streets. There was no room at the inn. For real.

To think things over, we went where habit took us and ordered a reviving whisky at the Bishop's. Since we were on the subject of cold places, I told John about my trip to Greenland. Unlike Alaska, this was a real place; and unlike Alaska, nobody had taken the trouble to think through the finer details of running a hovercraft service in the bleak Greenlandic climate.

Unhappy
Landings

Chapter 12
Unhappy Landings

Russ: Greenland, October 2005

Greenland is not a place you stumble upon or pass through on the way to somewhere else. From London, the earliest flight to Copenhagen is perfectly timed to miss the daily five-hour flight to Kangerlussuaq in the south of Greenland. So an overnight stay in Denmark is necessary, after which there is a series of flights on progressively smaller aircraft to increasingly remote airfields until the last leg from Qaarsut to Uummannaq can be completed only by helicopter. The unpredictable and rapidly changing weather regularly disrupts flight schedules and one delay in the precarious chain of connections results in a stopover in a local hotel. Against all odds, just two days after leaving London, I finally checked in to the Hotel Uummannaq.

I knew a few things about Greenland. I knew it was the world's largest island and the land of the midnight sun. I had often heard it said – ok, maybe once or twice, which is probably about how often I had ever thought about it – that Iceland is green and Greenland is icy. I knew it was a Danish dependent territory. I also knew that there is something strange about the appearance of Greenland on a world

map in that the distortion of the Mercator projection makes it look bigger than China. There are about 56,000 Greenlanders, which is approximately the population of Merthyr Tidfyl, a town with an area of 43 square miles. Greenland has an area of 836,330 sq. miles which means that rounded to one decimal place, its population density is officially 0.0.

Halfway up the west coast of Greenland on the last leg of my protracted journey, I stared down from the helicopter at an astonishing chunk of rock. Rearing up out of nowhere, it pointed skyward, the fresh snow-plain running out behind it like a bridal train scattered with coloured jewels of brightly painted buildings. This mountain was called Uummannaq which also gives its name to the town, the fjord and, apparently, a song by KT Tunstall. From the air, I was habitually scanning the coastline for a likely landing place; so far I had seen nothing but sheer rock.

Geographically, there is no doubt that it was an ideal place to run a hovercraft service. After the time it had taken to get there, it seemed to me like the remotest place in the world. But then it began to dawn on me that the dozen or so tiny villages scattered around the fjord were even more isolated. For Greenlanders, Uummannaq is actually a throbbing, sophisticated metropolis, the commercial and communication hub of the entire fjord, an area of 2,000 square miles which is about the size of Luxembourg (but there the similarities end – the fjord is a whole lot more rugged and has fewer coffee shops).

Uummannaq has three important 'H's: its own heliport, a good harbour and the only hospital in the fjord. From time to time, most villagers inevitably need to travel to Uummannaq but helicopters are expensive to operate. A local retail firm, the Greenlandic equivalent of the Co-op, had recognised an opportunity for an alternative means of transport and intended to operate the hovercraft from Uummannaq five days a week covering different routes around the fjord. The longest of these, going north and west, would mean a 160-mile round trip in a day. The longest single leg was 34 miles, from Ukkusissat to Illorsuit, in mainly exposed waters.

As soon as I arrived, I called the craft's owners to discuss the arrangements for training. I was anxious to allay the misgivings which had been niggling at my mind since the helicopter ride. I was told that a suitable landing place had been found – it even had a

hangar! No need to worry; everything was organised. When the last freighter of the year arrived in harbour the next day, the hovercraft would be on board. Everything was going well.

The hotel was pleasant, the view from my room showed a panoramic harbour scene straight off a travel poster. I set off in the sunshine to explore the town which was still surrounded by water, not yet ice. The brightly coloured cabins prettily arranged on a dramatic mountain-side gave the place a cute picture postcard look. Rosy-cheeked Inuit people were out and about, wrapped snugly in furs; children played in the snow. Spraglebugten Bay in the west of the island is the location for Danish TV's 'Santa's Castle' and it was easy to see that Santa Claus would fit in very nicely here. I was also heartened to notice that there were a good few cafés and bars in Uummannaq town. It's always nice to have an option to go out in the evening instead of festering in a lonely hotel room.

My optimism continued as the craft was duly delivered, as promised, without mishap. The drivers, Knud and Henrik, also arrived punctually ready for training. With the hovercraft, a Griffon 2000TD (see appx. 8) standing on the dockside beside the ship we had a few hours to assemble it, to unfold the side-decks and commission its systems so that we could use the ship's crane to lift the craft into the water before it sailed away for the last time that year. The craft had suffered some minor skirt damage in transit which we needed to repair before going to sea. Still with no clear idea of where the landing was meant to be, we arranged to take it to a local boatyard where it could be craned ashore every night.

With that all finished, I walked as far as I could around the island, looking for a landing spot and found nothing. Nobody seemed to know the whereabouts of the mythical landing area and hangar. Hovercraft are often operated successfully straight off unprepared beaches: all they need is a smooth sloping shore with enough space to land clear of the water. On the island of Uummannaq, if such a place existed, then I hadn't yet come across it.

At 1,170m tall, which is three times as high as the Empire State Building, the mountain was always a strong presence. It seemed to have many faces: with the snow clouds building up behind, it loomed and brooded, but glowed softly when a carpet of sunlight settled over it. In a clear sky and a fading light, it was a stark silhouette of a closed fist. To some, it is a gigantic phallus, but it reminded me more of a blancmange, which is less poetic but probably much more interesting to a psychoanalyst.

After a couple of days Nils, the chief project manager for the hovercraft owners, arrived in town. He was a sharp-dresser: flashy gold cuff-links and company tie-clip; a smart long overcoat over an expensive suit. In the city this would be nothing special, but in Uummannaq where nearly everyone wore seal skins, fetching polar-bear trousers or brightly-coloured hi-tech ski-wear, he stood out.

'Nils,' I said, 'can you show me the landing site that you mentioned? I've walked around and around the island but I can't find it.'

Nils seemed happy to oblige. We set off through the snowy town to a spot on the edge of the harbour where, in a gap between buildings, Nils proudly pointed to a huge boulder which, like many other similar such boulders, rose vertically out of the water to a height of about two metres. The only feature which made this particular boulder stand out from the crowd in any way was that it had a flattish top. I had seen it myself without noticing it, and never in a million years would have considered it as a landing site. I was lost for words. Landing a hovercraft there would have the same chance of success as balancing a coin on a floating lemon. I felt stumped.

'So, Nils,' I said, clutching at straws, 'I guess you are planning to cut a gradient into it, or maybe build a concrete ramp up to it? So the hovercraft can get up there?'

'No, the landing place is ready just as it is,' he said with disheartening finality and a definite hint of stubbornness. 'Next week, we will start to erect the hangar.' He pointed to a heap of steel beams I hadn't noticed before, piled beside the rock. 'And the service will begin the following week.'

I had to quash this idea here and now, leaving no room for uncertainty.

'Nils, I'm sorry, this is impossible. It will never work. You'll never be able to land a hovercraft here.'

Nils was not happy – he didn't really want to discuss the situation but seemed insanely set on the fact that the service would be running in a week even though he had made no preparations. We began a frustrating few days travelling the length and breadth of the island, Nils with great reluctance, until in the end we did manage to shortlist two places, both of which were slightly less impossible, or a tad less outrageous, than any other place we had considered. But even with substantial adaptation and alteration, getting a hovercraft to land on either of them would mean stretching, if not transgressing, the laws of physics. The first had a good natural beach, rocky and just about workable, but no road access whatsoever. The other could be made into a ramp – it would just take a lot of dynamite. In my heart I knew, both of them were non-starters, but I had nothing else to suggest.

We had to get on with the training, with or without a landing site. As we only had the latter option, our daily training schedule revolved around craning the craft in and out of the water. This was in turn dependent on the arrival of the crane driver, a prickly, easily offended chap who was edgy enough when sober. On the mornings he was hung-over (usually from Tuesday to Saturday) he twitched with nervousness, seeming full of neurotic self-doubt and determined to take everything the wrong way – literally, including the craft hanging on the end of the hook, precariously swinging from one end of the dock to the other. It was an old crane, always working on its limits and the last few yards as the craft slowly neared the water, it was at full reach with alarm bells ringing, the driver tensely gripping the controls while I tried to make encouraging noises and keep up a confident carefree expression – after all, it was only my livelihood and reputation hanging off that hook, having yet another close brush with the harbour wall.

Once the craft was in the water and we had all taken a lot of deep breaths to recover our composure, there followed the terrifying walk of death down to the craft, a steep descent on a set of treacherously icy concrete steps with a handrail which tended to come away from the wall as you grabbed it. One slip to hypothermia. I have experienced many different commutes to work; this one was the shortest but without doubt the most harrowing!

Greenlanders are generally at home on the water; they know about boats. Their highway is the open sea, their roads are the well-used routes across the fjords based on generations of local knowledge. Boats are the main form of transport in the summer. The fact that the trainee drivers were extremely competent and qualified boat handlers with an ingrained instinct for the water meant that they had a huge head-start in the process of learning to drive a hovercraft. Nevertheless, there are some aspects to master which are unique to hovercraft.

Each day would start with a pre-operational check which I used as the basis for technical training to prepare the drivers for undertaking routine maintenance, repairs, trouble-shooting and safe handling. Once underway, we tackled the issue of Trim. Trim is a big deal. It basically means keeping the craft level and does not feature so much in the world of boats. A badly trimmed craft will drag on one side which not only wears the skirt but also makes the craft difficult to control. A well-trimmed craft stays level and flies smoothly and efficiently across the surface. Trim comes in three flavours: pitch, roll and yaw. Pitch (movement fore and aft) is controlled by ballast and elevators. Ballast can be fuel or water which is transferred between two tanks; elevators are horizontal vanes behind the propeller which work in the air-flow like rudders. Roll is controlled by the skirt-shift mechanism. Yaw means that you are 'sideways on' and not pointing in the direction you are travelling, which can be an unpleasant and disorienting sensation. Yaw is controlled by the rudders. Trimming the craft is a means of control in order to help change direction, adjust to different surfaces and to assist manoeuvres. Getting a feel for Trim is a key skill in the art of hovercraft driving and the phrase 'Check your trim!' soon becomes an oft-repeated mantra.

It is usual for one of the trainees to shine above the rest and this was the case with Henrik. He was a good driver thanks to a lot of experience with boats. A sharp-witted chap, he quickly picked up the rudiments of driving. Knud was another story. He might have been a good driver – he certainly had the experience – but there was a big snag in that if he went out in the evening, you probably wouldn't see him the next day, and maybe not even the day after that. Then, after one particularly lost weekend, we didn't see him again.

By now the ice inside the harbour was thick enough to support the parked craft and we were able to leave it there overnight. One evening after returning from several hours' driving, I was showing the crew how to make a skirt inspection. We were crawling under the side-decks of the hovercraft when we found ourselves lying in an increasingly deep pool of icy water. Trying not to panic, we quickly climbed out of the inspection hatches in the side deck to find the craft's weight had cracked the ice under it and was slowly sinking into the water. I had heard of cases of hovercraft becoming trapped in the ice like this, the water re-freezing around the skirt components. Needless to say, we decided to move the craft to an area of thicker ice, just in case.

We were getting no further with the landing place – there was nothing else we could do within the parameters of time and budget. By now, I was also beginning to sense a growing resistance among the locals to the idea of a hovercraft service. After a discussion with the owners, we agreed to suspend the training until they had made some more permanent arrangements for a landing.

Russ: Greenland, January 2006

In the New Year, I made the long trip back to Uummannaq. I felt enthusiastic about having a second crack because I knew it was a great place for a hovercraft service. It was heartening to think that by now there should be some new infrastructure in place which would mean we could get the project underway this time.

Although the journey was even more protracted, with the bad weather causing delays, I actually arrived more rested than before because of an unexpected overnight stop in the comfortable and welcoming Hotel Arctic in Illulissat which is on a UNESCO World Heritage Site and looks out over one of the world's mightiest glaciers. I decided that this view came second only to that of the Windermere Hotel in Darjeeling which gives a grandstand panorama of the Himalayas and at night, on the terrace, one is left with the impression of looking down at the mountains while floating among the stars. My optimistic mood took a serious knock, however, when I called Nils and received his terse instructions: 'You'll train the drivers to operate the craft from the beach at Qaarsut and land on the ice in the harbour at Uummannaq.' His tone suggested that there was no point in further discussion. So much for the new infrastructure.

Although they had done nothing to provide a landing site, the owners had instead appointed a Hovercraft Operations Manager. I tried to see this as a positive sign and looked forward to meeting him but once I did, I felt far from reassured. Malik was a strange, inscrutable man who always seemed to have something else on his mind. The fact that he spoke no English or Danish and I spoke no Greenlandic made communication problematic, to say the least. If I asked one of the crew to translate, their faces soon took on a puzzled frown and the answers they reported back to me did not seem to make sense despite their best efforts. But the more he was questioned, the vaguer he became. His job was really quite straightforward: to get the hovercraft service up and running, ensuring that all the systems met the safety requirements of the Danish Maritime Authority (DMA) in order to get the all-important operating certificate. But all my helpful ideas seemed to be falling on deaf ears and the man from the DMA was due any day.

When he finally arrived we arranged to meet at the hotel. As Marine Surveyors go, this one was a reasonable man who seemed to want to work with us. He had a big rule-book and his job was to enforce it. It so happened, however, that he had a bad case of flu and was understandably anxious to get himself tucked up in bed with a cup of hot Lemsip and a Scandi-Noir novel. With streaming eyes, he croakily relayed his findings which amounted to a dismaying list of shortfalls surely leaving Malik in no doubt that we were miles away from starting a hovercraft passenger service in Uummannaq. For once, I whole-heartedly agreed with the surveyor; his words left me feeling vindicated. It was a relief to hear another voice echoing all that I had been harping on about. The man from the DMA reiterated my objections to using the beach at Qaarsut as a landing site, pointing out, as I had, that it did actually have a metre-high ice shelf all along

the shore, like a small cliff, which made it impassable. Under no circumstances would the DMA allow passengers to embark or disembark on ice so all in all there seemed little hope for the project.

On a scale of one to ten, where one is indifferent and ten is devastated, Malik seemed to be at about two, putting him on par with someone who has broken the zip on his anorak. After the Inspector had left, leaving only a bin full of Kleenex and a strong smell of Vick, I suggested that we stay to have lunch in the hotel, imagining that this would be a good opportunity for the two of us to have a full and frank discussion about where to go next. I had an inkling that this was not going to happen when I returned from the bar with coffee to find that Malik had plugged himself into his iPod and was gazing out of the window where snow was falling rapidly. Falling on deaf ears. The phrase flashed into my head as it came to me that not only was Malik naturally taciturn and evasive, not only did we lack a common language... No, it was more than that. The times he had turned away as I talked to him, his distracted manner, his turned-in expression, all those times he ignored the ringing phone: suddenly all these moments combined to tell me something I should have known all along. Malik was deaf. I left him watching the snow and went off to think about the next day's training, which at least was something I did have some control over.

And despite all the uncertainty, our training schedule continued. It made no difference to me where we drove around the archipelago as long as we covered enough miles and put in the hours. Many of the trips seemed to revolve around picking up and delivering whale meat. One memorable evening, arriving back at Uummannaq, Henrik produced a severed whale fin from the cabin and proceeded to butcher it on the side deck while the rest of the crew looked on discerningly and apportioned it equally amongst them.

One evening, Henrik invited me to a party in his grandparents' home in Uummannaq. It was a family gathering and the small neat house was full of three generations of relatives and neighbours all milling around, eating and drinking. They made a game attempt at trying to converse with me, smiling warmly and introducing me around the room, although none of them spoke English. Henrik's grandmother passed me a plate of diced water melon as I tried to make out what his grandfather was saying about the hovercraft. I was pleased to see some fruit, and guessed that this was an expensive and exotic treat in such high latitudes – hence the tiny pieces. Not for the first time, I sensed misgivings were being expressed about the hovercraft as the elderly man spoke. I popped a piece of water melon in my mouth and tried to concentrate. As Greenlandic has no term of its own for hovercraft, the English is used so I found it easy to detect the word – it jumps out like a jack-in-the-box from the unfamiliar sounds of the native tongue.

But I was suddenly distracted by my taste-buds being thrown into shock and demanding some explanation from my brain. This was not water melon. In fact, this was the total opposite of water-melon. Instead of the refreshing burst of sweetness I was expecting, my teeth bit on something revolting. I tried hard not to reveal the inner

struggle this provoked. My instinct was to spit it out immediately. I stared back at the plate from which it had been offered. Each cube of pink was edged with a paler colour and grey-green rind. But it was chewy and fishy; not crisp and sweet but flaccid and rubbery. Not water melon, I realised, but raw diced whale-fin, with its layer of pale blubber and a wrinkly grey-green skin. Henrik's grandfather talked on animatedly and I wished I understood. But in the circumstances, what else could I do but chew and chew, hoping that at some point it would be small enough to swallow? After more frantic mastication, I realised that I would never reach that point – even if I swallowed it, I was sure it would reappear of its own accord.

Perhaps the old man thought I was being held totally rapt by his arguments, listening intently ready to add some pearls of wisdom to the debate. In any other circumstances, and with no language barrier, I am sure this would have been the case. But instead, when he had finished his spiel and was looking expectantly at me, all I managed was a cough and a strangled 'excuse me' before I dashed off to the toilet where I thankfully got rid of the morsel which still looked intact and un-chewed, impervious to all my attempts to process it.

The local opposition I had felt to the hovercraft service on my first visit was growing as time went on. There was nothing concrete, just rumour and a noticeable lack of momentum to the project – after all, there still wasn't even a landing site. I eventually got the lowdown from a young Greenlander I had met at the airport on the way in and then bumped into again in town. He invited me to his home to talk over coffee. Unlike the ordinary little house that Henrik's grandparents lived in, Torben's cottage was the epitome of Scandinavian style and tasteful cosiness. He and his wife were fair-minded and able to articulate the issues surrounding the hovercraft in perfect English. Helicopters can fly at about 120 knots, a hovercraft at 30 or 40 knots, but its running costs are a fraction of that of a helicopter; however, much of this bill was picked up by the Danish government who provided generous subsidies. To the Greenlanders, this attempt to establish a hovercraft service was seen as a cost-cutting exercise, a cheap and inferior alternative to the existing arrangements.

'If you lived on one of those remote islands on the archipelago and you had a sick child, which way of getting to hospital would you prefer?' asked Torben reasonably.

One day, a journalist from Greenland's national newspaper turned up at the hotel to interview me. I tried to give the straight facts as I knew them and not get too involved in comparing the hovercraft with the helicopter. The story, including my photograph, was put on the front page of the next edition. After that, I felt a bit like a hunted man, probably imagining hostility when there was none. Paranoia is an insidious stalker.

One day we visited the community of Niaqornat. The hovercraft was still a novelty and always drew an interested crowd as we landed on the ice on the outskirts of the village. From afar, the clusters of brightly coloured wooden houses looked idyllic, dotted higgledy-

piggledy here and there, each with its generous parcel of land, practical out-houses and racks for drying fish. Working dogs slept in the snow on the fringes of the pretty villages untroubled by the sub-zero temperatures. As we approached they barked and dragged on the chains which tethered them, bursting with unspent energy. The closer in we went, the more apparent it became that the people here lived hard lives in this bitter climate. At this time of year, nothing could be seen growing, no plants of any sort. We trudged on, skirting past the stinking dog compounds littered with half-chewed bits of carcass and piles of dog excrement which reeked of fish and stained the snow.

My waning optimism was beginning to slip onto the verge of depression. For one thing, I was very homesick. Although the crew were always friendly and hospitable, I was beginning to sense that their heart wasn't really in it. There was little to do in the evening: the bars and cafés I had been so pleased to see when I first arrived in Uummannaq were rough and depressing places to be, with drunks spilling onto the streets and lots of ugly fights. Several of the crew had warned me about the dangers of the streets at night especially on pay-day. One evening spent in a bar had been enough to convince me that

I was better off staying in, reading in my hotel room. My chosen book was called *Moondust* and was about the men who had walked on the moon. With its bleak themes of human insignificance within nature and the quest  for survival in an alien landscape I found I had many things in common with those twelve astronauts.

There's not much work in Greenland and not very much to do. The dramatic landscapes which take the breath away from visitors like me are probably invisible to the Greenlanders – you can't eat a view. Anyway, the country is in darkness for six months of the year. Food is in short supply, and unless it's imported it can only come from the sea. But sea conditions change very quickly from one day to the next: the fjord could fill with icebergs overnight. Sometimes the sea would freeze completely and the fishermen would have to lift their boats ashore and exchange them for snow scooters. However, it was not unusual for the wind to shift again quite suddenly, taking the ice away and the poor fishermen would have to re-launch their boats and put away their scooters. A few days later the ice would be back. Survival is the daily task.

We had so much time for training that the crew now almost knew more than I did about the craft. Sometimes we would be asked to make an emergency run to Uummannaq – a woman who needed to visit a relative in hospital, a man who wanted to register a death. The success of these trips convinced me afresh how versatile and useful the service could be if it ever got going. I had been keeping out of Malik's way but I learned from the crew that he had been making some pretty unbelievable claims for the craft. For instance, he had told the airport manager at Qaarsut that the hovercraft would be able to drive directly from the sea, up to the airstrip and disembark the passengers right outside the terminal building. If you are thinking this is a jolly good idea, you need to bear in mind that the airstrip was actually a narrow ledge cut into the flank of a mountain some 90 metres above sea level, only accessible via a steep, narrow, bumpy and winding dirt track, scarcely wider than a car. I felt sorry for Malik: isolated from the real world by his deafness, he seemed to have constructed a world of his own.

I contacted the office and told them I was coming home. On my last day, I went for a walk around the town. It was a still day with a fresh fall of snow. A young chap was fishing with a long-line through a hole in the ice. He had travelled there by a three-dog sled and already had quite a pile of fish lying in the snow. Zipped up in his padded overalls, he gave me a wide smile and a thumbs-up then the tugging line demanded his attention. I watched as he skilfully landed a beautiful fish. A haddock. A gleaming slab of twitching muscle, fading from silver to grey as it gave up the fight. I motioned to him that I would like to buy it and we made our exchange – a Krone or two for a freshly caught fish seemed like a good deal to me.

At the hotel, I presented the fish, which was at least two-feet-long, to the chef and asked him to cook it for me. I ordered a beer and sat looking out over the harbour where the Northern Lights had turned the snow to green and violet mother-of-pearl. I knew I would always remember that moment: the magical light, the prospect of going home the next day. I sipped my beer and looked forward to my fish. The lights were putting on a good show, brushing the mountainous skyline with feathery plumes of light so it was hard not to think that it was being orchestrated by someone or something. I ordered another beer. The fish was taking a long time. I guessed that the chef was cooking something special, something really tasty. Maybe in a nice sauce. The lights did more stuff and my stomach rumbled. I thought about ordering another beer but just then the waitress

arrived with my meal. At last. I picked up my knife and fork with anticipation and found myself staring down at a plate which held not the elegantly-sauced and seasoned very large fillet of my imagination but two small brown fishcakes partly obscured by a mound of mashed potato and frozen peas. I didn't have the heart, or enough Greenlandic to enquire what had happened to the rest of it.

I embarked on the long series of flights home, the first one over hundreds of miles of barren land, fringed by a startlingly blue ocean. I knew a lot more about Greenland by then: it's icy, it's empty; one step from those brightly painted wooden doors is a killer climate where people strive to be self-sufficient and sometimes struggle to do so. Battling with darkness on the outside, and sometimes on the inside as well.

I wouldn't see it now, but one day in March, the sun's light would creep back over the mountain for the first time that year and strike the heart-shaped rock.

Uummannaq means 'heart'. That was another thing I had learned.

Sweden 2012

Being homeless, cast out to roam the backstreets of Luleå, the sensible thing to do would be to make other enquiries for our accommodation. As it turned out, our decision to have a stiffening whisky in the Bishop's instead was exactly the right thing to do because if we hadn't done that, we might not have thought about asking in the hotel we passed on the way.

'We may as well try,' said John.

Sure enough, Father Christmas's fans didn't seem to venture down this end of town and yes, they had two rooms.

The new hotel had seen better days – but it was only for a few hours as we had worked out that we would have to leave at 3am to get to the airport for the early flight. Just as we had resigned ourselves to an early night, we got a call from Micke. Hearing we were still in Luleå, he offered us two tickets to a Blues Festival which was taking place at the Kulturhus that evening.

'Kulturhus' roughly equates to 'community centre' but it was not like any community centre I had known – not a scout-hut smelling of

If hovercraft can go anywhere, how did we end up here?

damp coats or a church hall posted with notices about tea-towel rotas. The Kulturhus was a sharp modern designer building of blond wood and glass, standing at the head of the fjord. It housed a restaurant, a music venue and a fantastic library with an expansive view of the water opening out right in front of the huge floor-to-ceiling windows.

In a strange land, there is nothing more gratifying than being welcomed into community life. Not only was Micke friendly and hospitable, but at the dance, I actually bumped into some of the men I had worked with about twenty years before: being hailed like an old friend after all this time gave me a warm buzz of belonging. The whole town was out, having a great time and throwing themselves into a wild evening as the music got faster and louder. Time and again, someone pressed a bottle of ice-cold Norrland Gold into my hand; the pretty woman behind the bar was Micke's sister, the blonde coat-check lady turned out to be his wife.

I found myself getting lost in the music but this introspection was not really permitted. Freed from their duties for a while, the two women made their way towards us.

'Can you lindy hop?' they enquired. I declared resolutely that no, I could not. Whatever it was, I knew I would not like it nor want to do it. John, always the honest type, looked uncertain.

'Like this,' they said, breaking into an energetic and vigorous sequence of movements which required the co-ordination of Ginger Baker and the muscular dexterity of Olga Korbut.

'You see? It's a sort of jiving. Do you do this in England?'

John looked doubtful. 'I shouldn't think so,' he admitted. I agreed – it was certainly not like anything I had seen – in public at least.

'It's a great band. Good Swedish blues,' I said, trying to deflect attention from the awful possibility of being made to lindy bop, or whatever you call it, and towards the admirable quality of Swedish music.

Micke's wife frowned. 'But they are Danish,' she pointed out. 'Don't you think their accents sound horrible?'

I tried to backtrack a little: it was a terrible faux pas to suggest that anything Danish was any good, or to mistake a Danish thing for Swedish. 'Well, yes, a little,' I admitted. 'A bit – er...'

'Ugly and horrible?' she supplied.

'Uh-huh.' In truth, all I could hear were strangled syllables of bluesy angst which were probably bewailing the injustice of having to get up so early in the morning. Swedish, Danish or pidgin English, the message was the same. The two women turned their attention to John. Not only had I failed to distinguish between Swedish and Danish but, out of the two of us, I was obviously much less physiologically equipped to lindy hop. At my last sight of him, he was being dragged unwillingly into the mêlée, subsumed by a flailing mass of limbs, like a moth in a Venus fly-trap. I felt sorry for him, but also guiltily relieved that it was him instead of me – though not guilty enough to do anything about it. In fact, I took the opportunity to slip away and look out at the view, at the long fjord, the floodlit ice where people were skating serenely to a different tune, and the pin-prick lights of snow scooters zipping and zig-zagging in the darkness.

It was nearly midnight when we left for the long walk to the hotel.

'So, tell me about India,' I said to pass the time. 'You went back, didn't you?'

John pulled his woolly hat down over his ears and began the extraordinary story of what happened next.

No-Go in Ghoga

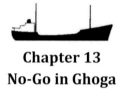

Chapter 13
No-Go in Ghoga

John India 1992

As I feared, the call from Bhavnagar was bad news. During a rough crossing from Surat, the craft had suffered damage and had been forced to land on a remote beach to disembark the passengers, who were taken on to Bhavnagar by bus. When the weather had moderated, the stricken craft had been towed back to Bhavnagar for repair, and was still not working.

Over a few days of polite enquiries the full situation unfolded. In order to make up for the lost revenue caused by the delayed start of the service, Modern India Enterprises (MIE) had chosen to continue running into the officially declared Monsoon Season when the weather gets rough and unsettled. The outward crossing had been extremely uncomfortable with passengers arriving seasick and frightened. During the return trip an engine cover had become detached and smashed one propeller, bouncing from that to the second prop where, just in case that wasn't enough, it had caused more damage. The smashed propeller had been replaced with a spare, but there were still problems. The craft remained inoperable, for unspecified reasons. It was under warranty so clearly something needed to be done.

Our plan came down to this. A team of three would go to India. The boss, JG, would travel out immediately and stay for a few days to provide assurance from the highest level that the company would help MIE in their hour of need. An as yet unknown miracle-worker would go for an open-ended period – as long as it took to fix the craft – and I would go for a couple of weeks to familiarise the aforementioned miracle-worker with the technicalities. But where could we find a person who would work on his own out there, perhaps for several weeks in difficult conditions, a good engineer, someone self-sufficient, who could use his initiative?

'Ask TC,' someone suggested. 'He'll do anything for the right price.'

Apparently, TC was something of a Legend, a Real Character, and a Bit of an Individual; and although his name sounded familiar, I couldn't remember where I had heard about him before.

JG didn't say much about TC except, 'Best to keep on the right side of him.'

When we eventually encountered each other at Mumbai airport, I was determined to be open-minded. I approached him nervously, wondering if I would meet his expectations. As it happened, he didn't have any.

'Who the fook are you?' he responded, briefly glancing up from wrestling with a leather strap on his battered case. He reminded me of a villain from a western, except with a Manchester accent. Thin and wiry; black hair, slicked back shiny with grease. But my eyes were drawn to his mouth in a sort of horrible fascination. Between thin red wet lips, hung the dog-end of a roll-up. I wondered if he knew it was there: it certainly looked like it had been appended for some time. When he spoke, he revealed an impressive set of tombstone teeth, unnaturally white and even.

'Er, John Barker? I'm er, here to… assist you on the trip. I've heard a lot about you,' I heard myself gush.

'Yeah, well it's all true,' he sneered, flashing the fluorescent gnashers again and making the wet dog-end wobble up and down like a wagging finger. 'And who are you when you're at home? You the joker who caused this mess?'

I laughed uneasily. 'Hardly.' What a tosser! I could see we were going to have a ball. We agreed to share a taxi but luckily there was no need to make further small-talk: my new friend simply closed his eyes and went to sleep, only waking when we arrived, just in time to berate the taxi driver for his high fares and careless driving, although he left it to me to pay him.

We were met at the hotel by MIE's new Operations Manager, a charming, jovial man whom I liked straight away. I was pleasantly surprised to find that he had arranged a sight-seeing day in Mumbai as the flight to Bhavnagar did not leave for another twenty-four hours. To my secret relief, TC cried off telling me that he'd seen enough of 'this shithole'.

In my host's suave and dynamic company, Mumbai seemed like a different city. Instead of squalor and deprivation, there was prosperity, vibrancy and colour. It was hard to believe that this was the same place: I had spent all my time here hardly glancing up long enough from each crisis to notice anything. Had my memories been wrong? Had my previous experience been just a bad dream?

No.

Our arrival in Bhavnagar put everything back in perspective. I was horrified at the sight of the hovercraft: it looked worn and tired, ten years rather than ten months old. The starboard prop was off and there was a grisly display of damaged and broken parts to view. The smashed propeller had been replaced but there were ominous vibrations and rumblings from the transmission. On the other side, things were far worse. The propellers were made up of four precisely shaped, laminated wooden blades bolted to a metal hub. The whole assembly was then carefully balanced. As only one blade had been badly damaged, MIE had commissioned a local carpenter to make a new one. To be fair, he had done a great job. It looked exactly the right shape and, under its coat of grey paint, indistinguishable from the original. But the shape was not the only thing it was necessary to get right. The wood he had used was heavier than the original, and the resulting imbalance was so bad it had bent the prop shaft and destroyed the bearings. If any of these highly stressed components failed, it would be extremely dangerous. There was no question that it would all have to be replaced.

Our task was clear now. We would need to fit a new transmission belt, bearings, and a new propeller and shaft. All these parts would have to be sent from England. JG left with everyone happy. TC and I would get on with the job by dismantling the craft, then when all the new parts had arrived, I'd go, leaving TC to his own devices. It all sounded good.

The people at Bhavnagar did not take to TC. I couldn't blame them: I was beginning to get a keen insight into his character myself. He didn't do small talk, never explained anything and had no time for collaborating. If you wanted to know if there'd been a call from the office, or whether that spare part had come then find out for yourself. If you didn't like it, you could fook off. The thinking behind all this was to make life as difficult for others as he seemed to believe it had been for him.

The fag was always stuck to his lip and mostly it was alight. He smoked anywhere and everywhere without any regard for others and as a non-smoker with a queasy digestion, I found it particularly off-putting when he smoked in the hot car. My attempts at politeness had long since faltered and I had learned that it was no good to expect him to pick up on indirect signals such as coughing, fanning the smoke away or glaring at him.

'Can you put that out please? I feel ill when you smoke in the car.'

TC jabbed at the window with his thumb. 'There's plenty of fresh air out there. You can get out and walk.' Before I stopped bothering with chit-chat, I once asked him about his wife back in Stockport and learned that she was much younger than him. Did she mind him being away so much? A stupid question – she probably jumped for joy the minute he was gone. He blew out a stream of smoke and narrowed his eyes. 'I dunno. I'm going off her anyway. She used to be alright but now she's getting a few ideas of her own.'

On the flight to Bhavnagar, he had been displeased to find we were sitting together. So had I. A woman struggled on with bags and a toddler. I helped her get her luggage stowed, watched sourly by my mate. As we took off, the little boy cried a little. 'Fooking kids,' he said. 'Shouldn't be allowed on planes. Mind you, I got my own back once. Took my lad on a flight to Manchester and I gave him a good pinching. Bawled his eyes out all the way through the flight. See if I care.' By now, I had learned not to express surprise or even answer.

When I phoned the Southampton office one day, Russ told me about the time TC had worked with him in America. Being thin and stringy himself, he hated fat people with a vengeance, just as much as he hated women, children and animals. The Project Manager of the American company was a well-respected and well-built gentleman whom TC had insisted on referring even in his presence as 'Lard Arse' which had drawn complaints from the management. TC was always Top Cat to me *(…the indisputable leader of the gang!)* but when I asked Russ what the initials stood for, he didn't know. 'I just thought it was short for 'That C***,' he admitted.

The time was approaching when none of this would be my problem. I had nearly done my two-week stint and TC would be left to his own devices as soon as I was on that flight out. I couldn't wait. To make sure my escape was arranged, I checked at the Bhavnagar office with the new man who had been put in charge of the repair, Mr Biswas. He nodded happily and asked for my passport to double check the details – he would borrow it for a day or two to 'do the needful'. The next time we met, I asked for it back. I sensed evasion. Had the flight been booked? Again I was given no straight answer. Yes, and no. He would let me know tomorrow. When tomorrow came,

Mr Biswas seemed to remember nothing of the conversation about my return flight, or the fact that he still had my passport.

'There is no hurry. You are being paid by your company.'

I was astonished. 'Mr Biswas, my two weeks are up. I have other commitments at home. I will be leaving as soon as possible. I should have gone already.'

Mr Biswas nodded genially. 'Yes, yes. But you must stay to finish this job first.'

'Can I have my passport back, please?' I responded, thinking I would sort out my own flight.

'Yes, certainly. I will give it to you as soon as the job is finished.'

'TC will finish the job,' I assured him tersely.

'But Mr TC is already upsetting the people here. He is very rude.'

I was stunned. Everything was suddenly clear. I was too angry to prolong my conversation with Mr Biswas and so seething with rage when I saw TC that I simply had to walk the other way in order not to give him the satisfaction of seeing me so riled.

After a while, I began to feel less angry. I had sympathy with Mr Biswas who was doing his best to sort out a situation not of his making and two pairs of hands were always going to get the job done more quickly. TC was actually a hard worker in his own particular way and he knew what he was doing. He would never allow himself to be hurried, never explain himself or show himself in the least bit stressed: if it wasn't good enough, he didn't give a monkey's arse, as he so charmingly put it.

'Still here?' he asked the next day.

I nodded. 'Get the job done quicker,' I pointed out.

TC gave me one of his narrow-eyed looks but said nothing.

Every day we commuted from Bhavnagar to Ghoga, a journey of thirty minutes each way. Working on the excrement-strewn beach at Ghoga, because this was the only place we had, I had started making some modifications to the engine-cover, the aim being to get more air through for cooling. One day we had to go into town to get some bits and pieces. The driver we had been assigned was truly terrible. The pavements in town were incredibly crowded but our man insisted that this is where he had to park – right outside the shop, not on the road. No matter that there were women and children and babies and street-sellers and the world and his dog in his path, it was a matter of pride that he would take us within an inch of our destination and they would just have to shift out of the way. There was some understandable hostility from the pedestrians at the driver's action. A man pulled his little girl out of the way, someone grabbed their bike from being run over, remonstrating angrily. TC laughed. 'He can't fookin' drive,' he said. 'It sticks out like a racing dog's bollocks.'

'What are you doing?' I said. 'For God's sake, park on the road, can't you?'

But it was too late. One old man had kept walking – he didn't appear to have heard the engine. Our car was bearing down upon him from behind when I saw him stop and raise his head, as if trying to ascertain the direction of the noise. He had a stick and was probably blind. He turned and moved towards the car just as the driver had been relying on him to leap out of the way.

'Look out!'

The old man swayed and toppled. The car had no choice but to swerve the other way, this time forcing some school-boys to leap into the road. A knot of people quickly gathered around the fallen man who was trying to get to his feet. He seemed bewildered but determined to retain his dignity. Some of those who were helping him broke off from their ministrations and came towards the car, shaking their fists, shouting. Shopkeepers came out onto the pavement to see what had happened. We were suddenly surrounded by people banging on the bonnet, barring our progress.

'Fookin' hell.'

An elderly man with a moustache emerged from the melée as spokesman; he leaned in through the window.

'You fool. You have nearly killed a man,' he said to the driver in English. The engine revved. I could see the old blind man walking away now, supported by some of the stall-holders. Someone found him a seat, a cup of *chai* was placed in his hand. I didn't know what to do. The driver was saying nothing, just staring straight ahead. TC was trying to look like he wasn't bothered. I found some Rupee notes in my wallet and handed them to the accusing gentleman.

'I'm sorry. Please give him this money.' The man took the notes with a look of surprise. I felt shabby. The westerner's usual get-out. We pulled away with the man still holding up the notes and frowning.

It was now impossible to continue our errand in this tense, ugly atmosphere. Bit by bit we edged through the throng as people began to drift away, losing interest. My head ached, I was hot and the anger I had felt earlier was now fermenting away inside of me. As we cleared the town, the driver picked up speed, driving even faster than usual as if to demonstrate that he had not been in any way affected by the demeaning skirmish. Trees flashed by as we sped towards Bhavnagar. I felt the anger like a bad taste in my mouth.

'Slow down!' I commanded. TC gave a nasty little laugh.

A dog appeared from nowhere. Like all dogs I had seen in those parts, he was a mutt, skinny, yellow-brown and medium sized. He came wandering out of the trees, tail up, nose to the ground in happy pursuit of some doggy scent, busy in his own world. The driver did not slow or swerve. The dog was straight ahead of us, contentedly sniffing and unaware of our approach. We still had time to miss it – just a nudge of the wheel would be enough.

'Mind the dog!'

I think the animal looked up in the split second the car hit; there was a lurch and a bump, hardly anything.

TC laughed. 'Got it!' In the mirror, I saw the driver's face suppress a smirk. We bowled on. I swung round to look out of the rear window. The animal was now just a small squashed hump of entrails on the road. The anger inside of me boiled over, taking me by surprise.

'You just killed that dog!' I yelled. 'On purpose! You stupid, stupid brainless idiot! Don't ever drive me anywhere again! You've just lost your job! I never want you driving me anywhere again!' I found myself batting him round the neck and shoulders again and again with my hands. If it hadn't been so awkward attacking him from the back seat, I could have killed him. TC, sitting in the front passenger seat, covered his head with his arms in mock protection, laughing hilariously.

'Fookin' hell! What's got your goat?' The driver swerved and cried out in protest as I laid into him with a particularly heavy blow. TC continued his high-pitched laughter. I stopped abruptly. Enough.

When we got back to the hotel I stalked off leaving TC still beset with bursts of inane laughter which caused his shoulders to shake, while the driver stared straight ahead, defiantly expressionless. No doubt the two of them had a good laugh about it all as I stomped up to my room. When I knew him a little better, I noticed that it was a tactic TC often employed, this siding with one against another, making underhand and subversive comments. Divide and rule.

It was the last time I saw that driver. I was serious when I'd said that I would never get in his car again: if I was going to be held captive, then it would be on my terms I decided. The next driver wasn't much better, as my colleague cheerfully pointed out most days.

Still we worked on. The repair on the beach was going well. I had designed what are known technically as 'scoopy bits' to fix on to the engine cover and redirect some cooling air through the system to counteract the overheating which had been the root of the accident. For the job of making them, I bought some sheet metal and rivets at the local market and secretly enjoyed this side-project, keeping well out of TC's way while he worked on through the job list at his own unhurried pace. We seemed to have reached a peaceable equilibrium by this point. The maxim 'the least said, the better' was never truer. One night we ate dinner together and I let TC ramble on about his past adventures, never really sure how much to believe. But one story struck a chord.

'I was kidnapped in Nigeria,' he said. 'Someone bottled out so I said I'd go instead - for the right price.' I looked at him closely, wondering if he knew that I was that someone.

'What happened?' I asked, casually taking a sip of water and wishing it was beer.

'They came swarming all over the craft, half a dozen jokers, all tooled up, shouting their mouths off. I was having a kip and I wasn't best pleased. Told them to shut up. Next thing I knew there was a gun-barrel up my nose. 'What d'you lot want?' I said. 'Drive the hovercraft or we'll shoot you,' they said. So I told them: 'If you shoot me you won't have anyone to drive the fookin' craft.' They hadn't thought of that. So next they say, 'Okay, if you don't drive the hovercraft, we'll blow it up.' 'Please yourself,' I said. 'It's not mine.' They didn't know what to do then. After a few hours of going round in circles, I said, 'I'm going.' And off I went. Left the other poor sucker there.'

The fragments of this story, which I had heard before, suddenly made sense now I knew the main character so well. I saw quite clearly what had happened. I guess you could call it the exact opposite of 'Stockholm Syndrome' when, instead of the victim developing such affection for the kidnappers that they did not want to escape, the kidnappers felt so irritated by the victim that they let him leave. A successful kidnapping rather depends on at least one person wanting the victim back. They probably had whip-round and paid him to go – perhaps it could be called Stockport Syndrome.

After a month, two weeks past the date I should have left for England, the end was in sight at last. It was time for a test drive.

Low tide was as low as I have ever seen, miles and miles out. We had a spin around and all seemed to be going gratifyingly well. So far so good. Taking a break, we parked the craft a long way out, near the water, not bothering to bring it right up to the beach. Some of the Bhavnagar mechanics, who had come out for the ride, looked concerned.

'Oh, no,' said one. 'It cannot be left there. Most important. When the sea comes in it will flood the craft.' I was at a loss to understand what he meant by this – certainly, I hoped it didn't mean what I thought it did.

'Why should that be?' I queried.

The man shrugged. 'It has always been so.'

'You mean it leaks?' We had been there over a month and no-one had mentioned this rather fundamental problem.

'Oh, well, yes,' he assured us, shaking his head.

In a flash, I saw my flight home slipping out of reach once again. In my mind, I had been almost there, heading west again with a cold beer in my hand. For once, TC and I were in agreement about what to do. We decided there and then that we would take the craft round to Bhavnagar Docks, about an hour's journey, and have it craned out of the water so we could assess the problem. This matter could not be left unaddressed. We were expecting some leaks but as we stood back to watch the craft being lifted, we were still astounded by what we saw. Water poured out of the bottom, cascading noisily out from a dozen different places all over the hull.

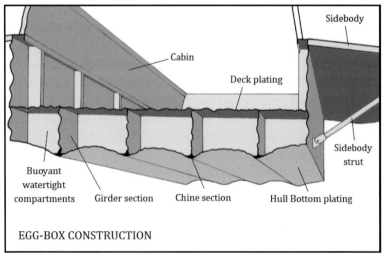

EGG-BOX CONSTRUCTION

The hulls of our hovercraft were made from welded aluminium sheet. The hull plating was generally as light gauge as possible to save weight - on smaller craft as thin as 2mm (that's about as thin as it's possible to weld) and up to 3-4mm on the larger twin-engine craft. This plating was welded to the chine to spread the landing loads into the long structural girder sections which run the length of the craft. If the hull bottom plating is penetrated, in theory only one or possibly two compartments will be flooded, providing a huge reserve of buoyancy. It is these dozens of watertight compartments in the hull that give it the name 'egg-box construction'. But this one was more of a colander.

We stood in silence, absorbing this new shock. My premonition that I wouldn't be going home in the near future had proved right. Calls were made to Southampton and it was agreed without question that we should stay on. With the original repair completed, we could at least now work at the docks in Bhavnagar rather than on Shitty Beach, as I thought of Ghoga. We were also nearer to the hotel, so that meant that the daily commute of terror was also mercifully shortened. Talking to the Bhavnagar crew, I was able to piece together a possible scenario which would explain the damage. Some of them said that the craft was often overloaded with too many passengers and at low tide, the craft had to hover over miles of rolling sandbanks. This is no problem for an experienced driver. But for a novice pilot, driving tentatively and poorly-trimmed over this undulating surface will mean that the hovercraft is not properly hovering – the bottom of the craft continually impacts the sand, causing damage – and worse when overloaded. The repair was a simple matter of welding up the holes, something I was relieved to hand over to the shipyard who completed it within a few days. This meant that our job there was finally done.

The next day, TC was gone. I hadn't anticipated any fond, tearful farewells between us, but we had struck up a way of working towards the end which at least might have warranted a goodbye handshake.

But I was glad I had stayed on; we'd done the best we could and we left the craft in good order. My passport was returned without ceremony and I was a free man once again.

With another day to wait for my flight, I went into Bhavnagar and bumped into Yamir and Gadin, the two pilots who had taken me lion hunting. They were as friendly and eager to chat as ever. Fortunately, they still worked in Bhavnagar Port so it had little effect on them that the hovercraft had been temporarily out of action: they certainly had enough work in their regular roles. They told me about a job they had to do further up the coast, in Alang Shipyard.

This shipyard is a famous place and Yamir and Gadin played an extraordinary part in its operation. To call it a shipyard is a great misnomer. The word conjures up an organised, built-up facility with sheds and hangars and dry-docks, full of cranes and heavy equipment for building and repairing ships. Alang turned all that on its head. It was actually the world's largest ship-breakers, a graveyard where one half of all the ships ever built anywhere will one day end up. The reason the ship-breakers happened to be at this place was not due to its facilities, because there were none, but to the fact that this stretch of coast has miles and miles of empty, gently shelving sandy beach and a large tidal range. Beyond this, there is a vast sprawl of a town where the breakers and their families live.

My pilot friends explained that sometimes they had to beach condemned ships and it so happened that they had one such job lined up for that night's tide. When they asked me along, I agreed readily.

At midnight, we were given a ride in one of the dockyard's launches to that night's victim. The tropical night was impenetrably black as we motored quietly among the hulking shapes of waiting ships which shifted restlessly on their chains, like nervous elephants in a circus. Some were weakly lit, some only detectable by the slightly denser nature of their blackness, the creaking of the hawsers or, as we drew closer, mysterious boomings and scrapings. The vessel to be scrapped was a nicely made Scandinavian cargo ship, still in good working order. Although building a ship of that size would take the skills and expertise of hundreds of workers, it seems that only three of us were needed now on her final voyage. The bit I had been dreading, the thing that had nearly caused me to say no to the expedition, was scaling the flimsy ladder up the side. I hated heights, a weakness I tried to hide by setting off determinedly, firmly trying to think of something else, something other than the growing gap between me and the ocean, or how many times I would bounce against the hull on the way down if I let go. This gung-ho approach sustained me until nearly half way when the ship gave a gentle roll, precipitating the reaction I had feared: I froze. Neither going up nor coming down seemed a viable option, and I couldn't think of another one. Luckily, I had chosen to go second so the example of Yamir ahead of me and the thought of Gadin coming up behind me propelled me into a sudden fast, clumsy ascent which ended in an inelegant scramble over the guard rail and a final flop onto the side deck.

I can vouch for the saying 'empty vessels make the most sound'. Every move we made seemed to ring through the old ship. The interior was tatty and rust-streaked but I could see she once afforded comfortable accommodation and was a good strong vessel. She probably had hundreds of thousands of sea-miles under her belt. I felt sad to see her brought so low in this eerie place, so far from home. We could have chosen a cabin in which to snatch a little rest but the Indian night was too enticing to waste, the experience so strange, that I could not use up time on sleep. Yamir and Gadin were good company, especially after my weeks of TC's joy-sapping presence, and we spent the time chatting about aliens and UFOs while polishing off a bottle of Black Label. It was the first drink I'd had in a long while and I found myself spilling out all the resentment I had been feeling, expecting them to take my side. I related how I'd been held against my will, about the dog and even about TC's kidnap experience. Gadin lit a cigarette and shrugged. He had a different view.

'This man, TC,' he said, 'is part of your destiny. He took a bullet for you and you should be thankful.'

'Not knowingly,' I pointed out. 'And he wasn't hurt. He didn't care.'

'But you would not have fared so well. He took hold of the situation and walked away. He's a survivor. He was meant to go in your place.'

'He has no respect for anything. He laughed when the dog was run over.' We passed the bottle around again and for a while we lay watching the stars in silence. I thought how odd it was that I should be here in this place with two strangers who were briefly friends. Their outlook was so different, as if everything was already ordained leaving no place for resentment or regret.

After a while Yamir said, 'The dog will be born again. Nothing is wasted. Nothing is lost.'

A little before 2am, at high-water, we started the engines for the last time. I was unsure what to expect. Stripped of some of its fittings and empty of cargo, the ship was unnaturally high in the water with the prop only half-submerged, making it feel unnervingly tippy. Slowly, Yamir cranked up the engine until we were at maximum speed and we headed in, knowing that the black unlit coast lay somewhere before us. It went entirely against all natural instincts. I braced myself for some sort of impact but in the end it was all very undramatic – there was hardly a bump as the old ship made way for its few final metres, decreasing speed all the time until the soft sand drew her to a standstill. There she sighed and leaned gently as if aware of her fate.

With our part of the job done, we launched a life-boat to get ashore, which entailed another death-defying ladder stunt, but this time without the added excitement of the ship rolling. As we beached the life-boat, we could see the evidence of earlier industry, a jumbled barricade of huge engine blocks, wheelhouses and monstrous machinery. As the sky lightened we wandered through a boat-trader's heaven of covered stalls and little shops selling huge brass binnacles, sextants, teak decking, cleats, winches the size of barrels, scions of rope of every size and hue. If only I'd had a shipping container at my disposal, I could have made my fortune at the next Beaulieu Boat Jumble.

The sun came up and picked out the yard now slowly coming to life as the newly arrived ship attracted a stream of workers, swathed in cloths, ready to break our vessel apart, robbing what was left of her brass finery, dragging off entrails of rope and chain. I knew that by the time I boarded my London-bound plane later in the day, the industrious workers would be wielding cutting torches and angle-grinders until every last nut and bolt was reclaimed, cleaned up and ready to be used for something else. The last remaining planks and pipes would be taken using hammers and brute force. This is India, I thought. Nothing is wasted. Nothing is lost.

If hovercraft can go anywhere, how did we end up here?

Sweden 2012

Back from our night out, we calculated that we could allow ourselves about two hours of sleep before leaving for the airport to catch the plane to Stockholm for the first leg of our journey home. Some might say that it was the effects of the Norrland Gold but I would say it was more likely sheer exhaustion which caused both of us to sleep through the alarm and wake an hour and a half later with a horrible start. All the way through the dark snowy drive to the airport I was worried about missing the flight. In fact, our timing was perfect: when we finally arrived all the queues had gone, meaning that we sped through the tedious process of check-in and arrived at the gate with a comfortable few minutes to spare. Then we found that the plane was delayed by an hour.

The dismay that John had felt in India as water cascaded from the hull of the Indian craft reminded me of a trip to Ireland.

'I had a leaker once,' I said. 'A bloody sieve.'

To Sea in a Sieve

Chapter 14
To Sea in a Sieve

Russ, County Mayo, Ireland, 1995

Jeff Bird came to Ireland with me. It was all at very short notice – I knew it would be a 'think on your feet' assignment, and that's what Jeff is good at. He has a calm, logical way of sizing up a problem and going at it from a different angle. He had once driven to Ireland on a life-saving mission with a large fuel tank strapped to the roof of the company Austin Montego. But that's another story. In this one, we set off in his Volkswagen van to drive to Ireland where we would meet up with the lorry transporting the hovercraft.

The lorry arrived five minutes after we did and the people of Killycross were out in force to have a look. Bikes with their wheels still spinning lay on the pavements where boys had abandoned them to climb onto the parapets for a better look. Middle-aged ladies with shopping baskets elbowed their way in to get a peep of it.

'Would you look at that now. A rare sight. What is it one of them is called now?'

'Sure, it's called a hovercraft. It's a boat that hovers on air, so it is.'

'God save us. And look at yer man there, no better than he should be, coming over here, playing the big I am.'

This remark was directed at the customer, Roly Cormick, to whom I had been briefly introduced by our sales manager some time ago. The idea of running a hovercraft service here in the very west of Ireland had been trickling on for over a year, as these things do, then suddenly it was full speed ahead with no time to really think about arrangements. But at least Cormick was here: I could see him unnecessarily directing the traffic (which amounted to two cars and a tractor) so that the lorry could take the narrow turning after the town bridge.

The craft, a Griffon 1500TD (see appx. 5) had been the only one available, lying idle by the Thames in Greenwich, used from time to time as a back-up for the ferry service to Canary Wharf. I had meant to get up there to check it over thoroughly, but in the end, I'd only had time to give it a cursory once-over and to speak briefly to Albert, one of the Thames Watermen. We looked at the craft which was showing its age, parked on a patch of scrubland next to a sagging fence. 'Still goes a fucking treat,' he assured me, noticing the look of doubt on my face.

I explained that I was going to take it to Ireland. Having spent all his life in Rotherhithe, Albert looked like he thought this was probably a bad idea. 'What d'you wanna go there for?' He indicated our own surroundings, the warehouses and wasteland beyond the river. 'Look at this place. We got it all here, 'istory, buildings, lots of nature!' As if to prove his point, a duck flapped over our heads and skidded to land on the mud in front of us. 'See what I mean? I fuckin' love nature.'

Now here was the craft, somewhat cleaner and easily identifiable from the large 007 emblazoned across the side-body – nothing to do with James Bond though, just the yard number.

Roly came over and shook my hand. 'Well, the whole town's out,' he said.

'So I see.'

'It's all good publicity,' he beamed, as Jeff and I hurried to undo all the straps and have it ready for the crane which had apparently been spotted by one of the locals just ten minutes away.

I could tell by Jeff's face that he wasn't any happier about all the fuss than I was.

'We'll need some time to get everything ready,' I said. 'The side-decks will need unfolding, there are the fixings to put on the skirt. I'd rather leave rides till tomorrow.'

'Now you wouldn't want to be disappointing all these people surely?' beamed Roly, slapping me on the shoulder with a hand he had spare because he wasn't doing any of the work.

Quite honestly, I couldn't have cared less. It's a long drive from Southampton to Fishguard – who could have suspected Wales was so big? – and the bed-and-breakfast above the pub had been a bad choice, mainly because of the lock-in. At 1am just after I had finally fallen into a light sleep, the barmaid accidentally sat on the panic button behind the bar. The alarm seemed to be directly linked to a point right above my bed. Suffice to say, I found that my startle reflex was alive and kicking – I believe I actually rose six inches above the bed, making the shape of an electrified starfish before dropping like a stone back on the mattress. Then the noises went on and on: ragged singing, furniture bumping, fists banging on car bonnets, raucous shouting, the Garda arriving and remonstrating in Gaelic. Jeff, who had been 'sleeping' in his van in the car-park, fared worse: he was actually down there, in the centre of the maelstrom.

Then we drove two hundred miles and found ourselves here, at the centre of this circus, so no, I really didn't much care if a few people were disappointed. Add to that the dispiriting discovery that there was no convenient landing area which meant the crane would have to put the craft straight into the water.

The crane was driven by Mary Murphy's youngest nephew. His name was Wayne. I was told this by a pair of teenage girls who stood arm in arm watching us like a pair of seraphim, far preferable to the dozen or so lads who were trying to 'help' and asking endless questions. Unfortunately, my feigned interest in Wayne must have been too convincing, because it prompted a detailed account of his life (starting with his ancestors) and all his best characteristics plus a few of his forgivable failings. The fact that he was the spit of Tom Cruise was, I felt, neither here nor there, but I was pleased to hear that his crane-operating capabilities were top-notch.

'He's done lots of tricky jobs so he has. Lifting a little hoverboat will be nothing to him.'

'He's here!' squealed the second girl. They unlinked arms and disappeared into the crowd. I was pleased to see that the crane was on time – Roly had told us that every minute of it was costing a 'king's ransom' to hire. The plan was to lift the craft off the lorry onto the dockside, whereupon Jeff and I would work like fury to get it ready to launch, and the crane would then lift it into the water, there being nowhere else to put it on land. Unfortified by tea or anything to eat since breakfast, we shouldered our way through the crowd to talk with the crane driver, only to find him already flanked by several of his admirers. Having no idea of what Tom Cruise looked like, I didn't spend time on assessing the likeness, merely felt a momentary surprise that such a famous actor would have a lumpy nose and spots. However, he seemed capable enough, nodding sagely as we explained our plan and made one or two sensible suggestions himself.

It was the hottest summer in Ireland for one hundred years. Huge green spider crabs high-stepped around the quay as we worked. The crowd had fallen back, but had not gone home. There was quite a party atmosphere as they sat and waited on the grass around the bridge or hung about on the dock shooting the breeze. Roly went among them bigging up his plans for the hovercraft, how it would transform the lives of the poor people of Enniscroy, how the children would no longer miss school if the weather was bad, the doctor would be able to get there at any time of day, in any weather. Sure it would be a great asset to the community and he was a fine fellah to be setting it all up.

The assembled craft was deposited safely in the water to a smattering of applause as Wayne's little band of admirers, his Auntie Mary and the rest of his extended family, demonstrated their appreciation of his craning skills. Wayne looked modest. It should have been time for tea, but worryingly, people were now forming queues on the little strip of beach. There were at least 50 and the craft was a 15-seater.

'What's going on?' I asked Jeff. The lorry was revving loudly, pulling away with difficulty through the straying crowd. I looked round for Roly and found him talking animatedly to Wayne the Crane who was gesticulating expressively from his cab. As the crane then pulled away, Roly came forward with a woman hanging on his arm as they picked their way over the shingle. 'This is Cora. She's looking forward to a little spin.'

'Oh, will you look at that!' she exclaimed. 'It's an 007!'

She had obviously just arrived: there is no way I could have failed to notice a very loud, excitable, elaborately coiffed, busty woman dressed in a zebra-striped track suit and pink high-heels. Roly was already helping her, with some difficulty, onto the craft. Her squealing embarkation precipitated a near-riot as others pushed forward and clambered on board. Are you taking it out? How fast can it go? Can I drive?

'He's promised them all a ride,' Jeff said.

'What?'

'Last night in the pub, he promised everyone a free ride today. The lads told me.'

Suddenly, it was imperative to start up the craft just to avoid being swamped by enthusiastic boarders. When I had a chance to look, I saw we were an unlikely little band. If ever a crew was motley, this one was. There was me, Jeff, who had been practically prising people off the side-decks, Roly and his zebra-clad wife, carroty-haired twin boys each holding the hand of a large man with cauliflower ears whom Jeff hadn't felt like arguing with, the four pushiest and mouthiest of the pushy mouthy lads, a man holding a camera who had been standing watching us for two hours and had spoken to no-one but himself, and a Catholic priest in full get-up.

Off we set. 'This is just a quick spin to test everything out, to check the systems,' I explained. With that, the engine stopped. We were 10 metres from the beach. I guessed straight away that the air intake was probably blocked and it so happened I was right. I could have explained this, had not a terrible screeching started up behind me.

'Oh for the love of God, we'll all be drowned! The thing's broken down and with us stuck here in the middle of the sea. Oh, Lord, Father, what can we do? Roly, go and do something...'

'It's only...'

'We're sinking, so we are! We'll all...'

'Actually, a hovercraft is much safer than a boat if it breaks down,' I explained. 'It can't sink, you see, because of the buoyancy tanks. We haven't broken down anyway, I just need to tweak this pipe which must have got trodden on in the crush, to let the air back in...'

My words were lost in the alarming din.

'Father, say a prayer, we're all sinking...'

The Father, an owl-eyed, cheery little man, patted her hand. 'Now isn't this just the situation our Lord was in on the Lake of Galilee? He was in a boat, not a hovercraft, but just like this vessel, his boat was in trouble and Jesus woke and what did he do?' Checked the air intake? I wondered. But apparently not. 'He rebuked his disciples for their lack of faith.'

No-one else was the least concerned. The ginger twins stared impassively at the hysterical woman. The lads ignored her completely, still going for the record of greatest number of pointless questions in one hour. The man with the camera continued to enjoy his chat with himself, even having a few private chuckles. Imagine being shipwrecked with this lot, I thought, like one of those 'Trapped' movies where a small group of diverse people start to break down under pressure. I'd seen films about people trapped in boats, burning buildings, trains and ski-lifts – why not a hovercraft? Zebra woman would be the first to be eaten. The mouthy lads would actually run out of questions, the priest would lose his faith. It would be the big quiet man who emerged as a true hero, leading us all to safety. *The Poseidon Adventure*, Hovercraft style.

A minute later we were off again. The engine sounded fine.

It was 1995 and there was plenty of EU money sloshing around for member countries at its far-flung edges, and Roly had set his beady eyes on some of it. We were way out west on Killycross Island where you will find the second highest sea cliffs in Europe above a long curved golden beach. Fuchsias grew in the hedgerows. If Killycross Island was small, Enniscroy was minute – an islet, shaped like a pin-headed three-legged horse. There was a small community of about a dozen houses. No electricity or running water and the only way on or off was on a small open boat across the 400 yard fast-flowing Bull's Mouth Channel, and even then only at high water.

The craft was going well, the sea was flat and the sun was out. We sped up one of Enniscroy's creeks to the head where a barely adequate beach was exposed at this level of tide. Houses straggled along the sides of the inlet. Again, the entire population was out to watch our arrival, it's just that this time they would have all fitted in a mini. They spoke to each other in Gaelic. Roly had told me that there were octogenarians on Enniscroy who had never left the island and we met a man called Stephen who was such a person. He was content with his small cottage and quiet existence, had never married and gave this as a reason for his longevity. He switched to English to tell us that in the early twentieth century, the population had risen to about 130 souls. There had been a post office and a school, both now closed. The handful of current Enniscroy children had to take the boat to school on Killycross and often had to miss lessons due to bad weather or the wrong tides. Helicopters were used in emergencies. As a transport link with Killycross, the hovercraft scheme had been in the wind for a while and there had once also been talk of providing a cable car service. Perhaps it was the estimated cost of £760,000 (over £10,000 for each of the then 73 residents) which put an end to that idea. Stephen didn't seem worried if neither scheme reached fruition.

One elderly couple took a particular interest in the craft. He was an ex-Spitfire pilot from South Africa, she was American. With no mains electricity, they powered their house on 12V generated by a windmill. But the transport problem was killing the community and I sincerely hoped that the hovercraft would be the solution.

Interestingly, no-one on the island seemed to have heard of Roly Cormick.

For the rest of the day, we kept on ferrying groups of people back and forth. Two nagging worries were starting up in my head and I could sense that Jeff was thinking the same. For a start, there seemed to be no natural landing area and certainly nothing purpose-built. The second worry was more immediate as I had the ominous feeling that the craft was growing slower and heavier as we went along. I nodded approval as Jeff made a surreptitious check inside one of the buoyancy tanks and looked grim. 'Bit of a leak?' I asked. 'She's a sieve, mate,' said Jeff.

'Shit.' We were nearing the Killycross drop-off point, such as it was. 'Only five passengers from now on, Roly,' I said. 'With us and you, that makes eight.' Roly looked displeased. 'Health and Safety,' I said. 'We haven't completed trials and pre-op checks. Wouldn't want an accident.'

By late afternoon we had made the round trip ten times. We hadn't eaten and we certainly hadn't unpacked because we weren't sure where we would be sleeping that night. But before we could attend to any of that, we had to decide what to do about the leak. If there was no landing place, the craft would have to stay in the water which wouldn't normally be a problem, as I had so confidently explained to all and sundry only a few hours earlier. There was no other solution but to turn out of our beds, if we ever found any, and check the water-levels through the night. The one piece of luck we had was that it was low tide from about 3 am so we could bail out the craft, leave it up the beach and at least be ready to start the day with a dry, light craft. There were about 20 buoyancy tanks, all of them rather awkward to get to. With no electric pump, we had to finish emptying each one by hand.

For the second night running we had almost no sleep.

Next day, it was pretty much the same routine, this time operating a shuttle for a succession of local dignitaries whom Roly wanted to impress. Not only was the promised slipway missing, but there were no arrangements in place for fuelling the craft – perhaps he thought it would run on Irish mist. Luckily, we had thought of it and brought jerricans with us. Roly's enthusiasm was contagious and apart from worrying about the state of the hull, we had an enjoyable day. People

liked the hovercraft. In theory, it was a very good plan especially if there was an EU grant available to fund it. All it needed was a slipway at either end of the route. Nobody commented on the sluggish performance – having nothing to compare it with, perhaps nobody noticed. By the end of the day, the poor old thing was on its last legs, about ready to sink into Killycross Sound without a trace. It was a relief to complete the final demo.

As we were getting the strops ready for the crane, Roly casually mentioned that the crane driver couldn't come today after all, not until tomorrow, our last day when we had planned to make the most of the sunshine with a visit to the beach of dreams. A golden crescent, virtually empty for miles on end, we had been looking longingly at it for the past three days, ready to throw ourselves into those Atlantic rollers.

'But you booked him for today, surely?' I said, stung by this disappointment.

'Oh, I did, but you know people round here are unreliable. It takes a lot to pin them down.'

'Isn't there anyone else?'

Roly pursed his lips. 'Not at the price, no.'

Next morning, which dawned as glorious as the previous ones, the lorry turned up promptly but Roly was missing. And so was the crane.

After an hour of waiting, worrying about the dwindling amount of time we would have left to drive across Ireland to catch the afternoon ferry, I decided it might be a good idea to try to contact our absent customer. I knew that Irish telephone boxes were green but I couldn't remember seeing one in Killycross. In the year 1995, people did not generally have mobile phones so I was surprised when the driver proudly pointed to one, a chunky black object, which was hanging in his cab with his rosary. He handed it to me. Not only was it the size of a house-brick but it weighed pretty much the same.

Then he started his engine.

'It's ok,' I said, confused. 'We don't need to find a phone box now.'

'Ah, but we need to drive up to the Church, you see. Sure, it's only outside the church that you get The Signal.'

It was true, the strength of the signal leapt up as we approached the church, as if it sprang from a direct line straight down the tower from some heavenly operator. It may have been an excellent signal, but Roly still wasn't answering.

'Would that be Roly Cormick you're phoning now?' asked the driver, rolling a cigarette.

'Yes,' I admitted. 'Do you know him?'

'I know he left for Blarney this morning. And without bothering to settle his bill.'

Somehow I wasn't surprised. 'Are you certain? Only he's meeting us here with the crane...'

'Oh sure, and I'm fecking Terry Wogan. Yer man's done a bunk, that's what it is.'

He tucked the rolled cigarette behind his ear and I handed him back the house-brick with a sinking feeling.

'Now then, should I phone my cousin Wayne?' asked the obliging driver. Wayne was tracked down with the help of his Auntie Mary who cycled down to the snooker club to get him. With the celestiallyboosted signal we were able to hear both parts of the conversation... Or perhaps it was just that Wayne was shouting as loudly as the driver, in which case we were hearing him directly from Aunty Mary's kitchen. 'That tight bastard, fecking eejit, still hasn't paid me for the last job... I told him I wasn't coming out unless I had the cash. Sure he plays the fine fellah about town, but he's a crook, I'll tell yer. That's not his wife, neither, she used to work for the bookies in Ballycroy...'

We got the picture.

'He says he'll do it this time as long as he's paid up front for both jobs,' said the lorry driver, paraphrasing the long conversation and hoisting his phone back into position. 'Cash.'

Wayne was rolling into town within ten minutes, not even bothering to finish his game.

The crane cost £80 – knowing Wayne, this was a fair price. Jeff and I literally emptied our pockets and pooled what cash we had left. 'Good job I didn't have that last Guinness,' said Jeff dolefully. We were a few coppers short – it really was that close – but Wayne was philosophical. 'Sure, it's not your fault,' he said. 'Feckin' bastard.'

Weighed down with cash, Wayne did his stuff and the craft was soon safely strapped to the back of the lorry. Poor old thing, she'd

done enough. Luckily, the lorry driver said he would wait for his money until we got to Southampton.

Roly Cormick disappeared without trace. Hovercraft often attract people of his type: dreamers with big plans and no appetite for small details. An eye for a profit but not willing to make the investment. Wanting the acclaim but not the hassle. They talk the talk but in the end, they can't walk the walk.

If we'd bought another round of Guinness, 007 might be still stuck in Enniscroy, rotting away in a field. Instead, it came back safely and after a little TLC, went on to support a civil engineering operation in Germany.

The people of Enniscroy did not get a hovercraft service. A shame because with a little thought to infrastructure, it could have revived a community.

'Who is Roly Cormick, anyway?' I asked Wayne as he climbed back into his cab.

'Depends who's asking' said Wayne. 'If you ask Roly, he's a banker. But people round here,' he said as he started the engine, 'say he's more of a wanker.'

Ireland had been for us a place of missing things: slipways, cranes and customers. Now we set off to make the long drive home, the last thing we wanted to add to the list was a missed ferry.

Sweden 2012

Arlanda Airport, Stockholm, 2012

We left Luleå in darkness on one of the shortest days in the year. In Arlanda we sat on the mezzanine drinking strong coffee and convincing ourselves that at least the darkness here in Stockholm was a bit thinner.

White Christmas *was playing as we boarded and for me this brought about my moment of unravelling. There is such a moment in every trip, when the vigilant tension which has held you upright for weeks enabling you to deal with the problems, anticipate the unknowns and keep alert to all the things that could go wrong suddenly falls away and home does not feel so very distant after all.*

The boss had been right – it had been a routine job, nothing had gone wrong; today was the eve of Christmas Eve and we were flying south.

Back Before Dark

Chapter 15
Back Before Dark

Russ, Svalbard 2009

I thought I had done the north. There had been a time when it meant any place beyond Watford Gap. Then I had discovered the real north: snowy wastes of Sweden, Finland, Alaska, Greenland – they all felt pretty northerly. But Longyearbyen is really North. From Tromsø, near Nordkapp, the most northerly point on the mainland of Norway I had flown on north for nearly two hours, finally arriving at the island of Svalbard, in the Spitzbergen archipelago.

Longyearbyen is the nearest and most accessible community to the ice of the Arctic Ocean and the perfect base for an Arctic hovercraft operation. It is an important centre of research and the home of the internationally respected UNIS – The University Centre of Svalbard. There was an old-fashioned feel to the town, with cold-war architecture and remnants of an industrial past in the obsolete machinery and fenced off compounds still visible around the town. The hostel in which I was staying was originally accommodation for the Russian miners who worked there during the war. The place had the atmosphere of a frontier town, especially as many people carried a gun. It gave the young men an extra swagger as they walked around with a rifle slung casually over their shoulder. No-one was allowed to go out of town unarmed as polar bears were a constant threat.

The hovercraft which I had come to commission, a Griffon 2000TD (see appx. 8), had a unique conception. Two scientists on opposite sides of the world, Yngve and John, both sharing a fascination with the Arctic, one with the idea and expertise, one with the vision and capital to make it happen. Dr John Hall was an expert on the Alpha Rise, an Arctic mountain range bigger in area than the Himalayas but much less well-known because it is underwater. His interest with the Alpha Rise stretched back to the 1960s when the subject of his PhD thesis was the theory that it existed as a result of a massive meteor impact several million years ago. To test this premise, he needed to analyse sediment from the area and compare it with deposits from the rest of the sea-bed: if his theory was correct, the samples from Alpha Rise should be much older. But his ambition had been hampered by the expense of setting up scientific expeditions in such hostile latitudes. Meanwhile, halfway across the world, fellow scientist Professor Yngve Kristofferson was rather out of his element, unenthusiastically looking around Universal Studios with his family, feeling bored and wishing he was somewhere else. He happened to see a hovercraft in a movie which reminded him that he had once hired a small hovercraft which worked well on the Arctic ice but was not really robust or big enough for that type of terrain. Now, after seeing the movie, the idea was rekindled.

That evening, Yngve phoned Dr Hall to discuss the idea and to his amazement, John Hall said: 'Why don't we buy a bigger hovercraft?' That's when they turned to Griffon.

The high cost of funding scientific research in such a remote place is inevitable if you have to rely on icebreaking ships for transport, costing tens of thousands of dollars a day to run; and even ice-breakers will be halted by the thickest ice. Wheeled or tracked-

vehicles can only get so far before encountering 'leads' which are patches of open water between ice-floes.

The hovercraft was a very good solution but not without some problems of its own. For instance, low temperatures will cause some skirt fabrics to stiffen and thus wear out more quickly so it is necessary to use specialist materials which will stay supple in spite of the cold. With cautious handling, the hovercraft can easily traverse the thick ice and most of the leads. But it isn't easy. Some ice ridges are impassable and can stretch for many miles. Any vehicle is hampered by fog, an ever-present hazard, and even in clear visibility, under an overcast sky the contours of the terrain can be impossible to make out. The hovercraft is the least problematic vehicle to use in such challenging terrain but it is by no means a magic carpet.

There were distinct advantages in buying the hovercraft outright and cutting out the need for sponsorship. Seeking funding from backers and investors is a time-consuming business, as is keeping them happy enough to maintain their sponsorship. A hovercraft, as an independent mobile research platform, could operate at a fraction of the cost and undertake research for purely scientific reasons.

This craft was designed to accommodate two or three scientists and a raft of specialist equipment. With Norwegian efficiency, it was delivered as deck cargo to Longyearbyen in midsummer, craned onto the dockside where we assembled it and launched it into the fjord, driving it to a good beach-landing less than a mile away. Here there were some wooden sheds to house stores and equipment, making it easy to undertake the final preparations to go to sea and test the craft. It was June and the islands were surrounded by open water: to reach the permanent ice, one would have to travel yet another 100 miles further north of the archipelago.

Setting foot in Svalbard I experienced the beauty of the Arctic for the first time. But it wasn't until the next morning when I saw the QE2 anchored in the bay that I began to appreciate the monumental scale of the place: the famous ship looked like a toy boat in a bath tub.

These large cruise ships are a very common sight in the Arctic. While the environmental regulations are becoming tougher each year, the size and number of cruise ships is growing too. Ironically, climate change is instrumental in this increase as it is already slowly reducing the amount of summer sea-ice, making the coastal waters more accessible to cruise ships. On the positive side, the tourists who come tend to be there because they are already interested in the environment, particularly the wildlife – the sheer numbers make bird-watching impressive here. There have also been moves to get visitors inland and away from the sensitive coastal breeding areas. Everyone secretly wants a close-ish encounter with a whale or a polar bear; and although you would be lucky to spot an Arctic fox, reindeer can always be easily found.

Most operators inform guests about environmental guidelines and regulations: the smaller coastal cruise ships are especially hot on valuing the environment and often have well-qualified experienced naturalist guides who make sure that tourists are escorted around in small groups to lessen the impact. But this is not the case for some of the larger cruise ships where there are many more tourists per guide. It is surprising the number of ways these can bring pollution and disruption, from CO_2 emissions and discharge of sewage, grey-water waste, and ballast water, to biocides from anti-fouling and disturbance to breeding grounds. Vegetation is worn away by the sheer numbers of trampling feet. It is not uncommon to see cigarette butts and other rubbish strewn around.

I was never more aware of being a long, long way from home – there were so many legs to the journey and it took such a long time. I have often noticed that when one is surrounded by strangers, the mind often tries to persuade you that there are familiar faces in the crowd: that woman there, she looks a bit like Auntie Doris, around the eyes. The man in the red North Face jacket parking the snow scooter could be the man who works in the bank. When I went into the local store on my first day of looking around, I came across a couple who were the absolute spit of my near neighbours, Matt and Sharon, whose garden backs onto mine. We stop and chat if we pass in the street, we exchange Christmas cards, take in each other's parcels and Sharon once gave me some goldfish for my pond. Our eyes met over a postcard carousel, flicked away and then locked.

'Russ?'

'Matt!'

'Sharon. It's Russ.'

It would be satisfying to say that we continued the conversation just as if we were standing outside the Post Office, rather than three thousand miles from home in Latitude78° N with a stonking great glacier just a few hundred yards away.

'Cold enough for you?'

'Brrr, yes, wrap up warm today.'

'We're just off for a walk, you know – blow the cobwebs away.'

'Good idea.'

'How are the goldfish?'

'Doing well! You must pop round for a –'

'Cup of tea, yes, we should.'

'Well, see you around!'

Instead, there was just enough time to relay our separate purposes for being there – they were on the QE2 for a 'trip of a lifetime' – when they were rounded up by their tour guide and hurried on to make way for the next group. The ship was due to leave in two hours and there was still a lot to see. In all this haste, Sharon left her postcards on the counter. Not to worry, I thought, I'll drop them round some time. A week later I was able to pop them through the letterbox.

I thought I had seen stunning places before but nothing prepared me for our sea trial the next day. We headed about fifteen miles out of the relatively sheltered Longyearbyen Fjord, passed the bleakly named Dead Man's Point where the sea became rougher, and steered north into the wide-open sound. There we were ringed by dark grey mountains, mountains I knew were 20 miles distant but nevertheless seemed huge. Many of the high peaks had a snowy flourish at the very summit, a delicate curl carved out of rock by a million years of wind. On the flatter ranges a string of gauzy clouds rested lightly.

I learned that as well as sediment sampling, the hovercraft was being used as a platform for many other types of research: oceanographic surveys of temperature, salinity and current, measuring ice thickness, filming and taking weather observations as well as seismic profiling using sonar in the form of buoys which scan the seabed autonomously for months as the ice sheet drifts about. The data was recovered over a satellite phone link.

We continued our passage for almost a hundred miles in this stupefyingly vast and beautiful landscape until we arrived at the port of Ny-Ålesund. We saw one other vessel on this leg, a tubby little tug with a plume of smoke puffing out of the funnel, like a child's drawing of a boat. I was expecting to see little more than a group of huts and a

fuel dump at Ny-Ålesund; instead it turned out to be a civilised town with a small harbour, its own museum and even a hotel – The Nordpol Hotellet. We tied up at the fuel berth in the tiny marina and had time to walk around town while someone found the man to sell us some diesel. It was a pretty place. Outside the museum stood a granite bust of the explorer Amundsen.

Leaving the harbour with full tanks again, we turned towards the head of the fjord where the tongue of the glacier laps the sea. In windless calm and thin sunshine, we stopped the engine and sat in eerie silence, a little group, made insignificant by the towering mountains. The landscape itself was beyond superlatives – I could only look and look. We all know in our heads that we live on a planet, but at that moment I understood it for the first time. The landscape is brutal but also fragile and eye-wateringly beautiful. Seeing it with my own eyes, the thought that it could be lost was almost unbearable. Awe-struck we may have been, but nevertheless we set about doing what humans have always done and, undaunted by the looming mountains, the ghostly icebergs or the forbidding ocean, we carved a cosy little niche for ourselves and carried out a few domestic rituals. Yngve got some dinner on the stove and even poured us a small glass of red wine, all the time keeping a sharp eye on the icy giants which murmured and grumbled all around us. We ate in silence. I kept looking around me, anxious never to forget the moment. Not far away, three huge walrus basked in the sunshine on the beach, unbothered by our presence.

Underway again, we rounded back down the fjord where we encountered a research vessel belonging to UNIS. Staring up at the ship as we pulled alongside for a chat, I saw, and can still see, a row of cheerful young rosy-cheeked Norwegian faces, complete with blonde hair and woolly hats, smiling down at us from the rail.

John Hall had called the craft Sabvabaa which is Inuit for 'flows swiftly over it'. In the breeze which picked up, we lived up to the name, tumbling through the lively seas, heading back to Longyearbyen, the hovercraft a red spark in a monochrome landscape. We finally made it back at 2am. For me, this 14-hour journey seemed like a huge adventure and something I would never forget. We had passed 79.08°N on a round trip of over 200 miles. Then it dawned on me that such a trial was like a stroll to the post-box for these guys: they would be going 600 or 700 miles further than that, alone on the frozen ocean for months on end. It made me feel slightly pathetic. Sometimes, Yngve operated the craft alone. The level of self-sufficiency needed for this is mind-boggling: you might as well be hurtling through space in a tiny capsule for all the help available if you got into trouble. Yngve told me quite matter-of-factly that sometimes the craft would get stuck on a hummock or ridge, losing its cushion. He found the only way to recover from this predicament was to build a wall from ice-blocks, igloo-style, cut with a chainsaw, to close the gap between skirt and ground. This took hours of hard labour but only then would the craft hover again. After I left, the craft went on to cover more than 11,000 nautical miles, most of them over ice.

When Yngve dropped me back in Longyearbyen, I bade him goodbye and wished him luck with the expedition. 'You can come again,' he said. 'Because you don't talk at mealtimes.'

'Take care,' I said.

'Don't worry,' he replied. 'We'll be back before dark.' Only when I'd trudged wearily back to my bed in the hostel at the top of the hill and lay watching the sun streaming through the curtain-less window did it dawn on me what he'd meant: here, in the frozen north, the darkness would not arrive until September.

Footnote: In 2014 Professor Yngve Kristoffersen spent more than a year in the hovercraft on the Arctic ice; for some of the time he was entirely alone. A tremendous achievement. An account of this adventure can be seen in a documentary film by Neil Weisbrod called *Secrets of a frozen Ocean*.

Sweden 2012

Flying Home from Stockholm

It was still a bit early for spirits, but hey, it was almost Christmas and the drinks were complimentary. Soon a cramped window-seat had never felt so comfortable. John started to tell me about his trips to New Zealand, a destination I really envied him, one that had eluded me despite my best efforts.

'Of course, you know the story of how Auckland Airport became the world's oldest and longest-serving hovercraft operator,' I said, interrupting him. 'It all started with Sheepy Lamb.' The name took me straight back to my childhood.

It is my ninth birthday. I am lying on my bed reading *Tales of Modern-Day Pioneers*, a present from mum and dad. This story is about Lieutenant Commander Sheepy Lamb, 'the first hovernaut', who just two years earlier in 1960 had been in the driving seat of a Westland SRN6 hovercraft at the Auckland Air Show. He had come right across the world to demonstrate this British invention on behalf of the Hovercraft Society of Great Britain. It was a warm day and the airfield was crowded with visitors who had come to witness two exciting prospects – a hovercraft demonstration and a parachute display. The hovercraft was a novelty in New Zealand and a large number of admiring enthusiasts had gathered to watch it being put through its paces. Suddenly a frisson rippled through the crowd and Sheepy, waiting to begin his demonstration, became aware of people pointing skywards. One of the parachutists from the display team was seen drifting helplessly out over the tidal marshes which fringed the airport. Sheepy didn't hesitate. With no time to explain to his startled colleagues, he zoomed off in the direction of the parachutist, heading out towards the flat swampy tidal reaches where the unfortunate man was about to splash down in the oozy mud. In one sweep, Sheepy helped him into the craft and sped him to safety. Waving away the parachutist's exclamations of grateful thanks and the crowd's applause with airy nonchalance, Sheepy resumed his demonstration as if nothing had happened. The rescue greatly impressed the airport authorities – they could see its uses for the airport right there and then. There have been hovercraft on the airfield ever since.

'Oh, I know all about old Sheepy,' said John. 'JG was always banging on about him in New Zealand.' He resumed his story.

Sheepy Lamb
to the Rescue

Chapter 16
Sheepy Lamb to the Rescue

John, New Zealand 1999

We were taxiing to the gate after landing and JG was nearing the end of his tale about Sheepy Lamb's derring-do. I was more interested in getting off the plane after our twelve-hour flight. People started to reach for hand-luggage ready to shuffle down the aisle towards the open doors. The trip to New Zealand was seen as a plum assignment, one that I knew Russ envied. JG was an old friend of our agent in New Zealand, so he naturally claimed the trip but as he wouldn't have enough time to complete all the pilot training, I happily went along to help commission the craft and finish the job.

Waiting at baggage reclaim, JG explained that since Sheepy's legendary demonstration the Kiwis had never stopped being enthusiastic about hovercraft. They used SRN6s to begin with, building excellent facilities to accommodate the craft. Over the years, these expensive early craft were replaced by those which were smaller and cheaper to run. The airport is situated with the runway jutting out into the Manakau harbour, a vast, shallow tidal inlet. If a

plane goes down in the Manakau, the quickest way to reach it is by hovercraft. Nowadays, many international airports including Rio De Janeiro, Singapore, South Korea, Venice and Shannon in Ireland use hovercraft in both Security and Search and Rescue roles. It's a legal requirement to provide security around the centre perimeter of an airport and, like Auckland, many of them have flight-paths extending over shallow tidal water – perfect hovercraft terrain.

By the late 1990s, the old faithful Skima 12 (see appx. 3), built by Pindair in Gosport, was not surprisingly coming to the end of its service life in Auckland and a replacement was needed. In the rest of the world, the Skima 12 had been obsolete for nearly two decades since Pindair folded in 1983 so it is possible that the Auckland craft was the only one still running. Pindair's agent in New Zealand suggested a Griffon craft. And so it came to be that in 1999 we built a Griffon 2000TD (see appx. 7) for Auckland Airport Fire & Rescue Department, which is why we were there.

In the book of National Character, the words 'positivity' and 'enthusiasm' figure highly when describing Kiwis. It is therefore not surprising that commissioning went without a hitch. In driver training it soon became obvious that the least experienced pilot present was me. Some of the crew had worked for over twenty years driving hovercraft. The Manakau can be a bleak place in late winter with a brisk wind kicking up a nasty chop over the shallow water but these blokes knew the local conditions inside out. During an early test-run one of the old hands took the controls and confidently managed a 180° turn onto a narrow slipway without looking at all scared. Suffice to say I probably learned more than anyone.

An assignment with the boss meant being on best behaviour. JG is not a man who drinks or swears or stays up late. Most evenings we would have a nice dinner with our agent and maybe a trip out on Auckland harbour aboard a boat belonging to one of the crew. Then bed. One Friday evening, however, as I was happily watching back-to-back re-runs of *Upstairs Downstairs* in my hotel room, I got a call from JG. He sounded slightly agitated and I wondered what had gone wrong.

'B shift are down in reception,' he said. 'They're inviting us on a Pub Crawl.' Falling from his lips, the phrase had a slightly foreign sound as if it was the title of an obscure Maori initiation rite, perhaps one that is likely to be painful. 'What do we do?'

I pointed out that to refuse might put us in the wrong light: after all, we had Sheepy Lamb's spirit of spontaneity to live up to. It would be churlish and rude not to go. We had a duty to show that the English know how to party. It soon became evident that this was not a casual or impromptu pub crawl – B shift had hired a bus for the occasion and we were not their first stop. Neither JG nor I had eaten; I'm a lightweight and JG is pretty well teetotal. By our fourth stop, we were both beginning to turn green. For me, this was simply due to the sudden and unaccustomed alcohol intake of the last couple of hours, JG from the amount of orange and kiwi juice he had drunk – more than enough to ensure a lifelong protection from scurvy. Just the thought of returning to the hot, rowdy bus made my stomach heave. Somewhere between O'Hagan's Bar and Stumpers, we cut our losses, nipped out of the back way via the gents and took a taxi back to the hotel. I doubt that we were missed.

As a perceived 'trip of a lifetime', after the job was done, I took two weeks out to travel around. What I found was a sort of parallel universe England (with no mention of *Lord of the Rings* yet – it was still located firmly in Middle Earth until the films appeared), only with far fewer people and lagging about a decade behind. The bucolic scenery seemed familiar but the flora and fauna quite alien: imagine a Constable painting with triffids. And it's actively volcanic. Mount Ruapehu had recently erupted, disrupting air traffic worldwide with high altitude ash. But apart from randomly erupting volcanoes and occasional earthquakes, it was all very neat and orderly. The suburbs of Auckland were a sprawl of spacious plots with neat lawns around well-kept clapboard houses and a good line in pebble-dash bungalows. In the suburbs, Maori and English names were in equal measure, so Birdwood Road led into Waimoko Glen, Shakespeare Road into Taharoto Lane. Outside the city, the pastoral and agricultural landscape was dotted with small villages connected by hummocky B roads. It was often easy to forget that New Zealand is a rugged outpost at the bottom of the world: for example, getting off the bus at a small village I needed relief. In such a remote place in England, if there had been a public toilet at all, it would be grotty and graffitied. Here it was immaculate with, most impressively, three toilet rolls in each cubicle – not only a spare but a back-up as well. It was a small but pleasing detail which seemed to exemplify the Kiwi character once again.

John, New Zealand 2015

Sixteen years later, I found myself back in Auckland where the whole airport was being upgraded to cope with increasing traffic and to accommodate the new Airbus 380. The safety equipment was being upgraded too: there were new Rosenbauer fire tenders, new boats and their old Griffon 2000 was being joined by a shiny new one, the same model but now a Mk 3 (see appx. 8). I had to go and assemble the new craft with my Griffon colleagues Carl and Dan, then get the pilots familiar with operating it.

After two consecutive eleven-hour flights via Hong Kong, we put up at a hotel near the airport. Although it seemed slightly familiar, it was a while before it clicked that I was actually staying in the same place as before. The city had changed and expanded, with the suburbs now extending right out to the airport. That evening we strolled out to find somewhere to eat. It all seemed typically Kiwi: neat little bungalows with tidy gardens. A few cars parked up on the pavements, a straggly hedge here and there and the odd piece of litter but all very respectable. The next day we went out to the airport to meet the crew.

When we told them where we were staying, they seemed horrified. 'You don't want to stay there,' they advised us, as if we had moved into the Ghetto. 'Move further down town where it's safe. Epsom's nice.' When we went to Epsom, we could see the difference straight away: it was indeed neater and tidier with regimentally clipped hedges, slightly grander houses, pleasanter restaurants and all the cars parked just where they were meant to be. We felt much safer.

Some things about the place had changed, but enough had stayed the same to spark off long forgotten memories of the previous visit. Not only were there a lot of familiar faces around the base, but their old craft looked as good as new after sixteen years of constant use. Dave still ran the company which maintained all the airport equipment. He greeted me warmly, wearing a pair of Griffon overalls I had given him on my last visit since when I had probably got through about ten pairs myself; needless to say, his looked ironed and well cared for with a couple of neat patches on the knees; and they still fitted him. Self-sufficiency is another typical Kiwi characteristic.

'We are a long way from anywhere, so we have to look after ourselves,' explained Dave. It was true - unlike some customers who have regular crises, we had heard very little from New Zealand over the years until one day we'd suddenly received some pictures of the craft with a spectacular dent in the bow, right in the front – decidedly un-Kiwi. Over a cup of Typhoo, the crew now filled in the details of this story which I had heard only sketchily up until then.

They explained that as well as Search and Rescue, the craft had another very specialized role. With its extensive mudflats and sparse population Manakau harbour is a rich habitat for all species of birds. During recent years, the migration of black swans over the winter had increased significantly. These birds weigh about the same as a Beagle, and if Beagles could fly can you imagine the threat they would pose to air traffic? It was the job of the hovercraft to proactively chase the swans away from the runway area, a process known as 'bird-hazing'. During one such mission, one of the numerous wooden navigation posts which are used around the harbour to mark the winding creeks and mud banks suddenly revealed itself. The pilot had been concentrating so hard on swan-herding that he did not have time to stop. To his very great credit, he did have the presence of mind to straighten up the craft at the last second in order to hit the post head on. This may sound rather *kamikaze*, but in doing so, he made sure that only the front easily replaceable fuel tank was damaged. It was the first real prang that the craft had suffered but even then the pictures which they sent to us in Southampton came not with a request for a new tank, which would have been very expensive to build and ship, but for the drawings. They would build the tank themselves.

The accident had left a legacy: whenever I (or anyone) drove the craft, the person in the co-pilot's seat would say: 'Have you seen that post?' as soon as one came into view. This was not said in a jokey or ironic way, but as part of a new operating procedure adopted after a review of the collision. It was the co-pilot's job to point out the post, an idea which should give new hope and purpose to every back-seat driver. Then one day I met the man himself. The post-hitter. I would not have known if he hadn't confessed of his own volition because although the crew frequently engaged in quite merciless banter, none of the other pilots ever said a single word about it. Their view was that it could have been any of them. There was no blame, no-one pointing a finger. Another Kiwi character trait.

The airport was, as would only be expected, full of roomy, well-equipped hangars ideal for assembling the craft, but none of them was available. Was this a problem? Of course not. Everything had been thought through. An events company was hired to erect a tent to keep out the unsettled weather. The craft was removed from the shipping container which had been its home for several weeks and resplendently installed under a large white marquee like a VIP at a garden party. We also had our own yellow bus: a retro 1960s machine, although actually built in the early eighties, which had been lately used as a mobile emergency operation centre. It doubled up as a workshop-cum-tearoom, equipped with a little kitchen and a comfy seating area plus plenty of storage space for tools and parts.

There was lots of willing and competent help on hand to make things go so smoothly that the craft was completed ahead of schedule, ready for a test drive - down the runway to the slipway at the far end of the airfield. We took advantage of our mobile accommodation by riding in the old yellow bus by way of the perimeter road. Dave fired her up for the first time in who knows when, and we set off in good spirits like workers on a Sunday outing. After a few hundred yards, our carefree mood was suddenly curtailed by a huge bang and a jolt, which was a surprise as this sort of thing did not happen in New Zealand. Doors burst open and an avalanche of tools and equipment came sliding down the gangway, out of control. There was a prolonged, confused moment of squealing brakes, creaking, crashing and cursing, then I found myself on the floor. Dan, who had been standing, was hurled into the kitchenette and was lucky not to be catapulted through the windscreen. Fortunately, he managed to grab the pole on his way past, inadvertently ringing the bell as he did so. Being New Zealand, of course, it seemed that the polite ding-ding brought the bus to an immediate halt. Having established that no-one was hurt and nothing had broken, we set about tidying up and had a cup of tea. It seems the brakes had stuck. But here was an incident to rival the Hitting of the Post, providing a rich seam of discussion and reminiscence for years to come.

Trials were, as would be expected, entirely straightforward. The last one was the night trial, to check all the lights and navigation equipment worked properly. We had a few hours to kill before it got dark.

'Let's go over to Laingholm,' suggested Tony, the crew chief. 'There's a great fish and chip shop there. It's across the other side of the bay.' But Laingholm was a surprisingly elusive place which took us a while to find – although we could see parts of it, the first few

pretty wooded creeks we nosed into were dead ends. Eventually, we found the right one which led us to a little village tucked in behind the beach. It turned out to be a sleepy, bohemian place with an atmosphere which reminded me of Venice Beach, but a Venice Beach with a fish and chip shop. Frondy dark green jungle foliage sprang out against a brilliant blue sky and looking upwards through the dappled woods we caught glimpses of clapboard houses and beach cabins, bungalows with verandas and terraces, hand-painted signs to 'Artist's Studio' or 'Pete's Pottery'. Friendly loose-limbed locals in surfing T-shirts ambled by and formed a languid group around our strange yellow vessel which we had parked on the beach. There was an earthy green smell to the air, enriched by pot fumes and incense.

Tony offered a hand up to one of the girls, all braided blonde hair and faded shorts, and she climbed lightly on board followed by several other hippy chicks who only appeared to have two words of vocabulary: 'Wow' or 'Cool' but uttered these in many varying intonations as they sat dangling long brown legs over the side-bodies while the blokes, all cool surfing dudes, looked on, less impressed. Tony seemed to have forgotten about the fish and chips but the rest of us hadn't. After some nagging he set off to the chip shop, returning a long time later with not only fish and chips but the girl who worked there, who had helped him carry our supper and was promised a joy-ride in return.

By now, a soft dusk was stealing over Laingholm. It would be my first time driving this craft in the dark, not something I do much anyway. Now there was a crowd to please too. The creeks were quite tricky in places, fringed and crisscrossed with a riot of primeval vegetation in which nestled suburban gardens strewn with all the paraphernalia which comes with them: see-saws, ride-on lawn-mowers and garden furniture. But there was a temporary feel about these human habitations, as if the ancient earth was humouring them for a little while, like flies buzzing at a sleeping lion. I had been aware of this feeling ever since arriving in New Zealand, in the same way you can almost hear the footsteps of Roman armies ringing out on those long, straight Dorset roads. New Zealand, they say, is a young country geologically, but this just makes it seem more ancient, makes you more aware of how the land once boiled and split and crumpled, the raw materials barely disguised by thin coverings, jagged edges yet to be worn away. Now the planet was quiet for a spell, dozing and resting but one day it would sigh in its sleep, give a little twitch and all traces of the human race would be gone.

We had about ten people on board – the blonde surfing girls, a couple of the lads and the hippy from the chippy whose name I hadn't caught.

'August,' she said when I asked her to repeat it. She shrugged. 'My parents, you know.' She shook her head and watched as I fired up the craft, 'Oh, wow,' she said, 'This is going to be so magical!'

We eased into the creek, avoiding tree branches and dangling creepers, and headed into the bay. Our own lights were added to the fairy lamps strung among the trees; the cosy glow from living rooms and kitchens mingled with the steady gleam of the Southern Cross. Snatches of Pink Floyd emanated from a distant radio as we slid across the mud and over the shallow, clear water. The craft headlights were amazing, transforming the surrounding water into mercury, their beams shining right through to the bottom causing a series of silent explosions of silver sparks as little fish jumped in the sudden light.

August sat quietly until we were back where we started. We cut the engine and subsided onto the mud. I have taken many people for rides on hovercraft. Some ask lots of questions: Can I drive? How fast does it go? How much is it? Some don't like it, others like it too much. But August's comment was a first. 'Wow,' she said. 'That was a mystical experience.' And I had to agree.

After the trials were over we had a weekend off. This led to a revelation: Hobbiton is not CGI! I was a moderate *Lord of the Rings* fan – read the books and seen the films. Now we visited the movie set. The countryside all around Matamata is the Shire. Impossibly green rolling hills, knots of trees and meandering streams. To my great disappointment, however, the hobbit dwellings were no more than facades, just doors leading to nothing. We mooched around the gift shop full of Orc fridge magnets and Elven tea-towels. I bought a nice edition of *Lord of the Rings* to replace the old dog-eared one I had at home.

I had been trying to avoid it but inevitably I got roped in to that other NZ obsession: extreme sports, the stuff of the gap year student and the well-preserved newly retired. A visit to the Waitomo caves included black-water rafting, abseiling down into the caverns through a great fissure in the earth, being tossed like rag dolls down fast flowing water in a rubber ring, careering along in the pitch dark to stalactite-hung caves lit by glow-worms. On to Rotorua, or Roto-vegas as the locals call it, the world centre of rugged activity, to do a bit of luging, which basically consists of careering downhill on a tiny skate board crossed with a go-kart. Then on from that to a sort of giant swing situated high on a hillside where the three gondolas were winched up until we were only held from falling forward by our seatbelts at which point it is utterly impossible not to swear. As the swing dropped like a stone, the G force pulled at my face and a long-drawn-out scream was torn from my throat, I wondered why I was doing this. Perhaps one day a decade or so ago, a dynamic freshly-appointed Minister for Tourism had sighed in despair as he'd looked at the modest income generated by his newly acquired department and arranged a focus session.

'Ok, what's going on?' he demanded bullishly. 'What's the problem? Hardly anyone comes here.'

'Is it because it's a long way away, perhaps?' suggested someone defensively, pulling his cardigan closer around him.

Heads nodded. 'Certainly is. Helluva way to come. I wouldn't come all that way.'

'But we have so many good things, especially things that the Brits love.'

'There's a new series of *Dr Finlay's Casebook* repeats starting next week.'

'The flower-beds are tidy...

'Our public toilets are clean and always have two spare toilet rolls.'

'There's nothing dangerous here.'

'No, nothing... dangerous...' said the Minister, nodding his head slowly. 'But maybe that's just it!' He clicked his fingers. 'How about we offer people the chance to do dangerous things? Like.. like... I don't know... dangling on a long piece of elastic over a raging, boulder-strewn river?'

'Or getting them to throw themselves off a bridge in a little rubber boat into frothing, boiling rapids full of submerged boulders?'

'Climb things that don't want to be climbed.'

'Shouldn't be climbed!'

'A chance to put your life in danger, to make you feel alive!'

And so New Zealand's extreme sports industry was born; visitors began to flock to the island at the bottom of the world in search of an adrenaline rush. Now the tills ring and the coffers are full as tourists of every nationality rush around the miles upon miles of incredible scenery, the brooding, doom-laden mountains, the rushing, icy rivers, the majestic glaciers, and think: How can I endanger my life today?

And where are the Kiwis? Well if they're not manning the tills, many of them are watching re-runs of *Dr Finlay's Case Book* with a nice cup of tea.

By the time Dan and Carl were due to go home I only had a couple more pilots to familiarise with the craft. It had been my perfect trip: we'd all had a good time, in a lovely place with nice, enthusiastic people. A job well done, everything smooth, efficient and professional.

That morning, Dan and Carl said their goodbyes then went off to Departures while I went out on the craft with Tony and my student, Scotty, an experienced, confident pilot who was unfazed by the differences from the old craft. During a manoeuvre, he rolled the craft to one side using the skirt control and I waited for him to level up. He didn't. Why? It seemed that the skirt shift system had failed, leaving

the craft listing ten degrees from level and difficult to control. The only thing we could do was head back to base and investigate the problem. It's a simple system and it could only be a mechanical or hydraulic fault. We turned back, but after a few minutes, the engine stopped. No big thing, just a fuel problem. I got out of the cabin and dropped the anchor, then went back and opened the engine cover. Restarting a hovercraft engine after a fuel problem is a two-handed job. One person (Scotty) goes inside to turn the key, while the other (me) vigorously works the fuel priming pump (this has the highly technical term of 'wanking'). The engine fired momentarily but didn't pick up. On the third attempt Tony said, 'Something's burning!' and sure enough one of the electrical boxes was full of smoke. We opened it up revealing a goo of black melted stuff. Now I can cope with mechanical and hydraulic problems, but I have a complete blind-spot about electrics; to me, it's a black art.

We needed Dan! He knew the electrical system better than anyone. I looked at my watch. Had he flown yet? No, still half an hour to go. I made the call. He had checked in his bags and was waiting at the gate, ready to board. Until this point the craft had run every day without a single problem. Now we had three.

Meanwhile, we were left anchored with an inoperative hovercraft a couple of miles from the nearest slipway. Dead hovercraft are difficult to tow. Although they are light, the deflated, submerged skirt causes a lot of drag. Tow too fast and there is a high risk of damaging the skirt. You need a careful, sympathetic driver with a powerful boat. Where could we find such a thing? The driver was no problem: we were spoilt for choice from among the Fire & Rescue pilots. But the only vessel available was the other hovercraft, and hovercraft don't make good tugboats for all sorts of reasons. In fact, they are diametrically opposite to what is needed, but it was the only option available, so we decided to give it a try. They came whizzing out and we hitched up the tow. Very, very slowly we set off, so thoroughly bombarded with prop wash that we had to shelter in the cabin. An

hour passed before the slipway came in sight by which time we had travelled all of two miles. By now, it was low tide so the mud extended several hundred metres off-shore. As if this wasn't bad enough, the tide was still receding. We reached shallow water and the tow quickly became untenable, the drag of the skirt along the bottom stirring up clouds of mud. We had to drop the tow and put down the anchor with the shore still a quarter of a mile away.

In the airport, the intrepid Dan had worked his way backwards through the airport check-in procedure and was on his way to rescue the situation. He was ferried out to us and got down to work. The diagnosis was good. A loose fuse had got hot; its plastic casing had melted but hadn't blown. With a bit of cleaning and tightening up it would work. With the electrics back in operation, we needed to get the engine started. Another bout of vigorous pumping and it burst into life. Things were certainly looking up – now we just needed to get to shore as quickly as possible.

Heading for the slipway, I realised this was one I hadn't hovered up before - shorter and steeper than the one we'd been using all week. Approaching an unknown landing area is always a challenge. Speed, gradient, camber, wind direction – many factors affect a successful landing. The normal procedure is always to approach with caution, then if you are too tentative and the craft doesn't make it all the way up you can always have another go. Better than coming in too hot and crashing into something. I didn't follow normal procedure. The skirt shift wasn't working, so full control was compromised, with the craft pulling to one side. The tide had now just covered the mud presenting the worst conditions for an approach. In shallow water the air pressure under the craft displaces the water, creating a big bow wave that the craft can't climb over. This dictates the speed of approach. And the engine wasn't running properly. It was surging, losing power then picking up again. We were only doing about five knots, not enough speed to climb the slope. If we couldn't get up, we would just have to nose onto the slipway and either be towed up it or wait until high-water. I kept the throttle wide open, willing the craft on. Nearly there. The shallow water had given way to mud and the engine roared up to full power. I glanced down at the speed display and my stomach lurched: 16 knots! Far too fast. We shot up the slipway, swerved into a 180° turn and set down in the middle of the landing pad facing the way we had come, exactly where we needed to be. From a distance, the manoeuvre would have commanded great respect for my driving skills. The guys in the craft might have been impressed too if only I hadn't been yelling 'Shit! Shit! Shit!' at the top of my voice.

The skirt shift problem turned out to be a tiny fluid leak and easily fixed. The melted fuse was replaced. Dan flew home the next day. But although it initially seemed obvious, the fuel problem was not so straightforward. With only three of us on board we had moved all the fuel forward – this was necessary to trim the craft. There is a warning buzzer which sounds to warn of the possibility of starving the engine of fuel. The failure of the skirt shift rolled the craft to port causing the fuel-feed pipe, in this rare situation, to come clear of the fuel. Eureka! But hang on - unfortunately it still wasn't that simple. Despite getting the craft now flying level, the engine still kept stopping after a few minutes' running. This meant we had to begin the laborious process of finding air leaks. The crew were excellent engineers and set to working their way methodically through the fuel system. My flight was booked for late the next morning: I needed to pack and tie up all the loose ends. The engineers didn't hesitate – two of them would work on into the night until the problem was found.

The next morning, I checked out of my hotel and headed down to the hovercraft. Things were looking good. The lads had found a couple of loose connections and once they fixed them, the engine started promptly. With time ticking away, we went out for a test run, relieved to see that everything was going smoothly at last until we were twenty minutes out... and the engine started to surge at full throttle. Then it stopped. When the throttle was eased back, it ran fine. Open the throttle and again it stopped. Things were not right so I decided I had no choice but to stay on. There was a flurry of activity as we hurried back to base and made calls to change my flight, book a room, and let Southampton know that I would be late. Just as the plane I should have been on passed overhead, we found an air leak in the priming pump. With that bypassed, everything was fine. A final test run and all was well.

The next day, on the plane at last, I could see beneath me the two bright yellow smudges which were the hovercraft, parked side by side half way down the runway. I kept my eyes on them until the tilt of the wing blotted them out, leaving just a landscape of hills bathed in the sunlight of early morning with no human features except for the plane's shadow. Some lines from Tolkein had been tugging at my memory for days - something about a far green country and a swift sunrise. Then I remembered my newly purchased copy of *Lord of the Rings*. After a bit of a tussle, I retrieved it from the very bottom of my cabin bag. It was a nice edition with coloured plates and gilding, small but promisingly heavy.

I turned to the first page. I knew it was a long book, but that was OK because I was still a long way from home.

Sweden 2012

Flying into London

As John reached the end of his story, the second whisky reached my brain and our London-bound plane reached the edge of the North Sea. There was a change in the engine note, the plane banked and started its descent. With one half of my brain, I knew I was nearly home and London was spread out below me with its miniature Trafalgar Square and the Thames snaking along past the London Eye; but as I slipped into a doze, I was nine years old again and back in my bedroom at Lee-on-the-Solent.

The noise of the engine coming through the bedroom window is unmistakable. I know that if I jump on my bike right now, I will arrive just as the lights change to stop the traffic. Today my timing is perfect. I join the crowd on this hot hazy morning and see the two Military Policemen are already in their places on either side of the slipway. In a few moments, the hovercraft will drive up the slip before crossing Marine Parade West and into HMS Daedalus, through the wide metal gates which have been opened to receive it. It is just visible now, beyond this wide sweep of road with the art-deco edifice of Lee Tower in the distance. Now I can actually see the sinister shape of the SRN3 out to sea. It is easily distinguishable from the much smaller SRN6, impressive in its ugliness with its big distinctive pylon and fin and its lumpy, whale-like silhouette.

Here it comes. It is always this transition which fascinates me – how the insignificant distant smudge grows relentlessly into a space-age machine, the hum of the engines becomes a deafening roar, right here in this ordinary road.

There is a smell of kerosene in the air. I climb the bank and stand on tiptoe, waiting for that moment when the hovercraft will rise up and cross the threshold of land and sea as if they are not separate elements but one and the same thing.

I am nine years old and the world is full of promise. There's sure to be a bright future ahead for this would-be hovernaut.

Anorak's Corner
(Technical Appendix)

Anorak's Corner Contents

Appx.	*Craft*	*Chapter*	*Location*
1	Pindair Skima 4 Mk 2	1	Stoneleigh and Hamble
2	Pindair Skima 4 Mk 3	5, 6 & 8	Spain, Bangladesh and Pakistan
3	Pindair Skima 12	1 & 16	Gosport and New Zealand
4	Griffon 1000TD	8	Pakistan
5	Griffon 1500TD	7 & 14	Italy and Ireland
6	Griffon 2000TD Mk 1	3	Scandinavia
7	Griffon 2000TD Mk 2	3, 10, 11 & 16	Scandinavia, Nigeria, Alaska and New Zealand
8	Griffon 2000TD Mk 3	12,15 & 16	Greenland, Svalbard and New Zealand
9	Griffon 2450TD	3	Sweden
10	Griffon 3000TD	4 & 10	Thailand and Nigeria
11	Griffon 4000TD	9 & 13	India

Appendix 1: Skima 4 Mk 2

Builder	Pindair Limited
Length Overall m. (ft.)	4.8 (15'9")
Payload Kgs (passengers)	300kg (4)
Max (cruise) speed mph	34 (25)
Machinery	Three Husqvarna SM160 2-stroke petrol engines, one direct-drive to an axial lift fan and two belt-driven to axial propulsion fans.
Construction	Inflatable hull with rigid floorboards to support passengers and machinery. Passengers seated on a pair of removable, inflatable bench seats.

Appendix 2: **Skima 4 Mk 3**

Builder	Pindair Limited
Length Overall m. (ft.)	5.1 (16'9")
Max Payload Kgs (passengers)	300kg (4)
Max (cruise) speed mph	34 (25)
Machinery	One Hirth twin cylinder 40 bhp air-cooled 2-stroke petrol engine driving a single axial fan. A proportion of air is split off behind the fan to provide lift.
Construction	Inflatable hull with rigid floorboards to support passengers and machinery. Passengers seated on a pair of removable upholstered bench seats.

Appendix 3: Skima 12

Builder	Pindair Limited
Length Overall m. (ft.)	7.77 (25'6")
Max Payload Kgs (passengers)	900kg (12)
Max (cruise) speed mph	43 (35)
Machinery	One Chevrolet V8 petrol engine 160 bhp driving a single axial propeller from the rear of the engine and a single centrifugal lift fan from the front.
Construction	Aluminium hull with inflatable horseshoe buoyancy collar. Inward facing bench seats. GRP crew cabin and canvas or GRP rear cabin cover.

Appendix 4: Griffon 1000TD

Builder	Griffon Hovercraft Limited
Length Overall m. (ft.)	8.4 (27'7")
Max Payload Kgs (passengers)	1000kg (10)
Max (cruise) speed mph	40 (32)
Machinery	One Deutz 6 cylinder 190 bhp air-cooled turbo-diesel engine driving a single axial propeller from the rear of the engine and a single centrifugal lift fan from the front.
Construction	Aluminium hull with hinged aluminium side-decks. Inward facing bench seats. GRP crew cabin and canvas rear cabin cover.

Appendix 5: Griffon 1500TD

Builder	Griffon Hovercraft Limited
Length Overall m. (ft.)	10.15 (33'4")
Max Payload Kgs (passengers)	1500kg (15)
Max (cruise) speed mph	36 (31)
Machinery	One Deutz 6 cylinder 190 bhp air-cooled turbo-diesel engine driving a single axial propeller from the rear of the engine and a single centrifugal lift fan from the front.
Construction	Aluminium hull is based on a stretched 1000TD. Hinged aluminium side-decks. Inward facing bench seats. GRP cabin.

Appendix 6: Griffon 2000TD Mk1

Builder	Griffon Hovercraft Limited
Length Overall m. (ft.)	10.6 (34'9")
Max Payload Kgs (passengers)	2000kg (22)
Max (cruise) speed mph	50 (40)
Machinery	One Deutz V8 air-cooled 360 bhp turbo-diesel engine driving a single axial propeller from the rear of the engine and a single centrifugal lift fan from the front.
Construction	Aluminium hull with hinged GRP side-decks. Inward facing bench seats. GRP cabin.

Appendix 7: Griffon 2000TD Mk2

Builder	Griffon Hovercraft Limited
Length Overall m. (ft.)	12.7 (41'8")
Max Payload Kgs (passengers)	2000kg (22)
Max (cruise) speed mph	50 (40)
Machinery	One Deutz V8 air-cooled 360 bhp turbo-diesel engine driving a single axial propeller from the rear of the engine and a single centrifugal lift fan from the front.
Construction	Aluminium hull with hinged or bolted side-decks. Inward facing bench seats. Aluminium cabin. Developed to comply with most aspects of the IMO's Code for the Construction of High Speed Craft when it was introduced.

Appendix 8: Griffon 2000TD Mk3

Builder	Griffon Hovercraft Limited
Length Overall m. (ft.)	12.7 (41'8")
Max Payload Kgs (passengers)	2000kg (22)
Max (cruise) speed mph	39 (31)
Machinery	One Deutz V6 liquid-cooled 449 bhp turbo-diesel engine driving single axial propeller and a single centrifugal lift fan. The Mk3 was fitted with a liquid cooled engine as the air cooled engines were to be discontinued. All other aspects of the craft are similar to the Mk2.
Construction	Aluminium hull with bolted side-decks. Inward facing bench seats. GRP/aluminium cabin.

Appendix 9: Griffon 2450TD

Builder	Griffon Hoverwork Limited
Length Overall m. (ft.)	13.4 (44)
Max Payload Kgs (passengers)	2500kg (25)
Max (cruise) speed mph	40 (33)
Machinery	One Deutz V8 liquid-cooled 598 bhp turbo-diesel engine driving a single axial propeller from the rear of the engine and a single centrifugal lift fan from the front.
Construction	Aluminium hull with bolted side-decks. 4 seat crew cabin. This particular variant had a hinged rear cabin roof and a crane to lift snow-scooters inside. Removable seating for 12 was fitted.

Appendix 10: Griffon 3000TD

Builder	Griffon Hovercraft Limited
Length Overall m. (ft.)	15.0 (49'3")
Payload Kgs (passengers)	3000kg (30)
Max (cruise) speed mph	46 (40)
Machinery	Two Deutz air-cooled 360 bhp 8 cylinder air-cooled turbo-diesel engines each one driving an axial propeller from the rear of the engine and a centrifugal lift fan from the front.
Construction	Aluminium hull with bolted GRP side-decks. Two seat crew cabin forward. Main cabin houses 30 forward facing aircraft-style passenger seats with air-conditioning in all accommodation spaces.

Appendix 11: Griffon 4000TD

Builder	Griffon Hovercraft Limited
Length Overall m. (ft.)	17.9 (58'9")
Payload Kgs (passengers)	4000kg (60)
Max (cruise) speed mph	44 (40)
Machinery	Two Deutz air-cooled 450 bhp 10 cylinder air-cooled turbo-diesel engines each one driving an axial propeller from the rear of the engine and a centrifugal lift fan from the front.
Construction	Aluminium hull with bolted side-decks. Two seat crew cabin forward. Main cabin houses 40 forward facing aircraft-style passenger seats with air-conditioning in all accommodation spaces.